'Who the devil taught thee so much Italian?'

'WHO THE DEVIL TAUGHT THEE SO MUCH ITALIAN?'

Italian language learning and literary imitation in early modern England

JASON LAWRENCE

Manchester University Press
Manchester and New York

distributed exclusively in the USA by Palgrave

Copyright © Jason Lawrence 2005

The right of Jason Lawrence to be identified as the author of this work has been asserted by him in accordance with the Copyright, Designs and Patents Act 1988.

Published by Manchester University Press
Oxford Road, Manchester M13 9NR, UK
and Room 400, 175 Fifth Avenue, New York, NY 10010, USA
www.manchesteruniversitypress.co.uk

Distributed in the United States exclusively by
Palgrave Macmillan, 175 Fifth Avenue,
New York, NY 10010, USA

Distributed in Canada exclusively by
UBC Press, University of British Columbia, 2029 West Mall,
Vancouver, BC, Canada V6T 1Z2

British Library Cataloguing-in-Publication Data is available

Library of Congress Cataloging-in-Publication Data is available

ISBN 978 0 7190 6915 4 paperback

First published by Manchester University Press in hardback 2005

This paperback edition first published 2011

The publisher has no responsibility for the persistence or accuracy of URLs for any external or third-party internet websites referred to in this book, and does not guarantee that any content on such websites is, or will remain, accurate or appropriate.

Printed by Lightning Source

In loving memory of my mother, Lesley Kay Lawrence.

Contents

Acknowledgements *page* viii

Introduction 1

1 'Mie new London Companions for Italian and French': modern language learning in Elizabethan England 19

2 'A stranger borne / To be indenized with us, and made our owne': Samuel Daniel and the naturalisation of Italian literary forms 62

3 'Give me the ocular proof': Shakespeare's Italian language-learning habits 118

Conclusion: Seventeenth-century language learning 177

Appendix: John Wolfe's Italian publications 187
Bibliography 202
Index 219

Acknowledgements

Warm thanks to Dr John Pitcher for his careful supervision of my DPhil thesis in Oxford, from which this book is developed, and to my examiners, Professor Emrys Jones and Professor J. R. Mulryne. I would also like to thank: Christopher Wakling and Dr Jane Kingsley-Smith for reading and making insightful comments on earlier drafts of the book; Dr Simon Mealor for his assistance with the translations from French, and Dr Anna Zambelli Sessona for checking my translations from Italian; Dr Michael Redmond for drawing my attention to George Pettie's habits of translation. Thanks also to the anonymous readers for Ashgate and Manchester University Press, whose comments and suggestions have been very helpful in the revision of the book, and to Matthew Frost and Kate Fox at Manchester University Press. Parts of the section in Chapter 2 on Daniel and Italian pastoral drama have appeared in *Medieval and Renaissance Drama in England* 11 (1999), pp. 143–71, reproduced by permission of the editor, and a version of the section in Chapter 3 on Shakespeare's dramatisations of Cinthio can be found in Michele Marrapodi (ed.), *Shakespeare, Italy and Intertextuality* (Manchester University Press, Manchester, 2004), pp. 91–106. Thanks finally to my family, friends, and partner for their constant love and support throughout the writing of this book.

Introduction

> I am an Englishman in Italiane; I know they haue a knife at command to cut my throate, *Vn Inglese Italianato, e vn Diauolo incarnato*. Now, who the Diuell taught thee so much Italian? speake me as much more, and take all. Meane you the men, or their mindes? be the men good, and their mindes bad? Speak for the men (for you are one) or I will doubt of your minde: Mislike you the language? why the best speake it best, and hir Maiestie none better.
>
> I, but thou canst reade whatsoeuer is good in Italian, translated into English. And was it good that they translated then? or were they good that translated it? ... Had they not knowen Italian, how had they translated it? had they not translated it, where were now thy reading? Rather drinke at the wel-head, than sip at pudled streames; rather buy at the first hand, than goe on trust at the bucksters.[1]

JOHN FLORIO'S letter 'To the Reader' at the beginning of his *Second Frutes* (1591), a parallel-text dialogue manual for learning Italian, offers an impassioned response to the celebrated Italian proverb that describes the apparently pernicious effect that the country has on many of its English visitors. The proverb is introduced into England in exactly this context, in Roger Ascham's *The Scholemaster* (1570), where young English gentlemen are given a stern warning about the dangers of exposing themselves to 'the *Siren* songes of *Italie*'.[2] Ascham, however, is equally concerned by the manner in which this negative Italian influence is beginning to infiltrate into England itself in the second half of the sixteenth century:

> These be the inchantementes of *Circes*, brought out of *Italie*, to marre mens maners in England: much, by example of ill life, but more by preceptes of fonde bookes, of late translated out of *Italian* into English, sold in euery shop in London, commended by honest titles the soner to corrupt honest manners: dedicated ouer boldlie to vertuous and honorable personages, the easielier to begile simple and innocent wittes.[3]

It is the wide availability of Italian books, such as Petrarch's *Trionfi* and Boccaccio's *Decameron*,[4] in English versions rather than in the original language that most troubles Ascham, as Florio clearly recognises in the emphasis he places on translation in his retort. Indeed, Ascham regards this very process of translation as a plot instigated by 'the sutle and secrete Papistes at home', who have deliberately 'procured bawdies bookes to be translated out of the *Italian* tonge'.[5] A decade later the former actor and playwright Steven Gosson goes a step further, suggesting, in the 'first Action' of his polemical *Playes Confuted in fiue Actions* (1582), that it is the devil himself who is responsible for the infiltration of Italian books into England and their subsequent translation. He also draws attention to a new phenomenon, the presentation of stories from these books on stage, in the recently opened professional theatres:

> First hee sente ouer many wanton Italian bookes, which being translated into english, haue poysoned the olde maners of our Country with foreine delights. . . . The Deuill not contented with the number he hath corrupted with reading Italian baudery, because all cannot reade presenteth us Comedies cut by the same paterne, which drag such a monstrous tatle after them, as is able to sweep whole Cities into his lap.[6]

In the '2 Action' Gosson elaborates on his argument by demonstrating how the playwrights have used a variety of books with foreign origins to provide the plots for their dangerous new plays:

> I may boldely say it, because I haue seene it, that the *Palace of pleasure*, the *Golden Asse*, the *Aethiopian historie*, *Amadis of Fraunce*, the *Rounde table*, baudie Comedies in Latine, French, Italian and Spanish, haue beene throughly ransackt, to furnish the Playe houses in London.

Gosson's personal convictions are strengthened by the sincere renunciation of his former profession, despite accusations of hypocrisy against him. In the dedicatory letter 'To the Rightworshipful

Gentlemen and studentes, of both Vniuersities, and the Innes of Court', he explains that two of his own plays have been performed in London since the printing of *The Schoole of Abuse* in 1579: 'The one was a cast of Italian deuices, called, *The Comedie of Captaine Mario*: the other a Moral, *Praise at parting*.' His critics have insinuated that they were 'written by me since I had set out my inuectiue against them. I can not denie, they were both mine, but they were penned two yeeres at the least before I forsooke them.' Gosson's admission that he composes a comedy of 'Italian deuices', now unfortunately lost, in the late 1570s is particularly interesting, for in this period he is evidently a keen student of the Italian language under the tutelage of John Florio in London. Gosson writes a commendatory poem for the teacher's earlier Italian language manual, *Florio his First Fruites* (1578), revealing his appreciation of Florio's methods of instruction. This suggests that the 'deuices' included in his contemporary comedy may have been taken directly from an Italian source, rather than via an English translation.

It is ironic that the authors of the two most vehement rejections of the growing Italian influence in Elizabethan England are *both* students of the language. Ascham is careful to explain that his objections to Italy and its malign influence have nothing to do with the language itself, 'the Italian tonge, which next the Greeke and Latin tonge, I like and loue aboue all other'.[7] It is not certain when Ascham acquires his knowledge of the language, but he includes an Italian pasquinade in his *Discours and affaires of the state of Germanie*, written in 1553, shortly after a three-year sojourn at the court of Emperor Charles V. It may be during this period in Europe that he learns Italian, before the miserable nine-day stay he endures in Venice, memorably recalled in *The Scholemaster*. If his Italian is learnt while abroad, then Ascham's name can be unexpectedly linked to some of the most notable early English Italophiles. Sir Thomas Wyatt's interest in the language and its literature is probably first aroused on his embassy to Rome in 1527. William Thomas's extensive knowledge of the language and history of Italy is acquired during his prolonged stay in the country in the late 1540s, for reasons of personal safety.[8] Thomas publishes his influential *Historie of Italie* on his return to England in 1549, and in the following year issues the first English manual for learning Italian, his *Principal Rules of the Italian Grammar, with a Dictionary for the better understanding of Boccace, Petrarca, and Dante* (1550). The publication of Thomas's works coincides with the arrival of a first generation of immigrant Italian teachers in England, who are generally religious refugees from the burgeoning Counter-Reformation in Europe. This suggests that the stimulus for the growing English interest in Italy and its culture, which so worries Ascham some twenty years later, can be traced to the late 1540s.

It is uncertain, however, to what extent this initial wave of interest advances a more widespread knowledge of the Italian language itself. The range of pupils taught by the newly arrived language teachers, such as Michel Angelo Florio, Giovan Battista Castiglioni, and possibly Petruccio Ubaldini, in the 1540s and early 1550s is almost entirely royal or aristocratic.[9] With the exception of Thomas's *Principal Rules*, there are no printed Italian grammars available, and access to Italian books seems to be primarily by means of translations, which start to be printed in the 1550s, and increase in number throughout the 1560s and 1570s. By the time that Gosson is writing his invectives against the London stage at the beginning of the 1580s, however, there have been major advances in the means by which these Italian books and indeed the language itself are being made available directly to a wider English readership.

The final quarter of the sixteenth century witnesses a concerted use of the print medium by immigrant language teachers in England to make foreign-language texts, particularly in Italian, accessible to the reading public for the first time. These texts usually take one of two forms, both of which are designed to facilitate a direct engagement with the original language as opposed to translations, 'rather [to] drinke at the wel-head, than sip at pudled streames' as Florio puts it. Throughout the 1580s and early 1590s the stationer John Wolfe prints numerous texts in Italian with great accuracy from his print shops in London, including books written by the immigrant teachers and other more celebrated or controversial works often provided and probably edited by them. Wolfe's Italian publications and the editorial activities of his Italian colleagues, such as Iacopo Castelvetro, will be examined in the appendix to this book. The other type of text contains passages in the modern foreign language (most frequently French or Italian) printed in parallel with a literal version in English. The practical manuals for learning Italian, which all use the parallel-text dialogue form, first appear in print in the mid-1570s,[10] a few years before Wolfe starts producing publications in Italian. There is, then, a close correlation between this means of developing an ability to read texts in the original language and the growing demand for new Italian materials in England that Wolfe is clearly attempting to satisfy shortly after.

It is doubly ironic, given the emphasis on first-hand knowledge and the contemporary aversion to translations from Italian, that the techniques for learning a new language exemplified in the instruction manuals should depend so heavily on an active use of translation. Chapter 1 will demonstrate how teachers encourage their private students and readers alike to attempt translation exercises both from and into the target language as an essential element of their language-learning habits. Passages for translation in the manuals and for private lessons are often chosen from literary sources, with the vernacular poetry of Petrarch proving especially popular, which would presumably be much to the dismay of Ascham. The emphasis on literary texts in this element of the language-learning process highlights one of the principal reasons for wanting to acquire an understanding of Italian in the first place. The English desire to read Italian fluently in the sixteenth and early seventeenth centuries is predicated primarily on a specifically literary interest, from William Thomas's *Dictionary for the better understanding of Boccace, Petrarca, and Dante* appended to his *Principal Rules of the Italian Grammar* in 1550, throughout John Florio's fifty-year career as the most noted teacher of Italian in England:

> Yet heere-hence may some good accrewe, not onelie to truantlie-schollers, which euer-and-anon runne to *Venuti*, and *Alunno*; or to new-entred nouices, that hardly can construe their lesson; or to well-forwarde students, that haue turnd ouer *Guazzo* and *Castiglione*, yea runne through *Guarini*, *Ariosto*, *Tasso*, *Boccacce*, and *Petrarche*: but euen to the most compleate Doctor; yea to him that can best stande *All' erta* for the best Italian, heereof sometimes may rise some vse.[11]

The careful choice of examples of the best Italian poetry for translation exercises also indicates how the teachers want to familiarise their students with the highest stylistic achievements in the vernacular language. Ascham suggests in *The Scholemaster* that young men can most readily achieve an elegant written style in Latin by translating the works of Cicero into English and then back into Latin. The Italian teachers similarly tend to direct their pupils and readers towards the Italian works of Petrarch, whose Tuscan language and style are canonised in Pietro Bembo's *Prose della Volgar Lingua* (1525), for translation purposes. It is possible that Ascham himself learns

Italian by means of the celebrated system of double translation that he recommends for mastering Latin. A version of this technique is certainly used by Philip Sidney during his stay in Italy in the 1570s, as he seeks to improve his Latin, French, and Italian simultaneously. The strong emphasis on student translation in the modern language-learning manuals is evidently a conscious development of Ascham's pedagogical programme. Holyband's *The French Schoolemaister* (1573) and later *Italian Schoole-maister* echo *The Scholemaster* in name, but they also share, along with the manuals by Florio and John Eliot, many of its key methods of language acquisition. It becomes clear that Ascham's instruction manual for Latin, which vividly warns of the dangers of Italy and its books translated into English, unwittingly contributes to a rapidly expanding knowledge of the Italian language in London and beyond. In the years immediately following Ascham's death,[12] the recently arrived teachers of French and Italian modify his techniques for translation into their own private lessons and parallel-text manuals.[13]

The sudden proliferation of these manuals in the final quarter of the sixteenth century, which clearly allows more widespread access to the methods of contemporary modern-language learning, is the decisive factor in accounting for the growing interest in the Italian tongue and original-language books throughout the same period. Chapter 1 will focus on the printed manuals to examine the techniques exemplified in the parallel-text dialogue format, developed from an emphasis on practical language learning in private lessons. Before the advent of the instruction manuals there are only two means of learning Italian in sixteenth-century England: private tuition or travel. Both of these methods tend to be available exclusively to members of the aristocracy or gentry, at least until the latter part of the century, and, in the case of foreign travel, available only to men. The first generation of language teachers in England, who are all native speakers, find employment in private households. John Florio's father, Michel Angelo, is a tutor in the early 1550s in the residence of the Duke of Suffolk, where he teaches Italian to Lady Jane Grey and her husband Guilford Dudley. Giovan Battista Castiglioni is employed in an even more prestigious household, responsible for teaching Italian to the teenage Princess Elizabeth in the 1540s. He remains in Elizabeth's service for at least the first decade of her reign, and dedicates his own Italian poems to her in a volume printed by Wolfe in 1580.

INTRODUCTION

A second generation of Italian teachers, again predominantly native speakers, are even more successful at cultivating royal and aristocratic patrons. Iacopo Castelvetro, who works closely with John Wolfe for much of the 1580s, becomes acquainted with Sir Philip Sidney, Sir Francis Walsingham, and Sir Christopher Hatton in London, although there is no evidence that he instructs any of them in Italian. He does, however, acquire two royal students after his move to Edinburgh in 1592. Castelvetro appeals successfully to James VI of Scotland to allow him to teach Italian to the King and his wife, Anne of Denmark, using the example of Queen Elizabeth's renowned love of the language and Italian books as an incentive to learn:

> Pensai appresso di dovere havere onesta opportunità, in presentandoglielo, per essere egli scritto in italiano, di proferire insieme a Vostra Maestà il mio fedel servigio, intorno ad apprendere a lei, od alla Serenissima Reina sua consorte, la mia natia lingua; hoggi non pure stimata da qualsivoglia nation forestiere per la più bella, & per la più compiuta di quante se ne parlino, ma etiandio abbracciata da tutti i prencipi del mondo; & è noto ad ognuno quanto ella habbia giovato ad illustrar le molte altre virtudi della Serenissima Reina d'Inghilterra sua sorella, che non la scrive, ne la parla men perfettamente, che se nel cuore della bella Italia fosse nata, & tanto se ne compiace ella, che non istima quel suo servitore esser perfetto, che veramente non la possiede, essendo solita di dire, che l'italica favella, non solamente per la sua rara belta, ma anchora per la quantita di rari libri, che in essa & non in altra si leggono, merita d'esser d'ogni nobile spirito saputa; e se non fosse mai per altro, sol per potere intendere i nobili poemi, da pochi anni in qua venuti a luce, del gran poeta Torquato Tasso, di cui parlando il valente suo poeta du Bartas, dice. Dernier en age, premier en honneur.[14]

> (I later thought that I ought to take this sincere opportunity, in presenting to you a work written in Italian, also to offer my faithful service to Your Majesty by teaching either you or Her Highness the Queen your consort my mother tongue; a language which today is not only regarded by every foreign nation as the most beautiful, and most complete of any that are spoken, but is also embraced by all the princes in the world; and it is known to everyone how useful the Italian language has been in highlighting the many other virtues of Her Highness the Queen of England your royal sister, who neither writes nor speaks it less perfectly than if she had been born in the very heart of beautiful Italy, and so highly does she esteem it that she does not consider any courtier to be perfect who does not have

full command of it, being accustomed to say that the Italian tongue deserves to be learnt by every noble spirit, not only because of its unique beauty, but also for the number of rare books, that can be read in this and no other tongue; and if there were no other reason, at least to be able to read the noble works, which have appeared in the last few years, of the great poet Torquato Tasso, of whose talent the poet du Bartas said, 'Last in age, but first in honour'.)

If Castelvetro instructs both King James and his wife in Scotland, then it is clear that Queen Anne continues her Italian studies after the royal couple move to England in 1603. John Florio dedicates the expanded version of his Italian–English dictionary, *Queen Anna's New World of Words*, to the Queen in 1611, by which time he has become a Gentleman of the Privy Chamber and a personal adviser to her.[15] Florio's status as the pre-eminent Italian teacher in early seventeenth-century London can be demonstrated by the number of illustrious pupils he acquires. In addition to Queen Anne, his dedications reveal Florio's professional associations with Sir Edward Dyer, Henry Wriothesley, the Earl of Southampton, Roger and Elizabeth Manners, the Earl and Countess of Rutland, Lucy Russell, the Countess of Bedford, and her mother Lady Anne Harington, Elizabeth Grey, Countess of Kent, Lady Penelope Riche, and Lady Marie Nevill. As Frances Yates suggests, 'as a ladies' tutor, Florio seems to have been rather a success'.[16] Florio evidently attempts to share his refined tastes in Italian literature and culture with his aristocratic students as a fundamental part of their language-learning experience. John Pitcher argues that Queen Anne acquires 'a taste for all things Italian – books, music, gardens, and architecture' after her arrival in England, presumably with Florio's expert guidance.[17] For example, Cosimo II, the Grand Duke of Tuscany, sends the Queen some Italian books as a New Year's gift in 1611, including one celebrated play with which she is already familiar, as Lotti records:

> I libri piacquero assai, a Sua Maestà et ne volle di tutte leggere il titolo, et si connobe che la Maestà Sua haveva più cognizione del *Pastor fido* che degli altri.[18]

> (The books pleased Her Majesty very much, and she wanted to read the titles of all of them, and it was clear that Her Majesty had greater knowledge of *Pastor fido* than of the others.)

While cultivating the language skills and the literary tastes of his socially illustrious pupils is a significant and rewarding element of

Florio's professional life, it will not be the central focus of this investigation into the profound effect that his modern language-learning techniques have on habits of literary imitation in England at the turn of the sixteenth century. This book is more concerned with tracing how Florio's influence, both personal and by means of his Italian instruction manuals, is disseminated among a number of contemporary poets and playwrights, and the sustained impact that this has on a concurrent, renewed engagement with Italian literary forms.

Many of the literary figures to be influenced directly by Florio's methods are examples of the new types of Italian student to emerge in the final quarter of the sixteenth century. An increasing number of French and Italian immigrants in London both willing and able to teach their mother tongues leads to the establishment of private language schools in the capital, such as the one run by Claude Holyband, the author of instruction manuals for both languages. The ten commendatory poems in *Florio his First Fruites* (1578) are evidently provided by some of the students Florio is instructing in London, including one by the actor and playwright Steven Gosson, but only two of them are written by pupils designated as 'gentlemen'. This indicates a notable broadening in the social range of students able to learn the modern languages in London under the supervision of Holyband, Florio, and the like. At the same time language teachers start to proffer their services in the potentially lucrative student market at the two universities. In a letter written in 1580 Gabriel Harvey refers to an unnamed 'Italian Maister' who is instructing him and his brother John at Cambridge.[19] John Florio accompanies Emmanuel Barnes as a private tutor to Magdalen College, Oxford, in the mid-1570s, where his name is recorded for the first time after his return to England. It is clear that he cultivates other university students to study modern languages with him in Oxford. Matthew Gwynne of St John's College contributes commendatory poems in both English and Italian, under the pseudonym *Il Candido*, to many of Florio's works from 1582, having met and been instructed by him at Oxford. Another lifelong friend is the poet Samuel Daniel, who meets Florio shortly after his matriculation at Magdalen Hall in the early 1580s. An examination of the close connection between the language-learning techniques that Daniel first practises as Florio's student and the poet's own careful habits of imitation from French and particularly Italian sources that he maintains throughout his career will be one of the key elements of this book.

'WHO THE DEVIL TAUGHT THEE SO MUCH ITALIAN?'

It is likely that Daniel learns both French and Italian with Florio in Oxford. He is probably studying both languages simultaneously, although there is a marked tendency among modern-language students in the period to acquire some knowledge of French before attempting to master the Italian language as well. In Daniel's case this is reflected in an initial interest in French sources at the earliest stage of his poetic career, shortly after he visits Paris in 1586, before he progresses towards a deeper, sustained engagement with Italian models during and after a visit to Italy in the early 1590s. This draws attention to another distinctive trend in contemporary language-learning habits, that students frequently start to learn a new language just before travelling to its country of origin, where they can further develop their linguistic facility among native speakers. For much of the sixteenth century this method is available only to aristocratic travellers, who have already benefited from the attentions of a private tutor. For example, Henry Wriothesley, the Earl of Southampton, learns Italian with Florio before his visit to Italy in the late 1590s. In the final quarter of the century, however, European travel is an increasingly real possibility for university students, such as Daniel and Robert Tofte. Thus Daniel, a less socially prestigious student of Florio, can similarly concentrate on mastering French in the mid-1580s before visiting Paris. His early poetry, probably written just after his time in France, demonstrates that he has already acquired some knowledge of Italian with Florio, which is later much improved during his eighteen-month stay in Italy.

The pattern of Daniel's language learning is by no means unique among students who travel to Europe with specifically literary interests. Philip Sidney is commended on the quality of his French as soon as he reaches France in 1572,[20] but it is doubtful that he has an equal command of Italian when he first arrives in Venice the following year. Sidney is accompanied on his European journey by a native Italian speaker in his father's retinue, Lodowick Bryskett, presumably to facilitate travel arrangements in Italy and also to aid Sidney's familiarity with the language and its literature. While in Venice the English traveller seeks advice from his mentor Hubert Languet about improving his written style in Latin, and Sidney later suggests that the recommended translation exercises might also assist his fluency in both French and Italian. William Fowler, who probably meets Daniel in Padua in late 1591, has already studied law in Paris in the early 1580s before he travels to Italy a decade later to enrol at the University of

Padua. On each occasion Fowler has gained some knowledge of the language before he visits the country. His stay in Italy allows him to deepen his understanding of both the language and its literary traditions. Fowler's translation of Petrarch's *Trionfi* is completed in 1587, some four years before his trip, but the extensive acquaintance with sixteenth-century Italian sonnet writing, often printed only in verse anthologies, demonstrated in *The Tarantula of Love* is probably gained in Italy itself. William Drummond, like his uncle Fowler, spends time in France in 1607–8, but his equally impressive grasp of Italian is acquired alone in his study at Hawthornden a few years later, by means of his careful comparison of Italian books alongside translations of them in either English or French. Drummond provides an excellent example of successful self-tuition in Italian by means of his private reading rather than from personal instruction or time spent in Italy.

A visit to the country itself clearly has an impact on the traveller's ability to *speak* the language effectively, particularly if it has been learnt initially by studying a printed manual rather than from private lessons. The focus in this book, however, will be on how students develop a sound *reading* knowledge of the target language, as it is not strictly necessary to speak a language accurately in order to understand it sufficiently well to engage with its literature. It is possible, therefore, to argue quite plausibly for Shakespeare's gradual acquisition of an adequate reading ability in Italian, given the frequent indebtedness to Florio's manuals and his uncontested Italian sources in many of his plays, whereas it would be mere conjecture to assert that he could actually speak Italian with any degree of fluency. Critical speculation about whether Shakespeare's knowledge of Italian has its origins in a putative personal acquaintance with Florio is largely irrelevant, as by the early 1590s, when Shakespeare starts to learn the language, it is perfectly possible to study it alone with the aid of Florio's *First* and *Second Frutes*. Indeed, the method by which Shakespeare tends to use his Italian models, approaching them as source texts alongside English translations or adaptations wherever possible, seems to develop directly out of the insistent parallel-text focus of the bilingual dialogues in *all* the contemporary language manuals. One of the central premises of this book is that the techniques for acquiring modern languages prevalent in the late sixteenth century have a clear impact on both the broader reading habits and compositional practices of many of the authors who strive to learn Italian. The emphasis in the manuals and private lessons on the use of literary translation, both as a language-improving exercise and as a means of understanding a text in its original form rather than as a replacement for it, encourages a close engagement with specific Italian sources, which often becomes the starting point for an act of creative imitation. The intimate connection between these two processes will be demonstrated in a detailed analysis of the language-learning habits and methods of sonnet composition of two notable Italophile poets, William Drummond and Samuel Daniel.

While Drummond inherits many aspects of Daniel's earlier imitative techniques in constructing his sonnets in the 1610s, particularly their simultaneous attention to both the Italian and French sonnet traditions, it is evident that the two poets learn Italian in rather different circumstances. Daniel benefits from Florio's personal instruction while he is a student in Oxford in his late teens, and then has the opportunity to improve his language skills during an extended stay in Italy some years later. Other students who strive to learn the language while at university before travelling to Italy include the poets Robert Tofte, who meets Daniel there in 1591, and Francis Davison, who visits Italy in the mid-1590s and lauds Daniel as the 'Prince of English Poets' in his *Poetical Rhapsody* of 1602. Drummond, however, begins to study Italian by himself at home in Scotland only in his late twenties. Similarly, Gabriel Harvey is almost thirty when he copiously annotates a copy of *Florio his First Fruites* in a bid to achieve rapid fluency in Italian in the late 1570s.[21] It seems that Shakespeare is about the same age when he chooses to start learning the language, probably through self-study, in the early 1590s. The passages of Italian dialogue in *The Taming of the Shrew*, unique even in the plays with an Italian setting, are constructed almost entirely from the opening chapters of Florio's first manual.

The pattern for learning the language initially in the late teens at university is more prevalent among the Italian students to be discussed in this book than the alternative model of mature self-tuition. Although there is no direct evidence for how Edmund Spenser acquires his extensive knowledge of Italian, he probably begins his studies at Cambridge in the early 1570s. Spenser's earliest poems, the *Sonnets* and *Epigrams* printed in *A Theatre for Voluptuous Worldlings* in 1569, are translated from French sources. The former are based on du Bellay's *Songe*, printed in the same volume as *Les Antiquitez de*

Rome in 1558, while the latter are adapted from Petrarch's *Canzone* 323, using Marot's French version, *Des Visions de Pétrarque*, rather than the Italian original. This suggests that Spenser does not know any Italian when he arrives at Pembroke Hall in the same year. A decade later, however, he is certainly familiar with the language and one of the landmarks of sixteenth-century Italian poetry, as Gabriel Harvey refers in a letter of 1580 to his friend's ardent desire to imitate and overgo Ariosto's epic *Orlando furioso* in the earliest fragments of *The Faerie Queene*. John Milton is another Cambridge-educated poet who develops a good understanding of French and Italian, long before visiting both countries in the late 1630s. He is instructed in the two modern languages, as well as Latin and Greek, at his father's expense even before he goes up to Cambridge in 1625, as he records in the poem *Ad Patrem* printed in 1645. Milton writes several sonnets in Italian, probably in around 1630, and he is the only English poet actually to compose verse in the language, with the exception of the playwright John Marston, whose mother is at least half-Italian.

The youthful instruction in languages by personal tutors, which Milton receives before he goes to university, is the only means of learning available to young women in sixteenth-century England. Although Holyband encourages gentlewomen to attend his language school in London, most female students of Italian are taught privately in their family's households. The methods of instruction seem to be the same, irrespective of either the gender of the pupil or the nationality of the teacher. The continuing practice of using Italian poetry as a source for translation exercises can be demonstrated in the 1590s, in the English versions of two sonnets from Petrarch's *Canzoniere* by Elizabeth Carey, the teenage daughter of Lord Hunsdon. The sonnets are probably chosen by her tutor Henry Stanford, who teaches his young pupil both Italian and French. His method recalls that of an earlier native Italian teacher, Giovan Battista Castliglioni, who instructs the teenage Princess Elizabeth in the language partly by setting her passages from Petrarch's *Trionfi* to translate. The taste for the Italian language and literature that Castiglioni first inspires remains with Queen Elizabeth and even develops throughout her reign. A letter from the language teacher, Iacopo Castelvetro, to his friend Lodovico Tassoni, secretary to Duke Alfonso II in the Ferrarese fiefdom of Modena, written in June 1584, demonstrates the Queen's fondness for one particular contemporary Italian poet:

Nè mi resta altro caldamente pregarla di favorirmi di scrivermi, se il povero Tasso vada tuttavia componendo cosa alcuna, o no: che Vostra Signoria sappia, che un illustre cavaliere me l'ha domandato, dicendo che Sua Maestà gli ha imposto d'informasene; e componendo egli cosa che vaglia, mi farebbe un segnalatissimo favore a mandarmene un esempio, onde ne la prego quanto più posso e so, assicurandola che questa reina non stima meno avventuroso il Serenissimo nostro Duca per avere cotesto gran poeta cantate le sue loda, che sì facesse Alessandro Achille, per avere egli avuto il grande Omero; e mi dicono che ella ne sappia di già molte stanze a mente.[22]

(There only remains for me to ask you warmly to do me the favour of telling me whether the unfortunate Tasso is still composing anything, or not: you should know that an illustrious knight has asked me about it, saying that her Majesty ordered him to find out; and, if he is producing anything worthwhile, you would be doing me a most conspicuous service by sending me an example, so I beseech you to my utmost, assuring you that this queen does not regard His Highness our Duke any less fortunate to have had his praises sung by this great poet than Alexander the Great did Achilles for having had the great Homer to praise him; and I'm told that she already knows many stanzas by heart.)

Queen Elizabeth has apparently memorised stanzas of Tasso's *Gerusalemme liberata* (1581) within a couple of years of its first printing, and evidently knows about the unfortunate poet's prolonged confinement in the hospital of St Anna by the Duke of Ferrara.

Another prominent female student of Italian is Mary Herbert, the sister of the celebrated knight possibly entrusted with discovering more about Tasso's activities by the queen, Sir Philip Sidney. The Countess of Pembroke also translates part of Petrarch's *Trionfi*, but her skilful and highly accurate version of the entire *Trionfo della Morte*, probably dating from the early 1590s, demonstrates an expertise in Italian well beyond the level of an early language-learning exercise. The young Mary Sidney may benefit uniquely from the attentions of a female language tutor, as the Penshurst accounts record a payment to a 'Mistress Maria, the Italian', in 1572–73, when her older brother Philip is setting off on his extensive tour of Europe. Katherine Duncan-Jones suggests that the Sidney family employ another Italian 'Lodovico' (though not Lodowick Bryskett, who is travelling with Philip) as tutor to Mary's younger sister Ambrosia in the same period.[23]

Whichever of these two Italians is responsible for Mary Sidney's initial instruction in their native tongue, it is clear that she is both fluent in it and an able translator from it by the time Samuel Daniel dedicates the first edition of his sonnet sequence *Delia* to her in 1592. Daniel's successful appeal to the Countess of Pembroke for patronage, and his subsequent prominence among the group of poets connected to Wilton House, is founded partly on their shared knowledge of the Italian language and a profound interest in its literary traditions. The two poets are also at the forefront of a concerted attempt in the late sixteenth century to naturalise some of these major Italian literary forms into English prosody. Daniel and his patron are keen to demonstrate in their work, by using both translation and related techniques of creative imitation, that vernacular poetry in England can bear comparison with the verse of its most illustrious European forebears. This book will strive to demonstrate how the impetus for the fruitful engagement with Italian materials in English poetry and drama at the turn of the seventeenth century can be traced to the very processes by which the same authors encounter the language and its literature in the first place.

Notes

1 John Florio, *Second Frutes* (London, 1591), sig. A4r–v.
2 William A. Wright, ed., *English Works of Roger Ascham* (Cambridge University Press, Cambridge, 1904), p. 226.
3 Wright, *English Works*, pp. 229–30.
4 'Than they haue in more reuerence, the triumphes of Petrarche: than the Genesis of Moses: . . . of a tale in *Bocace*, than a storie of the Bible': Wright, *English Works*, p. 232. The vernacular works of Petrarch and Boccaccio enjoy a new wave of popularity in the decades leading up to Ascham's complaint. The Italian poems in the *Canzoniere* and *Trionfi* are first translated during the reign of Henry VIII, by Sir Thomas Wyatt, Henry Howard, the Earl of Surrey, and Henry Parker, Lord Morley, but it is only in the 1550s that these English versions reach print. The translations of Wyatt and Surrey, mainly from individual sonnets in the *Canzoniere*, appear for the first time in Richard Tottel's miscellany, *Songes and Sonnettes*, printed in 1557, and a further eight times by 1587. Morley's version of *The Tryumphes of Fraunces Petrarcke, translated out of Italian into Englishe*, which dates from the early 1540s, is printed in 1554. The prose tales in Boccaccio's *Decameron* are increasingly available in English versions in the years immediately before Ascham writes *The Scholemaster*. Edward Lewicke's verse translation of the 'History of Titus and Gisippus', a version of which had already appeared in Sir Thomas Elyot's *Boke of the Governor* in 1531, is printed in 1562; his

stories, however, are more popular in prose collections, drawn from a variety of Italian and French sources. William Painter's *The Palace of Pleasure*, printed in two volumes in 1566 and 1567, contains a series of tales translated from Boccaccio, along with others from recently printed Italian works, such as Matteo Bandello's *Novelle* (1554).

5   Wright, *English Works*, p. 230. Ascham makes a notable exception for Hoby's translation of Castiglione's *Il cortegiano*, which is the only Italian book to escape his censure: 'To ioyne learnyng with cumlie exercises, *Conto Baldesaer Castiglione* in his booke, *Cortegiano*, doth trimlie teache: which booke, aduisedlie read, and diligentlie folowed, but one yeare at home in England, would do a yong ientleman more good, I wisse, then three yeares trauell abrode spent in *Italie*. And I meruell this booke, is no more read in the Court, than it is, seyng it is so well translated into English by a worthie Ientleman Syr Th. Hobbie, who was many wayes well furnished with learnyng, and very expert in knowledge of diuers tonges.' Wright, *English Works*, p. 218.

6   Steven Gosson, *Playes Confuted in fiue Actions* (London, 1582).

7   Wright, *English Works*, p. 223.

8   See E. R. Adair, 'William Thomas: a forgotten clerk of the Privy Council' in R. W. Seton-Watson, ed., *Tudor Studies* (Longmans, London, 1924), pp. 133–60. Francis Russell, the second Earl of Bedford, similarly spends two years in Italy in the mid-1550s, during the reign of Queen Mary.

9   Michel Angelo Florio is employed in the household of the Duke of Suffolk in the early 1550s, where he tutors Lady Jane Grey in Italian; a manuscript copy of his *Regole de la Lingua Thoscana* dedicated to her survives in the British Library. There is another copy of his grammar book dedicated to Henry Herbert, the second Earl of Pembroke, in Cambridge. Florio's son John suggests in the dedication of his *First Fruites* (1578) to Robert Dudley, Earl of Leicester, that his father also taught members of the Dudley family, probably during the period of his brother Guilford Dudley's brief marriage to Lady Jane Grey. Castiglioni teaches Italian to Princess Elizabeth from the 1540s onwards. There is no firm evidence that Ubaldini teaches Italian, but he is patronised by Henry Fitzalan, twelfth Earl of Arundel, from 1562.

10 The immigrant French teacher Claude Holyband introduces the parallel-text form in *The French Schoolemaister* (1573). It is first used for Italian in his *Pretie and wittie historie of Arnalt and Lucenda, with certen rules and dialogues for the learner of th' Italian tong* (1575), later revised as *The Italian Schoole-maister*. Henry Grantham's translation of Scipio Lentulo's Latin *Italian Grammer*, which does not contain any parallel dialogues, is printed in the same year by Thomas Vautrollier, who also publishes Holyband's works. John Florio's *First Fruites*, described on the title page as 'a perfect Introduction to the Italian and English Tongues', is printed in 1578.

11 John Florio, *A Worlde of Wordes, or Most copious and exact Dictionarie in Italian and English* (London, 1598), sig.A3v–A4r. Gamberini emphasises this insistent connection between a desire to learn the Italian language and a desire to read the vernacular literature: Spartaco Gamberini, *Lo studio*

INTRODUCTION

   dell'italiano in Inghilterra nel '500 e nel '600 (Casa Editrice G. d'Anna, Messina and Florence, 1970), p. 17 and p. 133.
12 Ascham dies in 1568, and the unfinished *Scholemaster* is published posthumously in 1570.
13 Holyband arrives in England in 1564, and spends almost forty years teaching both French and Italian in London. Florio is born in England in 1552 or 1553, but is taken abroad by his father during the reign of Queen Mary. He returns to live in England at the start of the 1570s, teaching Italian and probably French in both London and Oxford. See Frances A. Yates, *John Florio: The Life of an Italian in Shakespeare's England* (Cambridge University Press, Cambridge, 1934), pp. 1–28, for details of his background and early life.
14 The letter introduces a manuscript translation of the *Ragionamento di Carlo V. Imperatore tenuto al re Philippo suo figliuolo* presented by Castelvetro to the King in Edinburgh in August 1592. The dedication is printed in full in John Purves, 'Fowler and Scoto-Italian Cultural Relations in the Sixteenth Century', *The Works of William Fowler*, iii (John Blackwood and Sons, Edinburgh, 1940), pp. cxxvii–cxxx. King James later recalls to Antonio Foscarini, the Venetian ambassador in London, that Castelvetro taught him Italian for four or five years in Edinburgh.
15 See the account of Florio's influence with the Queen noted by Ottaviano Lotti, the Florentine resident in London, after a meeting with her in January 1611: G. S. Garganò, *Scapigliatura Italiana a Londra sotto Elisabetta e Giacomo I* (L. Battistelli, Florence, 1923), p. 64.
16 Yates, *John Florio*, p. 220.
17 John Pitcher, ed., *Hymen's Triumph by Samuel Daniel* (Malone Society Reprints, Oxford, 1994), p. x.
18 Garganò, *Scapigliatura Italiana*, p. 67.
19 See Kathleen T. Butler, 'Giacomo Castelvetro, 1546–1616', *Italian Studies* 5 (1950), 1–42; p. 42. Castelvetro begins to teach students at Cambridge after he returns to England in December 1612 from Venice, where he was teaching Italian in the household of the English ambassador until his brief imprisonment at the hands of the Inquisition. His release is secured by the personal intercession of the ambassador, Sir Dudley Carleton, and his eminent former pupil, King James. Castelvetro's personal album for 1613, preserved in the British Library, records the names of sixteen private students at the university, half of whom are from King's College.
20 His travelling companion Lodowick Bryskett later recalls the impression that Sidney's excellent French makes: 'He was so admired among the graver sort of courtiers that when they could at any time have him in their company and conversation they would be very joyful, and no less delighted with his ready and witty answers than astonished to hear him speak the French language so well and aptly, having been so short a while in the country.' Lodowick Bryskett, *A Discourse of Civill Life* (1606) in J. H. P. Pafford, ed., *Literary Works of Lodowick Bryskett* (Gregg, Farnborough, 1972), pp. 160–1.
21 Harvey also owns copies of Henry Grantham's translation of Scipio Lentulo's *Italian Grammer*, printed by Vautrollier in 1575, Holyband's *Arnalt*

& *Lucenda* (1575), which he annotates heavily in 1582, William Thomas's *Principal Rules of the Italian Grammar* (1550), and a densely annotated 1561 reprint of the same author's *Historie of Italie* (1549), described as 'a necessarie Introduction to Machiavel, Guicciardin, Jovius'. See Virginia F. Stern, *Gabriel Harvey: A Study of His Life, Marginalia, and Library* (Clarendon Press, Oxford, 1979), p. 237. The Lord Chief Justice, Sir Edward Coke, possesses copies of the same four titles, as well as the 1611 edition of Florio's Italian–English dictionary, revealed in the library catalogue compiled shortly before his death in 1634. See W. O. Hassall, 'A catalogue of the library of Sir Edward Coke', *Yale Law Library Publications* 12 (1950). Henry Percy, the Earl of Northumberland, uses this edition of Florio's dictionary for his Italian studies during his incarceration in the Tower of London, as Gatti has demonstrated by analysing the annotations in his copy of Bruno's *De gli heroici furori* (1585): Hilary Gatti, *The Renaissance Drama of Knowledge: Giordano Bruno in England* (Routledge, London, 1989), pp. 42–3. Batho suggests that the Earl 'employed an Italian reader to assist him in his studies in the Tower', whom Gatti has tentatively identified as Francesco Petrozani: G. R. Batho, 'The library of the "Wizard" Earl of Northumberland, 1564–1632', *The Library* 15 (1960), 246–61; p. 255. The Earl clearly also uses printed manuals for his language studies, as he owns copies of Florio's *Second Frutes*, and Lentulo's *Italian Grammer* (1587).
22 The letter is printed in Angelo Solerti, *La Vita di Torquato Tasso* (Turin and Rome, 1895), ii, pp. 204–5.
23 Katherine Duncan-Jones, *Sir Philip Sidney: Courtier Poet* (Yale University Press, New Haven, 1991), p. 25.

I

'Mie new London Companions for Italian and French': modern language learning in Elizabethan England

THE INTRODUCTION outlined three models for acquiring a sound knowledge of the Italian language in sixteenth-century England. The employment of private language tutors, who are usually native speakers, in royal and aristocratic households begins in earnest in the 1540s with the arrival of a first generation of Italian immigrants in England. The pattern of aristocrats and gentlemen travelling to Italy to gain direct experience of the language and culture, often having studied at home before departure, develops throughout the 1500s, with a marked increase in frequency and the social range of travellers during the final quarter of the century. The seventeenth-century language teacher Giovanni Torriano reveals the continued popularity of these two methods for learning Italian almost a hundred years later: 'Sundry noble men, Earles and Countesses speake admirable well; some of which haue had the master in the house, some haue learnt it in Italy, but in that manner which I intimated before a while.'[1] Torriano's observations are part of a dialogue, printed in parallel Italian and English texts, in which the speakers address the question 'Should a language be learnt in the country itself?' He favours the method of instruction at home before travel, practised by many students from the late sixteenth century onwards. Florio reveals how one of his best pupils, the Earl of Southampton, to whom he dedicates his first Italian–English dictionary, speaks the language well even before he visits Italy in the late 1590s. He praises Southampton and his fellow aristocratic dedicatees' 'studies much in al, most in Italian excellence': 'Being at home so instructed for Italian, as teaching or learning could supplie, that there seemed no need of trauell: and now by trauell so accomplished, as what wants to perfection?'[2] Torriano goes on to focus on the language-learning habits of another prominent group of Italian speakers in seventeenth-century England: 'Besides there are Merchants an infinite number that speake out of hand; tis true that some of them speake vnbeseemingly accordingly as they haue more or lesse made vse of a Master or some good grammer.'[3] Instruction with a professional teacher in this instance would probably involve attendance at one of the private language schools in London, which become popular from the 1570s. The growing numbers of Italian and particularly French immigrants in the Elizabethan period leads to an increased competitiveness in the language-teaching market, with rival schools opening in the capital, and teachers seeking to recruit pupils from among the student populations in Oxford and Cambridge.[4] This competition also gives rise to the most significant development in the field of modern language learning in sixteenth-century England, the third method to which Torriano alludes. The proliferation of printed grammars and practical dialogue books for learning French and Italian in the final three decades of the century permits for the first time the possibility of guided self-study. The far-reaching impact of this phenomenon will form the primary focus of this chapter.

The foundation of language schools in London leads to a limited expansion of the social spectrum of students who have both the desire and the means to learn Italian, reflected in the broader range of English travellers to Italy towards the end of the century.[5] It is, however, the availability in print of language-instruction manuals that has the most immediate effect on opening up the methods of modern language acquisition to a wider reading public. Simonini suggests that 'the use of purposeful language books seems to have been for most Englishmen the most feasible approach to the learning of a foreign tongue',[6] and these books are certainly intended to offer an alternative and even a substitute to the methods of private instruction and travel. One of the short commendatory poems in the *First Fruites*, 'Ri. T. in prayse of Florio his Labour', makes exactly this point with regard to the advantages of book learning over the dangers of foreign travel:

> *If we at home,* Florios *paynes may win,*
> *to know the things, that trauailes great would aske.*

> By opening that, which heretofore hath bin
> a dangerous iourney, and a feareful taske.
> Why then each Reader that this Booke do see,
> Geue Florio thankes, that tooke such paines for thee.

The direct address to the readers of the manual in the poem is more than a formal entreaty, hinting at the significance of their role in the language-learning process. The act of reading itself becomes an essential part of the pedagogical method, as a key dialogue in the *First Fruites* clearly demonstrates. One of the two speakers, an Italian who has been resident in England only for a year, explains how he has acquired his English, having not understood a word of it when he arrived:

> How haue you done to learne to speake English so soone?
> I haue learned English by reading.
> May a man learne a language so soone, by reading?
> Yes sir, a man may learne it.[7]

Florio's first manual is intended primarily as a means for English men to learn Italian, but its parallel-text format allows it to be used equally by Italians wishing to acquire some English, as the letter 'A tutti i Gentilhuomini, e Mercanti Italiani, che si dilettano de la lingua Inglese' indicates. At the end of the *First Fruites* Florio includes sections on the pronunciation of both Italian and English, but these are certainly supplementary to the dialogues themselves. Even if the Italian character in the earlier dialogue has learnt to *speak* English by reading, the interlocutors in Florio's section on Italian grammar ('*Necessarie Rules*, for *Englishmen* to learne to reade, speake, and write true Italian') seem to place the ability to speak the language accurately below the successful acquisition of a reading knowledge of it:

> Truly sir, the profit which I haue reaped from out of the pleasant conceites of your Dialogues, is such, as would you but prescribe some perfect methode, for the true pronuntiation of the Italian tongue, as you have already induced me into a direct course, for the true interpretation of it (certainely) you should not onely pleasure me, but a great many moe of my Countrymen.[8]

The distinction between the ability to read and understand the language through self-study and the ability to speak it fluently is reinforced by a later Italian teacher, who suggests that students must not neglect an active engagement with the language even if they are unable to practise their oral skills:

> Others because they haue no opportunity to speak, will neglect the vnderstanding part, and such I could wish would imitate their Ancestors who haue translated very good Italian books, who happily could not speak the language.[9]

Torriano not only suggests translation from Italian into English as a suitable method for maintaining and improving language skills but also reveals that certain notable English renderings from Italian were made by translators who could not actually *speak* the language of the original texts. This is a significant revelation for a book which will be concentrating simultaneously on methods of language acquisition and methods of literary imitation from Italian sources, as it removes the necessity to prove that any of the writers to be considered could in fact speak Italian. The ability to understand the language and subsequently to make fruitful use of its literature need be predicated only on acquiring a reading knowledge of Italian.

It is possible to extrapolate from the manuals for both Italian and French a clear idea of the techniques and time frame required to obtain a good reading ability in the modern languages. It is immediately striking that all of the instruction manuals printed from the 1570s onwards employ both the parallel-text format and dialogues on familiar topics. Even if most also include sections on grammar and pronunciation, these often follow rather than precede the dialogues, suggesting an emphasis on practical aspects of the language in use as opposed to a prescriptive focus on matters of grammar alone.[10] This serves to distinguish the teaching of modern languages from the contemporary techniques used to instruct boys in the classical languages at grammar school, which concentrate on instilling a good grammatical sense in the pupil before progressing to any practical language exercises.[11] The methods of instruction for modern languages, however, may have been influenced by an alternative sixteenth-century approach to the teaching of Latin.

A connection between Ascham's *The Scholemaster*, printed posthumously in 1570, and the language manuals is suggested initially by the title of Holyband's first book, *The French Schoolmaister*, probably printed soon after in 1573. The latter is intended as an equivalent for learning French to Ascham's 'plaine and perfite way of teachyng children, to vnderstand, write and speak the Latin tong' as described on the title page of the first edition. In addition to the advice to tutors for 'the priuate brynging up of youth in Ientlemen and Noble mens houses', Ascham indicates that his method is 'commodious also for all such, as haue forgot the Latin tonge, and would, by themselues, without a Scholemaster, in short tyme, and with small paines, recouer a sufficient habilitie to vnderstand, write, and speake Latin'. It is the emphasis on the potential for self-study, even if it is aimed at recovering a prior knowledge of Latin in this instance, which has most resonance for the authors of the modern language manuals. They are also struck by Ascham's marked distaste for the rote learning of Latin grammar practised in schools. Ascham instead recommends the setting of rigorous translation exercises for the student, which are then corrected with reference to the original by the teacher in order to exemplify certain rules of grammar:

> And therefore, we do not contemne Rewles, but we gladlie teach Rewles: and teach them, more plainlie, sensiblie, and orderlie, than they be commonlie taught in common Scholes. For whan the Master shall compare *Tullies* booke with his Scholers translation, let the Master, at the first, lead and teach his Scholer, to ioyne the Rewles of his Grammer booke, with the examples of his present lesson, vntill the Scholer by him selfe, be hable to fetch out of his Grammer, euerie Rewle for euerie Example: ... This is a liuely and perfite waie of teaching of Rewles: where the common waie, vsed in common Scholes, to read the Grammer alone by it selfe, is tedious for the Master, hard for the Scholer, colde and vncumfortable for them bothe.[12]

The absence of the tutor from the learning process in the modern language manuals clearly necessitates an adjustment in method to transmit the tutor's role in a manner appropriate for self-study. The innovative use of the parallel-text dialogue form offers the closest equivalent. The correlation between practical language usage and grammatical exemplification advocated by Ascham can be achieved by constructing dialogues which correspond with the key rules outlined in the sections on grammar printed in the same volume. Giovanni Torriano indicates that this is the intent purpose of the bilingual dialogues printed in his *Italian Tutor, or a New and Most Compleat Italian Grammer*: 'Italian Dialogues, which containe in them the greatest part of the difficulties and knots of the Italian tongue, which after may be resolved and vntied by the help of a good grammer and the treatise of Particles.'[13] It is also clear that these parallel-text passages are intended primarily to offer students the opportunity to practise translation, which becomes as essential an element of the modern language-learning process as it is in Ascham's instructions for Latin. Ascham strongly espouses the method of double translation developed by Johannes Sturm, in which the student first translates a Latin passage, usually taken from Cicero, into English, and then, after an hour's pause, attempts to render his own version back into Latin. There is a contemporary example of this technique being extended to encompass modern language learning. In January 1574 Hubert Languet writes to Philip Sidney in Venice in response to the English traveller's recent enquiry about how to improve the standard of his written Latin:

> You ask me to tell you how you should develop your style. You will do very well, in my opinion, if you carefully read both volumes of Cicero's epistles, not only for the choiceness of his Latin, but also for the weighty matters which those epistles contain; ... Many think that it is most beneficial to select some one epistle and translate it into another language. Next, putting the book aside, translate it back into Latin, and then, taking the book again, see how closely you have approached Cicero's kind of expression.[14]

Sidney replies to his intellectual mentor a couple of weeks later from Padua, revealing how he intends to go a stage further in his language studies by attempting exercises in triple translation to work on either his French or his Italian simultaneously:

> Consilium tuum de stilo hoc modo exequar. Primum aliquam Ciceronis epistolam in Gallicum sermonem vertam, postea ex Gallico in Anglicum et sic iterum in Latinum continuo mota. ... Forsan etiam Italicum eadem exercitatione confirmabo, habeo enim epistolas a Paulo Manutio doctiss⁰ viro in linguam vulgarem traductas, et a quodam alio in Gallicam.
>
> (I shall follow your advice on style in this way: first I shall translate some letter of Cicero's into French, then from French into English, and then back into Latin again by an uninterrupted process. ... Perhaps I shall also improve my Italian with this exercise, for I have a translation of the *Epistles* into the vulgar tongue by the very learned Paolo Manuzio, and into French by someone else.)[15]

The form of translation encouraged in using the manuals is another variation on the method of double translation. John Eliot's letter 'To the Gentlemen Readers, students of the *French tongue*' in his

Ortho-epia Gallica explains precisely how the student should approach the bilingual dialogue texts in order to benefit most from them:

> A good course to take some fruit of this my booke, which if he will learne, he must get the true meaning of the French, conferring it word for word with the English, and when he hath so conferred it, that in reading he doth vnderstand the French well, let him begin after one months progresse a little and a little to lay his hand on the French to hide it, and looking only on the English, trie with him selfe how swiftly he is able to Frenchifie the English, and if he misse, let him reuise and correct himselfe still by his booke, till he be perfect and get some habit of the tongue that way. This I haue learned by long experience to be the readiest way to attaine the knowledge of any language.[16]

Eliot's instructions are intended specifically for English students of French, but are of course equally appropriate for those learning Italian, or indeed for native French and Italian speakers wishing to learn English. All of the Elizabethan language manuals make use of these parallel texts, including one, Holyband's *Campo di Fior* (1583), which prints its dialogues in four languages (Italian, Latin, French, and English) and thus significantly expands the reader's language-learning opportunities, as Sidney endeavours to do with his multilingual exercises in Italy.[17] This technique for using the dialogues can be seen as a deliberate development from Ascham's method in *The Scholemaster*. There the first step is for the master to explain 'the cause, and matter' of the lesson, before he construes and then parses the Latin passage into English for the student, who repeats the process for himself to ensure understanding.[18] The title and description of the dialogues in the manuals fulfil this first stage, and it is then left to the reader to use the parallel translation as the means of 'conferring it [the passage in the original language] word for word with the English'. This careful verbal comparison of the two languages is the equivalent of the acts of construing and parsing, intended both to teach the reader vocabulary and also to familiarise him with important grammatical properties of the language. Eliot envisages the 'conferring' stage continuing for up to a month; repetition is clearly a key element of the process, not merely to help the student to commit words to memory but also to guarantee a fuller understanding.[19]

Once the student has achieved a reading comprehension of the dialogue in the original, he is ready to progress on to translation exercises. The task for the translator using the language manuals omits the initial stage of translation into English in Ascham's model; rather he is expected to pass immediately on to the more difficult level of translation into French or Italian, covering up the dialogue in the target language as he works. By already providing English versions, the authors of the dialogues correspond to the teachers at a more advanced level of instruction; Ascham urges them to offer pupils their own translations from Cicero, which the students must then translate unseen and unaided into Latin:

> And for translating, vse you your selfe, euery second or thyrd day, to chose out, some Epistle *Ad Atticum*, some notable common place out of his Orations, or some other part of *Tullie*, by your discretion, which your scholer may not know where to finde: and translate it you your selfe, into plaine naturall English, and than giue it him to translate into Latin againe: allowyng him good space and tyme to do it, with diligent heede and good aduisement.... Whan he bringeth it translated vnto you, bring you forth the place of *Tullie*: lay them together: compare the one with the other: commend his good choice, & right placing of wordes: Shew his faultes iently, but blame them not ouer sharply.[20]

The teacher's comparison of original and translation to elucidate the successes and errors in the pupil's version can be replicated in the manuals through the reader's self-correction and revision of his translation against the uncovered original dialogue, exactly as Eliot recommends.

The careful composition of the dialogues in many of the manuals allows the authors to build into their translation exercises the next stage of Ascham's pedagogical programme. As the pupil's abilities in translation increase, the teacher should 'begin to teach him, both in nownes, & verbes, what is *Proprium*, and what is *Translatum*, what *Synonymum*, what *Diuersum*, which be *Contraria*, and which be the most notable *Phrases* in all his lecture'.[21] The ability to identify these six points in a given passage is a further way to aid correct word choice in the target language by increasing the student's vocabulary in specific and related fields. The structured use of synonyms, near synonyms and opposites is manifest throughout the most effective language manuals of the period. The opening two chapters of the *First Fruites* demonstrate Florio's conscious use of these pedagogical tools for learning both nouns and verbs. In the first chapter there is a list of seven nouns in Italian to refer to a woman, including synonyms and near synonyms ('*vergine, giouine, ouero massara*'), and the second demonstrates the present, future, and past tenses in operation through the contrary verbs of to love and to hate.[22] Florio apologises in his letter 'Vnto the friendly, curteous, and indifferent Reader' for the apparently random appearance of these dialogues, which he did not expect to be printed. This, however, belies the careful thought that he puts into making the opening dialogues appropriate and useful for the beginner in Italian, with a gradual increase in complexity throughout the manual. Even in the more advanced dialogues of the *Second Frutes* Florio retains the use of related verbal clusters to aid the learner's memory and understanding. The final chapter, the longest in the manual, is constructed entirely around the opposite views on love and women expressed by Silvestro (positive) and Pandolfo (negative), which allows Florio wide scope for the use of synonyms and contraries, particularly adjectives in this instance.[23]

The student who painstakingly follows Eliot's ideal method for the use of parallel texts in the manuals should eventually obtain a fluency in reading in the new language. The heavy emphasis on self-study and repetition in the process, however, clearly proves to be too much for some students. In the *First Fruites* Florio is highly critical of those English gentlemen who are unable to maintain a commitment to their language studies:

> I see certaine Gentlemen rather lownes, to tel the truth, that begyn to learne to spake Italian, French, and Spanish, and when they haue learned two woords of Spanish, three woords of French, and foure wordes of Italian, they thinke they haue yenough, they wyll study no more.
> Think you it be possible, that an Englishman may learne the Italian tongue, & that an Italian may learne the English.
> Yea sir, that it is possible.
> In what tyme thinke you?
> Therafter as he plyeth it; I haue knowen them that haue learned Italian in three monthes.[24]

According to Florio, the keen student can learn a new language in only three months. If using a manual, this would require a month or so 'conferring' the dialogues in both languages, and then a couple of months practising and repeating translations into the target language. It is not clear whether many students managed to achieve fluency in this way in such a limited period of time, but there is at least one contemporary record of a student's frustration at his inability to learn Italian from a manual as quickly as he would like to. The scholar Gabriel Harvey acquires and copiously annotates a copy of the *First Fruites* shortly after its publication in 1578, in which he laments his own lack of facility in the language in comparison to other noted Italian speakers at Queen Elizabeth's court:

> Quomodo Comes Leicestrensis, Dominus Hattonus, Eques Sidneius, multique praeclari Aulici nostrates fluentissime loquuntur Linguam Italicam. Cur non Axiophilus eadem iam iamque dexteritate? Triduo ille J. C. Cur non ego biduo, aut triduo Italus semilatinus? Qui vultum habet Itali, ut aiebat nuper Regina: cur non etiam os, et linguam? Florio quot fecit ex tempore florentes Italos? Me Florio et Tomaso contesti inspirabunt, nobis linguis flagrantem. Hoc age. Ubi amor, ibi oculus . . . Repete, repete; ut fervidus lanista!
>
> (How the Earl of Leicester, Master Hatton, Sir Philip Sidney, and many of our outstanding courtiers, speak the Italian tongue most fluently. Why can Axiophilus [Harvey] not speak it with the same dexterity? In three days he learnt the principles of Roman law; why can he not therefore pick up Italian, which is half Latin, in two or three days? He who has the face of an Italian, as the Queen recently remarked: why should he not also have the mouth, and tongue? Florio, how often have you instantaneously created blossoming Italians? Florio and [William] Thomas in close connection will intensely inspire me with their language. This shall I learn. Where there is love, there does the eye fasten itself . . . Repeat, repeat; as the ardent trainer of a gladiator would do!)[25]

Despite his vain desire to master Italian in a matter of days and the reservations about his linguistic ability, Harvey manages to acquire a competent reading knowledge of the language quite rapidly; according to annotations in his copy of Livy, he has read Machiavelli's *Discorsi* in the original by 1580.[26]

A concerted engagement with the Italian language by means of Florio's manual and William Thomas's *Principal Rules of the Italian Grammar* (1550), as Harvey attempts, would be strongly directed by their particular interest in opening up the broad field of Italian literature to an English readership. Thomas appends to his grammar *A Dictionary for the better understanding of Boccace, Petrarca, and Dante*, facilitating his readers' efforts to confront the greatest writers of the Italian *trecento* in the original language. Florio deliberately introduces his English readers to Ariosto's *Orlando furioso* (1532) in chapter twenty-five of the *First Fruites*, 'Of wrath, with certaine fine sayings of Ariosto, and other Poets', actively encouraging them to seek out and study the celebrated Italian poem:

> Certis this is a braue saying, and learned, did Ariosto write it?
> Yea sir, you may reade it in his woorke that is called, Orlando furioso, at the thirtye song.
> The first tyme that the booke commeth to my hands, I wyl see if it be true.[27]

It is striking, therefore, that Harvey demonstrates some knowledge of Ariosto's epic shortly after reading Florio's dialogue; in April 1580 he refers in a printed letter to his friend Spenser's desire to 'emulate, and hope to ouergoe' the *Orlando furioso* in the nascent *Faerie Queene*.[28]

The chapter contains extensive quotation and Florio's translation of five stanzas of Ariosto's poem, including three on the theme of jealousy from the start of canto thirty-one. The printing of the original and English versions in parallel columns would allow the reader to engage in a series of advanced translation exercises from a literary source. The student can either translate from Italian verse into English by covering up Florio's translation, or from English into Italian using Florio's literal version as a source text, although he makes no attempt to reproduce the rhyme scheme of the *ottava rima* stanza in English. Florio also provides extracts from Petrarch and Alciati in this chapter, and it is a technique that he continues to utilise in the *Second Frutes*. The final chapter of the later manual contains further extracts from both Ariosto and Petrarch, including a substantial quotation and translation from the latter's *Trionfo della Pudicizia*, this time replicating the *terza rima* in English. There is little contemporary evidence of students attempting the more complex task of translation from English back into the original language (as both Eliot and Ascham recommend in their instruction methods, although notably only from prose sources). There are, however, a number of surviving renditions into English verse from Italian which suggest that the exercise of studying and translating literary sources is a widely used means of improving a student's accuracy and fluency in modern languages, employed both in the manuals and by private language tutors. It is a method that has been almost entirely overlooked in critical accounts of sixteenth-century language-learning techniques.

'She drew out her Petracke, requesting him to conster hir a lesson': Petrarch and the Italian sonnet as language-learning tools

The favoured source for these literary translation exercises from Italian is Petrarch, with passages taken from both the *Canzoniere* and *Trionfi*. Lyly's *Euphues and his England* (1580) provides an intriguing demonstration of the use of Petrarch's poetry in the language-learning process. In Lyly's narrative an English woman Camilla has written a letter to her Neapolitan suitor Philautus rejecting his amorous advances. She then has to develop an ingenious plan to deliver the letter to him discreetly: 'This letter *Camilla* stitched into an Italian Petracke which she had, determining at the next coming of *Philautus*, to deliuer it, vnder the pretence of asking some question, or the vnderstanding of some worde.' When Philautus visits her in an arbour shortly afterwards, Camilla manages to pass on the letter to him, despite the presence of other gentlewomen:

> With that she drew out her Petracke, requesting him to conster hir a lesson, hoping his learning would be better for a scholemaister, than his lucke was for a Phisition. Thus walking in the ally, she listned to his construction, who turning the booke, found where the letter was enclosed, and dissembling that he suspected, he saide he would keepe hir petracke vntill the morning, do you quoth Camilla. With yat the Gentlewomen clustred about them both, eyther to hear how cunningly *Philautus* could conster, or how readily *Camilla* could conceiue. It fell out that they turned to such a place, as turned them all to a blanke, where it was reasoned, whether loue came at the sodeine viewe of beautie, or by long experience of vertue, a long disputation was like to ensue, had not *Camilla* cut it off before they could ioyne issue.[29]

Despite Camilla's apparent inability to understand Petrarch in Italian by herself, her trick certainly emphasises the appropriateness of using this particular volume of poetry as the means of concealing a letter of amorous rejection. Philautus' strong feelings of unrequited love clearly align him with the frequently despairing poetic voice of his fellow Italian in Camilla's book. Although Camilla's language lesson is in effect only pretence, the episode in Lyly gives a valuable insight into contemporary practice. In this fictional scenario the teacher is a native Italian speaker resident in England, the pupil a young English gentlewoman, and the text for grammatical construing and philosophical explication a passage chosen from Petrarch's vernacular poetry. Camilla's lesson does not extend as far as the translation of Petrarch into English, but otherwise it bears an uncanny resemblance to the most striking historical example of literature-based language learning in the sixteenth century.

Queen Elizabeth's aptitude in foreign languages, both Classical and modern, is frequently remarked upon. One of the earliest writers to praise Elizabeth's language scholarship is Ascham, who reads Latin and Greek with her as a princess and then again during the first decade of her reign:

> Pointe forth six of the best giuen Ientlemen of this Court, and all they together, shew not so much good will, spend not so much tyme, bestow not so many houres, dayly orderly, & constantly, for the increase of learning & knowledge as doth the Queenes Maiestie her selfe. Yea I beleue, that beside her perfit readines, in *Latin, Italian, French,* & *Spanish,* she readeth here now at Windsore more Greeke euery day, than some Prebendarie of this Chirch doth read *Latine* in a whole weeke.[30]

Ascham's studies with Elizabeth stretch over a period of almost twenty years, but he records that she already has some knowledge of all these languages when he first tutors her in the late 1540s.[31] This indicates that language instruction was already an important part of the education of the teenage princess, and it is evident that personal tutors were employed to teach her the modern as well as Classical languages. The identity of her Italian tutor is revealed in another writer's contemporaneous praise of the Queen's linguistic abilities:

> Dirò ben questo, che fra l'altre sue reali virtu, ella è . . . cosi esperta in diuersi sorti di linguaggi forestieri, che se in tutti fosse nata & nodrita, non potrebbe piu ageuolmente spiegarui in suoi altri concetti. Ma in particolare possede ella ottimamente la nostra piu tersa & piu elegante fauella: di cui suo principal precettore è stato il S. Gio. Battista Castiglioni, hora gentil'huomo della Camera priuata di lei: il quale è cosi ornato di generose maniere, & di cosi nobil & honorate creanze, che meritamente per questo & per lo suo valore è carissimo à cosi gran Reina.[32]

> (I will say this, that among her other royal virtues, she is . . . so expert in a variety of foreign languages, that had she been born and brought up speaking all of them, she would not be able to express her high conceits with any greater fluency. But in particular she speaks per-

fectly our most terse and elegant tongue: for which her principal instructor has been Master Giovanni Battista Castiglioni, who is now a Gentleman of her Privy Chamber. He is so generous and of such noble and praiseworthy manners, that for these and for his valour he deserves to be held in such high esteem by so great a Queen.)

It seems certain that Castiglioni's instruction begins in the 1540s, if Elizabeth has already acquired some Italian before Ascham first meets her in 1548. The Italian's continued favour some twenty years later suggests the positive impression he makes on the young princess. While there is little biographical information about Castiglioni,[33] there is one surviving manuscript that may give a valuable insight into an aspect of his pedagogical method. This is Elizabeth's translation of the first ninety lines of Petrarch's *Trionfo dell' Eternità*. There is no definite evidence to confirm either the date or circumstance of the translation, but it is possible to extrapolate from it a number of factors which suggest that this version has its origin as a language-learning exercise. The passage chosen is from the final poem of the *Trionfi*, in which Eternity finally triumphs over Time itself. Elizabeth, however, translates only the first ninety lines of the poem, which stress the need for God's grace because of the mutability of time and transience of life on earth. Despite Ascham's later complaint in *The Scholemaster* that Italianate Englishmen 'haue in more reuerence, the triumphes of Petrarche: than the Genesis of Moses',[34] this extract does not seem inappropriate from a theological and moral perspective for the scholarly attentions of the princess. There may, however, be more practical considerations to explain Castiglioni's choice of this passage as an appropriate text for a language exercise. Petrarch's ruminations on time display an insistent emphasis on different verb tenses (present, future, and past) and associated vocabulary (today, tomorrow, yesterday) in Italian, which would be essential for any student of the language to master. The task of translation seems designed to reinforce exactly this kind of fundamental linguistic knowledge:

> O mente vaga, al fin sempre digiuna,
> a che tanti pensieri? Un'ora sgombra
> quanto in molt'anni a pena si raguna.
> Quel che l'anima nostra preme e 'ngombra,
> dianzi, adesso, ier, diman, mattino e sera,
> tutti in un punto passeran com'ombra;
> non avrà loco 'fu' 'sarà' ned 'era',

ma 'è' solo, in presente, et 'ora' et 'oggi',
e sola eternità raccolta e 'ntera.
                                    [61–69]

Oh happy wandering mind, aye hungering to the end,
What mean so many thoughts? One hour doth reave
That many years gathred with much ado.
Tomorrow, yesterday, morning and eve,
That press our soul and it encumber so,
Before him pass shade-like at once away,
For *was* or *shall be* no place shall be found
But for the time of *is, now* and today,
Only eternity knit fast and sound.
                                    [60–68][35]

An analysis of this extract from the princess's translation suggests that it may not have been entirely effective as an exercise in language reinforcement: Elizabeth omits certain key verbs and qualifying words in her rendition ('fu', 'dianzi', 'adesso'), largely because of the difficulty of trying to compress the original into English pentameters. Otherwise the translation is an accurate line-by-line account of the Italian, although it does not attempt to reproduce the *terza rima*, substituting simpler alternating rhyming quatrains. This is characteristic of sixteenth-century English renditions from Italian verse, which tend to simplify the original rhyme schemes for a naturally non-rhyming vernacular. In this instance, however, it suggests that the teacher is more interested in examining his pupil's linguistic accuracy than in developing the expression of her poetic facility. Some of the most literally translated passages demonstrate the princess's slightly ponderous phrasing,[36] and there is a marked tendency towards repetition: for example, Elizabeth has already used the verb 'reaves' only ten lines before she chooses it again to render the Italian 'sgombra' in line 61, and the adjective 'wandering' is given twice for different Italian words ('vaga' in line 60 and 'pellegrine' in line 85). This latter example leads to the most revealing aspect of the translation in relation to its origin as a language-learning exercise, the evidence of occasional verbal misunderstanding. The translation of the phrase 'mente vaga' as 'happy wandering mind' indicates clearly that the princess has assumed that the adjective derives from the verb *vagare*, 'to wander'. This is an understandable but false association, however, as 'vaga' actually means 'longing', or in this instance the even stronger 'desiring'. This is implied in the accurate rendering of the rest of the line in English, 'aye hungering to the end', suggesting that the mind's desires must remain unfulfilled in life, and making a nonsense of the additional adjective 'happy' in this context.

A comparison between Princess Elizabeth's literal but limited *Triumph of Eternity* and a later sixteenth-century manuscript translation from the *Trionfi* by another female writer may lend further weight to the argument that this earlier version has its provenance in the language-learning process. In the early 1590s Mary Herbert, the Countess of Pembroke, translates Petrarch's third poem, *Il Trionfo della Morte*, in its entirety.[37] This is another close line-by-line rendition of the original, but one which skilfully sustains the Italian *terza rima* for over three hundred and fifty lines and consistently achieves a fluency in English conspicuously lacking in the previous vernacular translations:

> Theis arte's I us'd with thee; thow ran'st this race
> With kinde acceptance; now sharpe disdaine,
> Thow know'st, and hast it sung in manie a place.
> Sometimes thine eyes pregnant with tearie rayne
> I sawe, and at the sight; Behould he dyes:
> But if I help, saide I, the signes are plaine.
>
> [II, 109–114]

> Questi fur teco miei ingegni e mie arti:
> or benigne accoglienze et ora sdegni
> (tu 'l sai, che n'hai cantato in molte parti),
> ch' i' vidi gli occhi tuoi talor sì pregni
> di lagrime, ch' i' dissi: 'Questo è corso,
> chi non l'aita, sì 'l conosco ai segni'.
>
> [II, 109–114][38]

The impressive precision of Herbert's version in both form and language suggests an origin beyond mere linguistic exercise,[39] intended rather to demonstrate the possibility of reproducing this intricate Italian form successfully in English verse. The introductory remarks to a third manuscript translation, this time of all six *Trionfi* by the Scottish poet William Fowler from the late 1580s, help to reveal the almost patriotic poetic agenda that inspires the later vernacular renderings from this particular Italian source:

> I wes spurred thairby and pricke fordward incontinent be translatioun to mak thame sum what more populare they ar in thair Italian originall; And especiallye when as I perceawed, bothe in French and Inglish traductionis, this work not onelie traduced, bot evin as it war

mangled, and in everie member miserablie maimed and dismembered, besydis the barber grosnes of boyth thair translationis, whiche I culd sett doun by prwrif.[40]

A similarly patriotic note is struck in another English poem adapted from Petrarch in the same period as the Countess of Pembroke's translation. In around 1593 or 1594 Elizabeth Carey, daughter of Sir George Carey, Lord Hunsdon, and Elizabeth Carey, translates two sonnets from Petrarch's *Canzoniere*. In the first of these, 'Ladie adorn'd with all perfection trew', based on Petrarch's sonnet 146, Carey makes telling alterations to the geographical references in the final tercet of the original to stress the wit and learning of her native England:

> full of your name yf that my verses might
> I would have fild Thyle, Tanais, Bactria Nile
> Atlas Olympus Calpe I would haue dight
> but since those thoughtes are vaine I'le them exile
> And fill that land which ever hath byn yet
> the cheifest place for learning & for witte.

> del vostro nome se mie rime intese
> fossin sì lunghe, avrei pien Tyle et Battro,
> la Tana e 'l Nilo, Atlante Olimpo et Calpe.
> Poi che portar non posso in tutte et quattro
> parti del mondo, udrallo il bel paese
> ch' Appennin parte e 'l mar circonda et l'Alpe.
>   [146, 9–14][41]

These translations have recently been discovered in a manuscript in the hand of her tutor, Henry Stanford, leading Katherine Duncan-Jones to suggest that 'they probably formed part of Bess Carey's tuition in Italian'.[42] She also conjectures that Elizabeth's father 'would have been well placed to procure someone of the calibre of John Florio', the foremost Italian tutor of the late sixteenth century, to instruct his teenage daughter.[43] The provenance of the manuscript, however, makes it more likely that Stanford himself is responsible for her tuition in Italian.

Carey's versions of Petrarch demonstrate that the setting of translation exercises from literary sources remains a popular language-learning tool until at least the end of the sixteenth century. The non-native Italian tutor Stanford employs the same method for instructing his young female student as Castiglioni almost fifty years earlier. The only substantial difference is in the choice of the *Can-*

zoniere rather than the *Trionfi* as a source text. If it is Stanford who selects these particular sonnets for his pupil to work on, then there may be both a specific and a general appropriateness in the examples chosen. Duncan-Jones argues that the two poems contain idealised self-portraits of Elizabeth, intended to display her physical, moral, and intellectual accomplishments to the family of her potential husband William Herbert: 'Both sonnets might help to capture the heart of her would-be mother-in-law, the countess of Pembroke, herself a subtle and versatile translator of Petrarch during the 1590s, as well as that of her young son.'[44] In more general terms, the sonnet itself seems especially suited to such translation exercises, given its compact fourteen-line form and transparent structural division into octave and sestet. Even if most English sonnet translations, including Carey's, favour the form of three quatrains and a couplet, it is still possible to reproduce quite naturally the habitual turn in argument after the eighth line in the naturalised English version, and to contain the sense of the original within the parameters of these distinct structural units.

It is striking that in the manuscript Carey's translations are surrounded by careful renditions of four French sonnets by Philippe Desportes, probably made by Stanford himself. Duncan-Jones suggests that these poems may also 'form part of his studies with the teenage Bess Carey, in which he sought to familiarise her with the best of recent French writing'.[45] Certainly one of the sonnets that Stanford translates, 'Pourquoy si folement croyez-vous à un verre', has already been imitated by Samuel Daniel in his sonnet sequence *Delia* (1592), indicating the contemporary popularity of Desportes in England.[46] It is possible, however, that these versions are intended to be used more directly in the language-learning process. The association of Italian and French sonnets in this manuscript strongly hints that literary translation is a prevalent means of instruction for both modern languages. If Stanford is teaching his pupil Italian and French simultaneously, he seems to be choosing examples from the respective sonnet traditions as sources for her linguistic exercises. The very accuracy of his versions of Desportes, in contrast to Carey's freer renderings of Petrarch, may indicate that they are intended to be read and studied by Carey as parallel texts alongside the originals, or even to provide source texts for translation into French at a more advanced level.[47]

The contrast between close translation and looser adaptation discernible in these respective versions of Desportes and Petrarch can be explained also by reference to different stages of the language-learning process. An important element in this attempt to demonstrate the widespread use of literary translation as a means of language acquisition is to make the argument for a fundamental connection between acts of translation and acts of imitation from the same sources. In his influential account of methods of imitation in the European Renaissance, Thomas Greene explains that *'imitatio* was a literary technique that was also a pedagogic method'.[48] *Imitatio* is encouraged at a more advanced stage of the humanist educational programme than translation itself, but it clearly develops out of this earlier process. Pupils should ideally progress on to imitation only after mastering the arts of *translatio* and *paraphrasis*. In the second book of *The Scholemaster* Ascham illustrates how his favoured method of double translation can be related to a series of further linguistic exercises. He rejects the practice of *epitome* out of hand, and expresses reservations about *paraphrasis* and the related practice of *metaphrasis*, but praises *imitatio* as an essential technique for achieving eloquence in a foreign language, particularly 'if yow be borne or brought vp in a rude contrie' with an unsophisticated mother tongue.[49]

Despite Ascham's doubts about the efficacy of *paraphrasis*, it is possible to demonstrate a precise relationship between this practice and the related acts of *translatio* and *imitatio* in the modern language-learning sonnet exercises. The habit of paraphrase, that is rendering a text into words slightly different from the original (either in the same language or in translation), provides a useful means for contemporary writers to mediate between close translation and the freer processes of adaptation and creative imitation. This may account for the relative freedom in Elizabeth Carey's rendering of sonnet 146, even if it is still a direct product of her language instruction.[50] It certainly helps to illuminate the practice of William Drummond in the composition of his sonnets.[51] A series of translations from two Italian sonnets in the Hawthornden manuscripts clearly shows the process by which Drummond gradually strives to distance himself from the original poems through a number of distinct steps. After copying out the two sonnets in Italian, one by Antonio Tebaldeo and the other by Pietro Bembo, Drummond first translates them 'In the same sort of rime', offering an accurate line-by-line account of the originals. He moves on to translations 'In frier sort of rime', substituting couplets for the Italian rhyme scheme, before progressing on to a third version 'Paraphrasticalie translated'. These final renderings display a greater freedom from their originals in terms of both form and verbal content.

Drummond's paraphrastic translation of Tebaldeo's sonnet 'O chiome, parte de la treccia d'oro' is the most interesting poem, as it shares characteristics with many of the sonnets printed in the first part of the *Poems: by W. D.* in 1616. Drummond favours the anglicised form of the sonnet, but for some of his poems he develops a unique version of the three-quatrain and couplet pattern, in which at least one quatrain is alternately rhymed while the remainder retain the Italian construction, where the first line rhymes with the fourth line of the quatrain. This is the case with Drummond's final rendering of Tebaldeo's sonnet (*ababcddceffegg*), which suggests that other printed sonnets in an equivalent form, such as sonnets I and VIII, may share their genesis in this process of conscious distancing from a specific source.

Paraphrastic translation also permits a greater poetic individuality to emerge, as the translator is not tied to reproducing an exact equivalent for all the words of the original text. In his third version of Tebaldeo's poem Drummond drops the image of the poet-lover as a bird trapped in the net of the beloved's hair ('il laccio, oue fui colto / Qual semplice augelletto' [2–3]), and adds references to the lady as a jewel and a flower (both a rose and 'vorlds lilie among violets' [4]).[52] While neither of these innovations is remotely original in sonnet literature, there is a third addition that is more characteristic of Drummond's poetic preferences. Ronald Jack argues that one of the fundamental similarities between Drummond and the Italian poet whom he imitates most frequently, Giambattista Marino, is that 'they even share an interest in mythology, at a time when conceits thus based were going out of fashion'.[53] Drummond's invented reference to Midas' golden touch to describe the beloved's blonde hair ('twitchet by Midas hand / In curling knots' [1–2]) strikes a note of individuality in this looser adaptation of Tebaldeo's sonnet. The deliberate movement away from the original by means of a series of progressively freer renderings in this example demonstrates the important connection between an act of translation and an act of imitation from the same source, mediated through linguistic paraphrase.

Although such mythological references might be out of date by the second decade of the seventeenth century, Drummond's marked fondness for them links him with a major English sonneteer of the 1590s with whose work he is certainly familiar. Samuel Daniel's *Delia*, first printed in an authorised edition early in 1592, is noteworthy both for its careful construction from a plethora of Italian and French sources and for its range of mythological allusions. Often, as with Drummond's reference to Midas, these allusions are Daniel's own interpolations into sonnets with clear European sources. In sonnet XV ('If that a loyall hart and faith vnfained'), which is constructed from Petrarch's sonnet 224 and Desportes' translation of it in *Les Amours de Diane*, Daniel inserts a reference to the poet-lover's 'Vultur-gnawne hart' [8], alluding to the punishment of both Prometheus and Tityus in Hades. In the following sonnet, 'Happie in sleepe, waking content to languish', Daniel invents an allusion to 'the *Hydra* of my cares renuing' [9]. This poem first appears among the twenty-eight sonnets by Daniel appended to Thomas Newman's unauthorised edition of *Astrophil and Stella* in 1591, and it is significant as the only early sonnet to be derived solely from an Italian source. Daniel's opening clearly registers his indebtedness to Petrarch's sonnet 212, 'Beato in sogno et di languir contento', which is sustained through the first five lines of the poem:

> Happy in sleep; waking, content to languish;
> Embracing clouds by night; in day time mourn;
> All things I loathe save her and mine own anguish;
> Pleased in my heart moved to live forlorn.
> Nought do I crave but love, death, or my lady.
>
> [1591, 1–5][54]

Daniel, however, does not translate line for line, but transposes elements from the Italian sonnet. Daniel delays Petrarch's memorable image of chasing the summer breeze ('seguir l'aura estiva' [2]) until the third quatrain, and instead brings forward references to night and day and the poet-lover's perpetual anguish to emphasise them at the beginning of the poem:

> Cieco et stanco ad ogni altro ch' al mio danno,
> il qual dì et notte palpitando cerco,
> sol Amor et Madonna et Morte chiamo.
>
> [212, 9–11]

(Blind and weary to everything except my harm, which I trembling seek day and night, I call only Love and my Lady and Death.)[55]

Daniel chooses to ignore Petrarch's reference to pursuing a lame ox in the second quatrain, substituting the more vivid image of the many-headed Hydra of his cares. He returns directly to Petrarch's second tercet, however, to construct the time-conscious lament of his final couplet:

Weep hours! grieve days! sigh months! and still mourn yearly!
This must I do because I love her dearly.
                                          [1591, 13–14]

Così venti anni, grave et lungo affanno,
pur lagrime et sospiri et dolor merco.
            [212, 12–13]

(Thus for twenty years – heavy, long labour – I have gained only tears and sighs and sorrow.)[56]

It is necessary to stress the full extent of Daniel's borrowings from Petrarch in his original version of the sonnet for two related reasons. Daniel is a careful reviser of all of his poetry, and this particular sonnet exists in three significantly different forms. The revisions that Daniel makes to the poem from the 1591 version up until its appearance in the third edition of *Delia* in 1594 show a perceptible movement away from specific indebtedness to Petrarch's sonnet. This has led to certain misapprehensions about how Daniel approaches his sonnet sources. Richard Adamany refers to this sonnet as a prime example of Daniel's habit of 'borrowing single lines from a source and then departing completely to write a sonnet which in no way resembles the source'.[57] While this may be a fair description of the sonnet as it appears in the 1594 edition of *Delia* and the *Works* folio of 1601, it seriously misrepresents the earlier versions of the poem and Daniel's technique in relation to his Italian source. Daniel's revisions have the simultaneous effect of distancing the sonnet from its immediate source and creating a more obvious structural cohesion to the poem in its final form. The couplet is altered for the edition of 1592 ('Waile all my life, my griefes do touch so neerely, / And thus I liue, because I loue her deerely' [13–14]),[58] thus burying the allusion to Petrarch's second tercet. This process is taken a stage further in the 1594 edition, where lines 3 to 5 are completely reworked:

> My joyes but shadowes, touch of truth my anguish,
> Griefes ever springing, comfortes never borne:
> And still expecting when she will reles
>   [1594, 3–5][59]

Even if the 'shadowes' of line 3 play on the double sense of Petrarch's 'ombre' (still rendered as 'cloudes' in the unchanged second line), these alterations consciously remove any other traces of the Petrarchan original, replacing them with internal allusions. The 'griefes' and 'touch' of the first quatrain are now echoed in the couplet, and the description of these griefs and sorrows as 'ever springing' [4] and 'new-borne' [10] amplifies the retained reference to the Hydra-like cares of line 9. Dennis Mitchell describes the final version of sonnet XVI as 'a free adaptation of *Canzoniere*, 212, which it follows only in general outline and in the wording of a few verses'.[60] This detailed analysis of the different versions of Daniel's poem, however, is intended to show an initially much closer correspondence between the two, and to stress that it is only through a process of careful revisions that Daniel produces a structurally satisfying and coherent sonnet, independent of its original model. The successive alterations traceable in the printed versions of the poem demonstrate a technique for approaching and handling Italian sources that can be compared with Drummond's multiple translations of Italian sonnets, where a close act of linguistic assimilation is superseded by a series of progressively freer adaptations.

Drummond's heading for his versions of Tebaldeo's poem in the Hawthornden manuscript helps to illuminate another important aspect of his compositional practice that is shared with Daniel, and which develops out of the insistent focus on parallel-text reading in the language-learning process. While Drummond acknowledges Bembo's authorship of 'Si come suol, poi che 'l verno aspro e rio', the second sonnet in the manuscript, it seems that he is unaware of the author of the other poem, which is described in French as a 'sonnet qu'un poet Italien fit pour un bracelet de cheveux qui lui auoit estè donnè par sa mistresse'.[61] This description is taken directly from the sixth book of Etienne Pasquier's *Les Recherches de la France*, printed for the first time in the expanded edition of 1607. In chapter seven the author considers 'si la Poesie Italienne a quelque advantage sur la Francoise', and he reproduces Tebaldeo's sonnet with a prose summary, an imitation by Desportes, and his own verse translation of it, to suggest that there is no qualitative difference between poetry in the two languages. Drummond records that he reads Pasquier's *Recherches* in 1609, and it is certainly via this book that he encounters both the Italian sonnets that he chooses to translate. Pasquier also prints Bembo's sonnet along with his own prose and verse translations of it and two other verse renderings, by Ronsard and de Baif respectively. Significantly the Scottish poet's access to his Italian material in this instance is clearly mediated through a specific French source.

Drummond's attempts to learn Italian begin in earnest soon after in 1610, and are usually conducted by means of parallel-text reading with the aid of either English or French translations. It is likely that his versions of these Italian sonnets form a simultaneous part of his language studies. Although Pasquier prints various renditions of each poem in French verse, it is striking that they all maintain the Italian sonnet form. The formal experiments in Drummond's progressive versions are thus his innovation. Drummond knows French before he begins to study Italian, but it becomes evident that the poet is not using only the French texts as sources for his versions. The translations of Tebaldeo's poem demonstrate his direct understanding of the original. He renders the Italian 'semplice augelletto' [3] as 'simple bird' and then 'sillie bird', which are both closer than Pasquier's prose version ('petit oyseau'), as are the renderings of 'aspra fortuna' [11] as 'cursed Fortune' and 'il divin choro' [8] as 'Heavens quire'.[62] Neither of the French sonnets translates these phrases literally.

Drummond's ability to read the Italian and French versions simultaneously allows him to incorporate elements from both into his translations, particularly in the freer adaptations. Thus 'the net' and 'murthering dart' [9] that the innocent deer fails to fear in Drummond's second version are closer to Ronsard's 'rets' and 'un trait meurtrier' [11] than Bembo's original 'saetta, o d'altro inganno' [9]. The description of the deer in his first version as 'secure and solitar' [6], however, combines Bembo's original 'secura' [7] with Ronsard's more felicitous 'seul, et seur' [5].[63] For the paraphrastic translation of Bembo's sonnet Drummond's added emphasis on the change of season at the start of the poem develops out of the imagery of Ronsard's opening:

> As the yong hart, when sunne with goldin beames
> Progressith in the first post of the skie,
> Turning old vinters snowie haire in streames.
> [1–3]

> Comme un Chevrueil, quand le Printemps destruit
> Du froid Hyver la poignante gelée.
> [1–2][64]

If Ronsard provides the direct inspiration, his image is not slavishly reproduced in Drummond's version: the personification of Winter, whose icy hair is melted by the force of the sun, adds another dimension to Spring's thawing power. The French adaptation of the Italian original becomes a starting point for a more elaborate image in the final English version. This can be demonstrated further by reference to Pasquier's verse rendering of Tebaldeo's sonnet, where the image of the bird trapped in a net is dropped in favour of an image of the Gordian knot. Similarly, in his paraphrastic rendering of the same poem Drummond excises the image of the bird, to replace it with an alternative Classical allusion, that of Midas' golden touch. For each of these translations from an original Italian source, Drummond enriches his final and least literal version with material derived from intermediary French adaptations. The proximity of the Italian and French sonnets in Pasquier's volume demonstrates that, rather than favouring a source in one language over the other, this process of translation is accomplished most fruitfully by an equal engagement with both languages simultaneously.

There is a substantial body of contemporary evidence to suggest that William Drummond is not unique in his approach to translation. Indeed, one of the principal aims of this book is to demonstrate that the concurrent use of sources in different languages in acts of translation and imitation is a widespread phenomenon that develops quite naturally from the emphasis on parallel-text study in methods of language instruction. The following chapter will elaborate on this in an analysis of the complex genesis of Daniel's sonnet sequence *Delia* from its many Italian and French sources. It is also a habit discernible in prose translations of the late sixteenth century. Multilingual parallel reading is actively encouraged in both language manuals and certain literary texts printed in the 1580s, and this is reflected in the technique of various prose translators. In Holyband's *Campo di Fior* (1583) the dialogues are printed in parallel columns in four languages (Italian, Latin, French, and English), allowing readers to study any one of these languages with reference to their mother tongue, but also, if they wish, to read comparatively across all the texts. In 1588 John Wolfe publishes a trilingual edition of *Il Cortegiano*, with Castiglione's Italian original printed in parallel with Hoby's English translation and Chappuys' French version; the format is clearly designed to permit similar permutations of either two-way or three-way comparative reading.

While the proximity of the multilingual texts in these examples is deliberate, translators are often quite active in creating opportunities for such comparative reading as an important element of their own work. Frequently this involves close consideration of versions of the source in two languages simultaneously (usually the original and a translation, although not necessarily prioritising the former over the latter). One such example is George Pettie's English version of Guazzo's *La civil conversatione*, printed in 1581, which is ostensibly 'translated out of French'. However, John Lievsay's painstaking comparisons of the texts in all three languages 'indicate that even when he [Pettie] was working from Chappuys' text he had the Italian before him. He was alert enough, also, to catch and correct an occasional error in the French.'[65] Chappuys' 1579 French translation uses only the first edition of Guazzo (1574), so Pettie turns as well to the revised version in Italian, printed in 1580, to fill in many of the passages necessarily absent from the French, which are then clearly demarcated in his printed text:

> Gentle readers, I have supplied divers thinges out of the Italian original, whiche were left out by the French translator, with what judgment, I referre to your judgement. I have included the places within two starres, as you may see throughout the Booke.[66]

Pettie's thoroughness requires a meticulous comparison of the French and Italian texts in order to construct his complete English version. It also demonstrates his ability to translate directly from the Italian, even if fundamentally he prefers to work from the French, because of a greater fluency in that language. Pettie's linguistic preference, however, does not preclude a concurrent engagement with both Chappuys and Guazzo in the process of translation.

Pettie's technique is replicated later in the 1580s in Samuel Daniel's first published work. His *Worthy Tract of Paulus Iovius*, printed in 1585, is nominally a translation of Giovio's Italian *Dialogo dell' Imprese Militari et Amorose* (1555), although Joseph Kau argues that Daniel's version is closer to Vaquin Philieuil's French translation of 1561. Daniel certainly knows this edition, as he uses the supplementary material by Domenichi and Simeoni printed with it in his final chapter.[67] Daniel, however, who is already firm friends with Florio from their days at Oxford, is likely to approach these source texts comparatively, even if his principal use of the French suggests a greater confidence in that language than in his Italian at this stage. An analysis of Daniel's methods of assimilating European sources for his poetry in the late 1580s and early 1590s will demonstrate his sustained comparative approach. It will also emphasise his increasing fluency in both the Italian language and its literary forms, and an eventual reversal of the linguistic preferences deducible in this early prose translation.

The pattern of using more than source concurrently in English prose translations of the 1580s is also evident in contemporary Scottish practice. In his analysis of late sixteenth-century imitations from the Italian in Scotland Jack identifies 'the first problem in tackling a Jacobean adaptation' as trying to ascertain 'whether or not intermediary sources were used'. He goes on to suggest that 'research into translations made by the Castalians nearly always shows a detailed awareness of any earlier works'.[68] His chosen example is William Fowler's verse rendering of Petrarch's *Trionfi*, but his argument is equally applicable to prose translation. Fowler's partial manuscript translation of Machiavelli's *Il Principe*, probably dating from the 1590s, utilises both a French and occasionally a Latin version in addition to the Italian original: 'Fowler continues his multilingual pursuits by producing a Scots version of an Italian text, while relying on French and Latin translations.'[69] It is perhaps surprising, given his explication of Fowler's comparative method of translation, that Jack does not entertain the possibility that John Stewart of Baldynneis uses a similar technique in his adaptation of Ariosto's *Orlando furioso* in the 1580s.[70] After establishing Stewart's indebtedness to Desportes' French *abbregement* of the poem, Jack debates whether 'the primary source may very well be Ariosto himself' or either of two full French translations, both of which 'are so close to Ariosto that it would be very difficult to establish whether an author was employing them rather than translating directly'.[71] The likeliest answer would seem to be a third alternative: that Stewart works with Ariosto in both Italian and French, in addition to Desportes' adaptation, to construct his Scots version.

The potential advantages of a simultaneous use of a source in two languages are clear, as it offers the translator the opportunity for elucidation of obscure words or passages and an increased range of verbal choice, stemming from occasional variant readings between the original and the translation. This habit of close comparative reading, however, may have its origins in a more practical element of the language-learning process. Before the advent of dictionaries and grammar books for both Classical and modern tongues, learning a new language often involved by necessity the careful study of parallel texts in two languages. Greene explains how in fifteenth-century Italy 'Greek was generally learned by the arduous comparison of facing Latin translations, usually those done by Theodore of Gaza'.[72]

'WHO THE DEVIL TAUGHT THEE SO MUCH ITALIAN?'

A version of this technique obviously persists in the modern language-learning manuals of late sixteenth-century England, where the new language is ideally learnt by a careful comparison with the dialogues in the mother tongue. In Greene's example, however, an intermediary language is used in the process (Italian scholars learning Greek through their prior knowledge of Latin), and this model also affects later techniques for the learning of modern languages. The final section of this chapter will trace in detail the progress of Drummond's studies in Italian in the early seventeenth century, in order to illustrate his persistent use of an intermediary language (French), and equally to emphasise the profound impact that this language-learning method has on the associated techniques of translation and literary imitation apparent in Drummond's poetry.

'Italien bookes red by me': William Drummond's Italian studies

Drummond provides the most illuminating early seventeenth-century example of modern language learning through the medium of a strong literary interest. It is possible to reconstruct quite accurately both the method and the progress of Drummond's acquisition of European romance languages, thanks to his bequest of books and manuscripts to the library of the University of Edinburgh in 1627. Among his personal manuscripts are a catalogue of his library collection, compiled in 1611, and an invaluable annual list of everything that he reads between the years 1606, when he leaves Hawthornden for a visit to London and France, and 1614. It is in these years that the literary tastes so evident in the sources for his first collection of poetry, *Poems: by W. D.*, printed in 1616, are formed and nurtured. The 1611 catalogue clearly displays Drummond's interest in modern languages: over twenty per cent of the 546 titles are printed in French, and a further eleven per cent are in Italian.[73] It also suggests that he begins to collect books seriously on his visit to London and France between 1606 and 1608: of the sixty or so Italian titles in his 1611 library, eighteen are purchased by Drummond in London, a further thirty-nine in Paris, and only two subsequently in Edinburgh.[74] MacDonald's identification of almost 1,400 items in the collection at the time of Drummond's bequest to Edinburgh University in 1627 demonstrates that the number of both French and Italian books has nearly doubled in the intervening period.[75] There are twice as many French titles as

Italian ones, but this does not necessarily imply a significantly greater interest in contemporary French literature, as there are some twenty-five translations from Italian works amongst the French books.

The presence of these translations suggests that Drummond's knowledge of Italian literature is initially mediated through his knowledge of the French language, and a closer examination of his manuscript reading lists confirms this. There are no titles in either French or Italian among the predominantly English books that he reads while in London in 1606, although his perusal of Hoby's translation of *Il Cortegiano* (1561) and Pettie's version of Guazzo's *La civil conversatione* (1581) demonstrates an interest in the Italian courtesy book tradition. The first French titles appear in the list for 1607, which Drummond spends in Paris and Bourges, where he has evidently developed his understanding of French sufficiently to be able to read fluently. It is striking, though, that virtually half of these French titles are translations from other languages; thus, he reads a version of *Diana* from Montemayor's Spanish, and three translations from the Italian: Tasso's pastoral *Aminta*, Sannazaro's *Arcadia*, and Gelli's *Circe*.[76] This is a pattern that continues over the following couple of years, when French translations, such as Herberay's *Amadis de Gaule* and Belleforest's versions of Bandello in *Histoires Tragiques*, are read along with original French works. By 1609, when he is back at Hawthornden, Drummond's reading in French has become increasingly literary in its focus; in this year he tackles du Bartas, Rabelais, Passerat, Jodelle, and a significant part of Ronsard's poetry, including his epic *La Franciade*, in the original.

Drummond also turns his attention to the sixteenth-century Italian epic in the same year, albeit still by means of translation. He reads *Le Roland furieux* in French, which is probably Chappuys' verse translation of Ariosto's *Orlando furioso*, but which could also be Desportes' *Roland Furieux, imitation de l'Arioste*; he reads Ariosto in English too, presumably in Sir John Harington's translation of the entire poem, printed in 1591. It is through an English translation that he also becomes acquainted with Tasso's *Gerusalemme liberata*, reading Edward Fairfax's *Godfrey of Bulloigne*, printed in 1600, for the first time in 1609. It is a book with which Drummond is to become far more familiar during the next twelve months.

It is in 1610 that Drummond first focuses his attention fully on the Italian *language*. If he learns his French in France in 1607 and 1608,[77] then his method of learning Italian is entirely different. He never visits Italy, and his impressive knowledge of the language seems to have been gained alone in his library at Hawthornden. Drummond possesses an Italian grammar, printed in French and bought in Paris in 1607,[78] and a copy of Holyband's parallel-text dialogue and grammar book *The Italian Schoole-maister*, printed in 1597, both of which are recorded in the 1611 catalogue. He also owns a copy of Florio's Italian–English dictionary, *A Worlde of Wordes* (1598), although this book is not in the 1611 list, which suggests that Drummond is not using it to assist his Italian reading as early as 1610. His method of reading is exactly that encouraged by Italian language teachers such as Florio and Holyband.[79] Drummond's reading in 1610 is conducted almost exclusively by means of multilingual parallel texts. It is immediately striking that many of the Italian works that he tackles in this year have already been read in translation in the previous two years; thus Sannazaro's *Arcadia*, Bembo's *Gli Asolani* and Tasso's *Aminta* are all read alongside French translations with which Drummond is already familiar. There is no separate Italian edition of Tasso's play recorded amongst Drummond's books, which strongly suggests that the French version of *Aminta* in his library, which is now lost, is Belliard's translation, printed in parallel with the original Italian text in Rouen in 1598.[80]

There are other Italian books studied in 1610, which have not already been read in translation, but the method of approaching these texts is identical. Thus, Drummond reads for the first time Guarini's *Il pastor fido* in both Italian and French, as well as the first part of the vernacular poems in Petrarch's *Canzoniere*, alongside a recent French translation of them.[81] The only Italian book not to be studied in parallel form in this year is Lucrezia Marinella's *Arcadia felice* (1605), which appears to be the first text that Drummond reads in the original Italian without the aid of a translation.[82]

The single most interesting Italian book that is read in the original language in 1610 is Tasso's epic poem, *Gerusalemme liberata*. Drummond first reads Fairfax's translation of Tasso in the previous year, and it becomes evident that he turns repeatedly to *Godfrey of Bulloigne* when he attempts to read Tasso in Italian, as his copy of Fairfax is one of the most densely annotated books in the entire library. His reading list for this year notes that Drummond also reads Tasso in Latin and French,[83] but it is with the aid of the English translation that he carefully works his way through the Italian text. MacDonald registers eleven characteristic types of annotation in Drummond's copy of

Fairfax,[84] and the two most frequent strongly suggest that the reader is actively working with the English and Italian texts open in front of him simultaneously.[85] In the most common type of annotation Drummond records what is introduced by the English translator, what he omits from the Italian text, and where he differs markedly from Tasso. The next most frequent type of annotation is more of a value judgement, indicating where Drummond thinks that Fairfax improves upon or falls short of Tasso's Italian in his rendering, but this again requires a detailed, simultaneous knowledge of both texts and languages.

Another recurrent type of annotation in Drummond's copy of *Godfrey of Bulloigne* demonstrates how the reader also sees beyond the parallel texts directly before him. Drummond frequently records instances of literary indebtedness, and notes other authors' uses of identical or similar stories in the margins of the book. This kind of broad comparative reading indicates that the scholarly study of the foreign sources for English literature, so popular at the turn of the nineteenth century, was already an important aspect of contemporary reading habits by the start of the seventeenth century. For example, in the seventh canto of Fairfax's translation, Drummond registers the similarity between Tasso's old shepherd in Erminia's pastoral interlude and Spenser's Meliboe in Book VI of *The Faerie Queene*, who offers Calidore the same pastoral respite in canto IX. Spenser's poem is, slightly incongruously, listed as another of the 'Italien bookes' that Drummond reads in 1610. This may suggest, however, that he is approaching the English epic through the lens of the two Italian epics to which Spenser specifically alludes in the *Letter of the Authors... To the Right Noble and Valorous Sir Walter Raleigh*, printed in the 1590 edition of the poem. His close examination of Tasso in the same year, and his perusal of two translations of Ariosto in the previous one, would make the Scot supremely qualified to appreciate Spenser's extensive use of *both* Italian epics, as he works his way carefully through *The Faerie Queene*.

Drummond's copy of Tasso in Italian also contains some significant marginal annotations. MacDonald lists the copy of *Gerusalemme liberata* from the library as missing, but it has subsequently resurfaced in a private collection. Richard Hatchwell has discovered a copy of the *Goffredo, overo Gierusalemme Liberata*, printed in Venice in 1593, which contains Drummond's signature on the title page. The signature is interesting in that it seems to have been written over the name of a previous owner of the book. Hatchwell suggests that this was the poet Francis Davison, and that the hundred and fifty or so marginal annotations in the copy are in his hand, rather than Drummond's.[86] Davison is another noted Italianist, who spends two years in Italy between 1595 and 1597,[87] where he probably obtains the 1593 edition of Tasso. It is uncertain how or when the book passes into the possession of Drummond, but if it is, as seems probable, the copy of Tasso that he is using in 1610, then this reveals some important connections between Drummond, Davison, and the other English poet referred to in these annotations.

On four occasions in his marginal notes Davison mentions 'Daniels Rosamonde', clearly alluding to Samuel Daniel's *The Complaint of Rosamond*, and each time he registers the English poet's indebtedness to Tasso's Italian.[88] Daniel's poem is first printed in 1592 in the same volume as the *Delia* sonnet sequence. It is striking that, while modern criticism has attempted to record the manifold Italian sources for Daniel's sonnets,[89] the borrowings from Tasso that Davison discovers almost immediately in *The Complaint of Rosamond* have remained unnoticed by critics for four hundred years.[90] Drummond is in a good position to appreciate both the perspicacity of Davison's observations, having already read in 1609 Daniel's *Works* folio of 1601, containing both *Delia* and *Rosamond*, and Davison's admiration for the poet recorded in his *Poetical Rhapsody* of 1602, which he reads in the same year. This high regard is clearest in Davison's poem 'To *Samuel Daniel* Prince of English Poets', in which Daniel assumes the laurel crown from the recently deceased monarch Spenser. It is also evident in one of his madrigals (*Vpon her hiding her face from him*), which opens with an imitation of Daniel's second *Delia* sonnet:

> Goe wayling Accents, goe,
> With my warm teares & scalding teares attended,
> To th' Author of my woe,
> And humbly aske her, why she is offended.
> [1–4][91]

Many of Davison's poems in the *Poetical Rhapsody* display his own borrowings from Italian verse, and from the madrigals of Luigi Groto in particular, and it is likely that his high opinion of Daniel is partly founded on their shared interest in Italian literature. Drummond is another poet who constitutes part of the early seventeenth-century community of interest in Italian literary forms, and he is certainly influenced in this respect by the prior examples of both Daniel and

Davison. A version of one of Daniel's best-known sonnets from the *Delia* sequence ('Care-charmer sleepe, sonne of the Sable night') exists in Drummond's hand amongst the Hawthornden manuscripts, and indeed is erroneously printed as his own work in Edward Phillips's posthumous edition of Drummond's verse in 1656. The first part of the *Poems: by W. D.*, printed in 1616, contains a sonnet on the same theme ('*Sleepe, Silence* Child, sweet Father of soft Rest'), which is a translation and adaptation of Marino's recent sonnet addressed to Sleep.[92] Marino's poem itself derives from an earlier Italian model, by Giovanni della Casa, which is one of Daniel's immediate sources. The version of Daniel's poem in his manuscript indicates that Drummond is aware of *both* the continental and native traditions of the familiar apostrophe to Sleep in sonnets, when he includes a similar poem in his own sequence.

Another sonnet in the first part of Drummond's *Poems* ('Ah burning Thoughts now let me take some Rest') combines a range of sources in a manner reminiscent of Daniel's method of composition in *Delia*.[93] The first four lines are a close rendering of the opening quatrain of Petrarch's sonnet 274 ('Datemi pace, o duri miei pensieri!'), while the rest of the poem strongly recalls two linked sonnets from Daniel's own sequence:

> My high Attempt (though dangerous) yet praise,
> What though I trace not right Heauens steppie Wayes?
> It doth suffice, my Fall shall make me blest . . .
> He liues, who dies to winne a lasting Name.
> [6–8, 14]

> The mounting venter for a high delight
> Did make the honour of the fall the more . . .
> And though th'event oft aunswers not the same,
> Suffise that high attempts have never shame.
> [XXXII (1601), 3–4, 8–9]

Daniel's two poems (XXXI and XXXII in the edition Drummond reads) again derive from an Italian source, on this occasion a celebrated pair of sonnets on the fall of Icarus by Luigi Tansillo.[94] It is striking that Drummond is repeatedly drawn towards Daniel at his most Italianate, when he assimilates familiar sonnet themes from the *Delia* sequence into his own lyric verse.[95]

An examination of the sources for the *Poems* of 1616 highlights an almost exact correspondence with Drummond's range of reading in English and modern European literatures between 1609 and 1614, a period that coincides with the composition of his first volume of poetry. Drummond's methods for assimilating foreign sources have already been analysed in relation to his multiple translations of sonnets by Tebaldeo and Pietro Bembo. The gradual movement away from the original in successive versions of these early manuscript poems can be traced in the process of composition of other poems printed in the 1616 volume. Another rare sonnet based on an original by Bembo in the first part of the *Poems* ('Deare Wood, and you sweet solitarie Place') demonstrates many of Drummond's customary habits when translating. The poet alters the rhyme scheme of the original to fit his preferred pattern of an Italian quatrain combined with two in alternating rhyme and a couplet (*abbaababcdcdee*). He indulges his 'preference for adding mythological details' by inventing a reference to Thetis,[96] and often expands upon or introduces images into the poem. Thus, the simple expression of envy for the poet's solitude in Bembo's poem ('Chi mi t'invidia hor' [3]) is much more impassioned in Drummond's version:

> What snakie Eye growne jealous of my peace,
> Now from your silent horrours would mee drive?
>
> [5–6]

Where the Italian sonnet concludes with the poet's positive desire to return to the secluded wood, Drummond's couplet expresses the same desire in a negative key ('your dear resorts / I would not change with Princes stately courts' [13–14]). Drummond's poem is certainly a close adaptation of Bembo's Italian original, and yet the changes create a greater intensity in the longing for isolation in his rendering, elucidating well what Jack describes as Drummond's 'principle of originality through imitation' in the process of translation:[97]

> What sweet Delight a quiet Life affords,
> And what it is to bee of Bondage free,
> Farre from the madding Worldlings hoarse Discords,
> Sweet flowrie Place I first did learne of thee
>
> [9–12]

> Quanto sia dolce un solitario stato:
> Tu m'insegnasti; et quanto hauer la mente
> Di cure scarca, et di sospetti sgombra.
>
> [9–11]

(You have shown me how pleasant it is to be alone, and to have a mind free from cares and worries.)[98]

Having already studied *Gli Asolani* in Italian and French and translated the sonnet printed in Pasquier's *Les Recherches* in around 1610, Drummond turns to Bembo's *Rime* in 1612, as his fluency in reading Italian continues to develop. His growing familiarity with the Cardinal's work then feeds directly into the poetry that the Scot himself is composing at around the same time. It is possible to demonstrate a similar pattern for virtually all of the Italian, French, and even Spanish sources that Kastner has identified for the *Poems* of 1616. He traces modern European sources for almost half of the seventy-three poems in the first part of the volume, of which fifty-nine are sonnets. Only three of these derive from Spanish, from sonnets by Garcilasso dela Vega and Boscan, which Drummond begins to read in 1614. For the ten or so poems based on French sources, the most popular models are Ronsard, whom Drummond studies in detail in 1609, and Passerat, whom he reads in 1609 and again in 1612.

Drummond's marked preference for Italian materials is immediately striking. There are more than twenty poems with Italian sources in just the first part of the 1616 edition, which is double the number of poems with French originals, despite the preponderance of French texts in his library. Drummond's reading of Bembo in 1612 impacts directly upon his choice of poetic models, and the situation is identical with Petrarch and the other Italian poets that Drummond reads in 1610 and after. His close attention to Tasso in that year progresses into 1611, when he reads *Il Rinaldo* and four volumes of the *Rime* (1583–87), which provide models for four madrigals and sonnets, including one sonnet already translated by Spenser in his *Amoretti* (1595), which Drummond also reads in the same year.[99] Further poems are indebted to sonnets from the *Rime* of Sannazaro, with whose work Drummond continues to familiarise himself in 1611, and to the less well known *Le nuove fiamme* of Lodovico Paterno, first printed in 1561, read in 1612.

It is in 1613 that Drummond first encounters the Italian poet who is to make the most lasting impression on his poetry. He reads the *Rime* of Giambattista Marino in the Venetian editions of either 1602 or 1608, and the Italian's immediate and lasting influence can be felt throughout the *Poems* of 1616. Drummond's apostrophe to Sleep derives directly from a sonnet by Marino, as do another four poems in the first part of the collection. The figure increases substantially for the second part of the volume, where there are a further thirteen poems indebted to Marino. This is most evident in the *Madrigalls, and Epigrammes*, where Drummond turns repeatedly to Marino along with his two most illustrious immediate predecessors, Tasso and Guarini, as sources.[100] James Mirollo suggests that altogether there are 'some two dozen examples of complete or partial translation out of Marino' in Drummond's work, and that this constitutes the first sustained response to *marinismo* in English literature.[101]

The earliest single translation from the Italian's poetry, however, is made by Samuel Daniel, Drummond's forerunner as the most noted Jacobean Italianist.[102] The following chapter will focus on Daniel's reading habits in European literature, and the related genesis of his Italianate sonnet sequence *Delia*, to demonstrate that the technique for assimilating Italian verse into vernacular poetry practised by Drummond in the 1610s is inherited from a previous generation of Italophile English writers.

Notes

1 Giovanni Torriano, *The Italian Tutor, or a New and Most Compleat Italian Grammer* (London, 1640), sig. F4r.
2 Florio, *Worlde of Wordes*, sig. A3v. The dedicatory poem to Southampton by *Il Candido* (Matthew Gwynne) reveals that the Earl is travelling as the dictionary comes to the press, visiting Italy where he can 'see what here we heare, / And heare what here we learne at second hand' [9–10]: sig. B3r. The other male dedicatee, Roger Manners, the Earl of Rutland, is also described as being 'wel entred in the toong, ere your Honor entred Italie, there therein so perfected, as what needeth a Dictionarie?': sig. A3v. Lucy Russell, the Countess of Bedford, is praised equally for her modern-language skills, although she does not have the opportunity to visit Europe like her male counterparts.
3 Torriano, *Italian Tutor*, sig. F4v.
4 The printed dialogue books often reveal a competitive edge in suggesting the poor value for money of their rivals' teaching. In Florio's *First Fruites* a gentlewoman, who attends a school run by a Frenchman, complains that fees of a shilling a month are too high. The most prominent French teacher Claude Holyband charges a shilling a week for instruction, implying that, in Florio's opinion, he is significantly overcharging: John Florio, *Florio his First Fruites* (London, 1578), sig. 12r.
5 Of the ten commendatory poems written by pupils for Florio's *First Fruites*, it is striking that only the authors of the first two are designated 'Gent'. By the 1590s university-educated poets such as Robert Tofte and Samuel Daniel, who travels with his patron Sir Edward Dymoke, are able to make trips to Italy.

'MIE NEW LONDON COMPANIONS'

6 Rinaldo C. Simonini, *Italian Scholarship in Renaissance England* (University of North Carolina Press, Chapel Hill, 1952), p. 42.
7 Florio, *First Fruites*, sig. 50r. Chapter 27, 'Reasonynges vppon Learnyng, and Philosophie, and what Writers are, and what the profite of readyng, and learning of Science is', is the longest and most impassioned dialogue in the first manual.
8 Florio, *First Fruites*, sig. 106r.
9 Giovanni Torriano, *New and Easy Directions for the attaining of the Thuscan Italian Tongue* (Cambridge, 1641), sig. A3v.
10 In Holyband's *Pretie and wittie historie of Arnalt & Lucenda, with certen rules and dialogues for the learner of th' Italian tong* (1575), the grammar section follows the parallel-text versions of a story by Bartolommeo Maraffi, although Holyband places the story at the end of the volume when he revises it as *The Italian Schoole-maister* (1583). Both Florio's *First Fruites* (1578) and John Eliot's *Ortho-epia Gallica* (1593) launch immediately into bilingual dialogues. Holyband's *The French Schoolemaister* (1573) and Torriano's *The Italian Tutor* (1640) place the dialogues after the grammar. Florio's *Second Frutes* (1591) is clearly aimed at the more advanced student, as it uniquely contains no rules of grammar, unlike the earlier manual, which the author says was intended for 'the use of such as were but meanely entred in the Italian tongue': Florio, *Second Frutes*, sig. A3v.
11 The standard school textbook for Latin is William Lilly and John Colet's *A Shorte Introduction of Grammar . . . for the bryngynge up of all those that entende to atteyne the knowlege of the Latin tongue*, first printed in 1549 and soon prescribed for use in all grammar schools. Shakespeare gives a comic enactment of a Latin lesson based on this primer in the scene between young William and Sir Hugh Evans in *The Merry Wives of Windsor* [IV, i].
12 Wright, *English Works*, p. 184.
13 Torriano, *Italian Tutor*, sig. F3r.
14 Translation from Languet's Latin by James M. Osborn, *Young Philip Sidney, 1572–1577* (Yale University Press, New Haven and London, 1972), p. 126.
15 Albert Feuillerat, ed., *The Complete Works of Sir Philip Sidney*, iii (Cambridge University Press, Cambridge, 1923), p. 83; translation in Osborn, *Young Philip Sidney*, p. 135.
16 John Eliot, *Ortho-epia Gallica. Eliots Fruits for the French* (London, 1593), sig. B2r.
17 *Campo di Fior, or else the Flourie Field of Foure Languages of M. Claudius Desainliens, alias Holiband: For the furtherance of the learners of the Latine, French, English, but chieflie of the Italian tongue* (London, 1583). Many of the Latin dialogues are taken directly from Vives, with Italian translations from Toscanella. Holyband adds the French and English texts.
18 Wright, *English Works*, p. 183.
19 One of the speakers in the *First Fruites* emphasises the importance of repetition in the learning process, when he is asked to explain his ability to recall accurately so many 'sentences diuine and profane': 'Sir, I wyl tel you, I haue readde them often, and so I keepe them in memory, for when a man

wil keepe a thing in memory, let him reade it often.' Florio, *First Fruites*, sig. 28r.
20 Wright, *English Works*, p. 239.
21 *Ibid.*, p. 186. Ryan defines the six terms in English as literal, metaphorical, synonymous, slightly differing, opposite, expressions: Lawrence V. Ryan, ed., *The Schoolmaster (1570) by Roger Ascham* (Cornell University Press, Ithaca, 1967), pp. 18–19.
22 Florio, *First Fruites*, sig. IV.
23 Eliot demonstrates a similar technique in the opening dialogue of his manual, 'The Maner how to learne and teache strange languages'. His method of 'Nature and Art', which equates to learning first vocabulary and then grammar and syntax, is exemplified by two contrary lists of words relating to God and the Devil, which are then structured into complete sentences: Eliot, *Ortho-epia Gallica*, pp. 8–14.
24 Florio, *First Fruites*, sig. 50r–v.
25 Translation adapted from Stern, *Gabriel Harvey*, pp. 156–7.
26 *Ibid.*, p. 268.
27 Florio, *First Fruites*, sig. 43r.
28 Rudolf Gottfried, ed., *The Works of Edmund Spenser: A Variorum Edition*, ix (Johns Hopkins Press, Baltimore, 1949), p. 471.
29 Edward Arber, ed., *John Lyly: Euphues* (A. Constable, London, 1904), pp. 361–2.
30 Wright, *English Works*, p. 219.
31 Ascham is Elizabeth's personal choice as tutor after the death in 1548 of her previous teacher, William Grindal, a former pupil of Ascham at Cambridge.
32 Pietro Bizari, *Historia di Pietro Bizari, Della guerra fatta in Ungheria dall' invittissimo Imperatore de Christiani, contra quello de Turchi* (Lyon, 1568), p. 206.
33 Castiglioni is still active in England at the beginning of the 1580s, when he is involved in the publication of John Wolfe's first Italian text, his late friend Aconcio's *Vna Essortatione al Timor di Dio*, along with five of his own poems. The teacher explains the genesis of the volume in his dedicatory letter to the Queen: 'Hora fra certe mie scritture cercando, & essendomi venute à le mani alchune belle rime, e tra l'altre vna bellissima Canzone fatta in lode di V. M. S. m' è caduto nel pensiero di far con esse e con la detta operetta vn volumetto.' (Searching through some of my writings recently, and a few beautiful poems coming into my hands, including a most beautiful Canzone written in praise of your majesty, it occurred to me to make a small volume of them and this other work.) *Una Essortatione al Timor di Dio* (London, 1579–80), p. 4.
34 Wright, *English Works*, p. 232.
35 Guido Bezzola, ed., *Francesco Petrarca: Trionfi* (Rizzoli, Milan, 1984), p. 130; Leicester Bradner, ed., *The Poems of Queen Elizabeth I* (Brown University Press, Providence, 1964), p. 15.
36 'If none of all these things do stand in stay, / That heaven turns and guides, what end at last / Shall follow of their ever turning sway?' [17–19]; 'or, se

non stanno / queste cose che 'l ciel volge e governa, / dopo molto voltar che fine avranno?' [16–18]. Bradner, *Elizabeth I*, p. 14; Bezzola, *Trionfi*, pp. 127–8.

37 The translation survives in a single manuscript of poems sent by Sir John Harington to Lucy Russell, the Countess of Bedford. It also contains a selection of the Countess of Pembroke's translations of the *Psalmes*, so it is impossible to determine whether this is the only *Trionfo* that she translates, or merely the one considered most appropriate for reproduction in the manuscript.

38 Margaret Hannay et al., eds, *The Collected Works of Mary Sidney Herbert* (Clarendon Press, Oxford, 1998), i, p. 280; Bezzola, *Trionfi*, p. 88.

39 Mary Sidney may have been tutored in Italian some twenty years earlier at Penshurst; the accounts record a payment to 'Mistress Maria, the Italian' in 1572–73, when Mary was eleven years old. See Hannay, *Mary Sidney Herbert*, i, p. 255.

40 Henry W. Meikle, ed., *The Works of William Fowler*, i (William Blackwood, Edinburgh, 1914), p. 16. Fowler is referring to the notoriously free and expanded English version by Henry Parker, Lord Morley. *The Tryumphes of Fraunces Petrarcke, translated out of Italian into Englishe* date from the early 1540s, but are not printed until 1554. Fowler, like Morley, translates into rhyming couplets. The French version could be either that by Baron d'Opede printed in 1538, or another by Vasquin Philieul, printed in 1555. Jack suggests of translation at the Jacobean Scottish court that 'most frequently it was regarded as an act of patriotism': Ronald D. S. Jack, *The Italian Influence on Scottish Literature* (Edinburgh University Press, Edinburgh, 1972), p. 87. See also John L. Lievsay, *Stefano Guazzo and the English Renaissance, 1575–1675* (University of North Carolina Press, Chapel Hill, 1961), p. 55, for a similar account of English translation: 'The aims of the translators, however, were seldom exclusively artistic. For most, the driving impulse was an intense patriotism, a sense of the urgent national need to keep abreast with other countries and, if possible, to "overgo" them. It was *necessary* for England to have a polished language, . . . to produce in short order a literature that could stand without apology beside that of proud Italy, of France, of Spain.'

41 Katherine Duncan-Jones, 'Bess Carey's Petrarch: newly discovered Elizabethan sonnets', *Review of English Studies* 50 (1999), 304–19; p. 316. Robert M. Durling, *Petrarch's Lyric Poems* (Harvard University Press, Cambridge, 1976), p. 293.

42 Duncan-Jones, 'Bess Carey', p. 309.

43 *Ibid.*, p. 311.

44 *Ibid.*, p. 314. The second Carey poem, 'In fortune great a modeste mynde she beares' is a translation of Petrarch's sonnet 215.

45 *Ibid.*, p. 311.

46 Desportes' poem is sonnet XVIII of *Les Amours d'Hippolyte*. Daniel's version is first printed as the sixth sonnet appended to the surreptitious Newman edition of *Astrophil and Stella* in 1591, and again in a slightly revised form as sonnet XXIX in the authorised edition of *Delia* in 1592. For Desportes'

reputation and influence in England see Anne Lake Prescott, *French Poets and the English Renaissance: Studies in Fame and Transformation* (Yale University Press, New Haven, 1978), pp. 132–66.

47 Duncan-Jones, 'Bess Carey', p. 312, attributes the freedom of Carey's translations to her greater skill as a poet: 'However, though Stanford may have selected and provided the material to be translated, the pupil seems to have surpassed her tutor. The Petrarch versions are noticeably freer and more fluent than the faithful, but rather laboured and old-fashioned, renditions of Desportes.'

48 Thomas M. Greene, *The Light in Troy: Imitation and Discovery in Renaissance Poetry* (Yale University Press, New Haven, 1982), p. 2. Greene also suggests that 'educational precepts blended too gradually into literary counsel to permit a fine line between them' [p. 54].

49 Wright, *English Works*, p. 242 and pp. 264–5: 'All languages, both learned and mother tonges, be gotten, and gotten onelie, by *Imitation*'.

50 'o only creature of divinest hew / founded vppon true worth not shoes profane' [3–4]; 'o sol già d'onestate intero albergo, / torre in alto valor fondata et salda' [146, 3–4]. Duncan-Jones, 'Bess Carey', pp. 315–16; Durling, *Petrarch's Lyric Poems*, p. 293.

51 The final section of this chapter will explore in depth how Drummond acquires his impressive knowledge of Italian through rigorous self-study, and illustrate how his voluminous reading in French and Italian literature, often using parallel texts, correlates directly with the sources for his own poetry.

52 Leonard E. Kastner, ed., *The Poetical Works of William Drummond of Hawthornden*, ii (William Blackwood, Edinburgh, 1913), pp. 231–2.

53 Jack, *Italian Influence*, p. 142.

54 Sidney Lee, ed., *Elizabethan Sonnets* (Archibald Constable and Co Ltd., London, 1904), i, p. 98.

55 Durling, *Petrarch's Lyric Poems*, pp. 365–6.

56 Lee, *Elizabethan Sonnets*, p. 98; Durling, *Petrarch's Lyric Poems*, pp. 365–6.

57 Richard G. Adamany, 'Daniel's debt to foreign literatures and *Delia* edited' (University of Wisconsin PhD thesis, 1963), p. 15.

58 Arthur C. Sprague, ed., *Samuel Daniel: Poems and a Defence of Ryme* (Routledge and Kegan Paul Ltd, London, 1950), p. 18.

59 Maurice Evans, ed., *Elizabethan Sonnets* (Dent, London, 1977), p. 68.

60 Dennis S. Mitchell, 'Samuel Daniel's *Delia*: a critical edition' (Princeton University PhD thesis, 1969), p. 105.

61 Kastner, *Poetical Works*, ii, p. 231. 'Sonnet that an Italian poet wrote about a bracelet of hair, which had been given to him by his mistress'.

62 *Ibid.*, pp. 231–2; Marie-Madeleine Fragonard et al., eds, *Etienne Pasquier: Les Recherches de la France* (Honoré Champion, Paris, 1996), ii, pp. 1438–9.

63 Kastner, *Poetical Works*, ii, pp. 233–4; Fragonard, *Les Recherches*, ii, pp. 1436–8. Ronsard's poem is sonnet 59 of the *Premier Livre des Amours*.

64 Kastner, *Poetical Works*, ii, p. 234; Fragonard, *Les Recherches*, ii, p. 1436.

65 Lievsay, *Stefano Guazzo*, p. 63.

66 Sir Edward Sullivan, ed., *The Civile Conversation of M. Steeven Guazzo* (Constable and Co, London, 1925), i, p. 12.
67 Joseph Kau, 'Samuel Daniel and the Renaissance *Impresa*-makers: sources for the first English collection of *imprese*', *Harvard Library Bulletin* 18 (1970), 183–204.
68 Jack, *Italian Influence*, p. 77.
69 *Ibid.*, p. 88. The French source is D'Auvergne's translation of 1553, and the Latin translation is by Sylvester Telius, printed in 1560.
70 Stewart's version runs to only twelve cantos, focusing on the episodes between Orlando, Angelica, and Medoro.
71 Jack, *Italian Influence*, p. 60. Desportes' *Roland furieux* is printed in the *Premières Oeuvres* of 1573. Jean Martin's prose translation of Ariosto is first printed in 1543, and goes through a further twelve editions by 1582. Gabriel Chappuys' complete verse translation is printed in 1576.
72 Greene, *Light in Troy*, p. 148.
73 This is a markedly higher percentage than in Henry Percy's contemporary collection, where only two per cent of the eight hundred or so identified titles are in Italian.
74 See R. H. MacDonald, *The Library of Drummond of Hawthornden* (Edinburgh University Press, Edinburgh, 1971), p. 40.
75 There are 227 French books, compared to 118 in 1611, and 116 Italian books, compared to 61 in 1611. Notably there are also 27 Spanish books, where there had been only 8 in 1611.
76 All three titles are listed among the French books in the catalogue of 1611, although two of the books are now lost: *L'Arcadie... mise d'italien en francoys* is listed as the sixteenth French title; *Aminte, pastorale*, which is probably the parallel-text edition and translation by Belliard printed in 1598, is the eighty-third; Sauvage's translation of *La Circe*, printed in 1550 and purchased in Paris, is the ninety-sixth.
77 MacDonald suggests that there is a copy of Holyband's *The French Schoolemaister* (1573) in his library, although it is not recorded in the catalogue of 1611.
78 Jean Pierre de Mesmes, *La grammaire Italienne, composée en Francoys* (Paris, 1548).
79 Maraffi's *History of Arnalt & Lucenda*, printed in parallel with Holyband's translation at the end of *The Italian Schoole-maister*, permits this kind of comparative reading in a specifically literary context.
80 Another French edition in Drummond's collection, printed in Lyons in 1598, contains Giovanni della Casa's *Galatea* in French, Latin, and Spanish translations.
81 Drummond's library contains an edition of *Il pastor fido*, which also includes Guarini's *Madrigali*, printed in Treviso in 1603, and a French version, *Le berger fidelle, pastorale, de l'italien*, now lost, which is probably Roland Brisset's translation. Drummond also possesses a copy of Brisset's translation of Luigi Groto's pastoral play, *Il pentimento amoroso*, printed in Paris in 1598. His Italian edition of *Il Petrarca* is printed in Venice in 1596, and the translation used is *Le Petrarque en rime francoise auecq ses*

commentaires, traduict par Philippe de Maldeghem, printed in Brussels in 1600.

82 Marinelli's text is something of an anomaly too in terms of its subsequent literary fame, and the absence of a translation of it in either French or English probably accounts for the unassisted reading.

83 The Latin version is probably Scipione Gentili's translation of the first two cantos, and part of the fourth canto, all printed by Wolfe in 1584. The French translation may be Du Vignau's *La Déliverance de Hierusalem*, printed in Paris in 1595.

84 MacDonald, *Library of Drummond*, pp. 33–6. The copy of *Godfrey of Bulloigne*, printed in London in 1600, is now in the Hirsel Library, as part of the collection of Sir Alec Douglas-Home.

85 The publisher Christopher Hunt anticipates exactly this kind of close parallel attention in his letter 'To the Reader', printed in Carew's translation of the opening five cantos of Tasso's poem: 'In that which is done, I haue caused the Italian to be Printed together with the English, for the delight and benefit of those Gentlemen, that loue that most liuely language. And thereby the learned Reader shall see how strict a course the translator hath tyed himselfe in the whole work, usurping as little liberty as any whatsoeuer, that euer wrote with any commendations.' Richard Carew, *Godfrey of Bulloigne, or The Recouerie of Hiervsalem. An Heroicall poeme written in Italian by Seig. Torquato Tasso, and translated into English by R. C. Esquire* (London, 1594), sig. 2v. Sir John Harington also expects some of his readers to look closely at his version of *Orlando furioso* alongside the original text: 'But if anie being studious of the Italian would for his better understanding compare them, the first sixe bookes, save a little of the third, will stand him in steed.' Sir John Harington, *A Preface*, in Robert McNulty, ed., *Ludovico Ariosto's Orlando Furioso Translated in English Heroical Verse* (Clarendon Press, Oxford, 1972), p. 15.

86 Richard Hatchwell, 'A Francis Davison/William Drummond conundrum', *The Bodleian Library Record* 15 (1996), 364–7.

87 See Hyder E. Rollins, ed., *A Poetical Rhapsody* (Harvard University Press, Cambridge, 1932), ii, p. 44.

88 The annotations appear alongside the following passages in the Italian: IV, xxviii, 3–6, which corresponds to lines 113–119 in Daniel's poem, IV, lxxiv, 5–8 and IV, lxxvi, 1–6, to which Daniel alludes in lines 391–396. All of these passages describe the first appearance of the enchantress Armida in the poem. The fourth passage is XIV, lxiii, 5–8, the song of the false Siren, which corresponds to lines 257–259. See Sprague, *Poems and a Defence of Ryme*, pp. 42–51.

89 See particularly Lars-Hakan Svensson, *Silent Art: Rhetorical and Thematic Patterns in Samuel Daniel's 'Delia'* (Gleerup, Lund, 1980).

90 Daniel's description of the secret palace built to host Henry II's liaisons with Rosamond Clifford (lines 463–476) contains an apparently undetected ten-line translation of Tasso's account of the entrance to Armida's enchanted garden (XVI, i, 1–8).

91 Rollins, *Poetical Rhapsody*, i, p. 90. 'Goe wailing verse, the infants of my

loue, / *Minerua*-like, brought foorth without a Mother: / Present the image of the cares I proue, / Witnes your Fathers griefe exceedes all other' [*Delia* II, 1–4]. Sprague, *Poems and a Defence of Ryme*, p. 11.

92 Kastner, *Poetical Works*, i, p. 7. 'O del Silentio figlio, e della Notte, / Padre di vaghe imaginate forme' [1–2]. Giambattista Marino, *Rime* (Venice, 1602), i, p. 31.

93 Kastner, *Poetical Works*, i, p. 17. Jack, *Italian Influence*, p. 140, describes this technique as 'the art of the eclectic borrower'. Daniel's methods of composition and construction in his sonnet sequence will be examined in detail in the following chapter.

94 The two Tansillo sonnets, 'Amor m'impenna l'ale' and 'Poi che spiegat' ho l'ale al bel desio', appear consecutively in a number of anthologies of Italian verse, the earliest of which is the *Rime di diversi illustri signori napoletani*, edited by Lodovico Dolce, and printed in Venice in 1552.

95 Drummond also comes to possess a manuscript copy of Daniel's pastoral tragicomedy *Hymens Triumph*, performed at the wedding of his kinswoman Jean Drummond in London in February 1614, which the Scot intends to have printed in Edinburgh before he realises that it has already been published in London in 1615. The play is, in its sustained pastoral idiom, the most consistently Italianate of all Daniel's works, and, with its frequent allusions to both Guarini and Tasso's *Aminta*, it is easy to understand the pleasure the play would give the Italophile Scot as he reads his newly acquired manuscript for the first time. See John Pitcher, *Samuel Daniel: The Brotherton Manuscript: A Study in Authorship* (University of Leeds School of English, Leeds, 1981), p. 17.

96 Jack, *Italian Influence*, p. 135.

97 *Ibid.*, p. 135.

98 Kastner, *Poetical Works*, i, p. 38; Pietro Bembo, *Rime* (Rome, 1548), pp. 43–4; translation by Jack, *Italian Influence*, p. 124.

99 Kastner, *Poetical Works*, i, p. 196, argues that Drummond is familiar with both Tasso's original ('Bella è la donna mia') and Spenser's version ('Fayre is my love', *Amoretti* LXXXI) when constructing his own sonnet, 'The *Sunne* is faire when he with crimson Crowne' [p. 34], perhaps read together as parallel texts.

100 Drummond rereads Guarini's *Il pastor fido* in 1614; his edition of the play, printed in Treviso in 1603, also contains the *Madrigali*, which the Scot clearly uses as a source for his own madrigals.

101 James V. Mirollo, *The Poet of the Marvelous: Giambattista Marino* (Columbia University Press, New York and London, 1963), pp. 251–2. See Jack, *Italian Influence*, pp. 235–43, for a sustained analysis of the similarities between Drummond and Marino as imitative poets.

102 Daniel's 'A Description of Beauty, translated out of Marino' appears only in the posthumous *Whole Workes* edition of 1623. Drummond does come to possess a copy of this volume, but obviously he cannot have read Daniel's poem before working on his translations from Marino for the 1616 *Poems*: see Pitcher, *Brotherton Manuscript*, p. 18.

2

'A stranger borne / To be indenized with us, and made our owne': Samuel Daniel and the naturalisation of Italian literary forms

SAMUEL DANIEL is a poet who fits exactly Torriano's ideal pattern for learning modern languages.[1] He begins to study both French and Italian at university in England with the assistance of a private tutor (and personal friend), and then makes separate trips to the countries to deepen his knowledge of each language and its literary traditions. Daniel's initial interest in French verse is gradually superseded by a more profound engagement with Italian literature, which has its earliest stirrings under the guidance of John Florio and develops throughout the poet's career. This chapter will demonstrate how Daniel consistently attempts to naturalise Italian poetic forms into English verse, from his earliest poetry in the *Delia* sonnets (1592) through to the last verse to be printed in his lifetime, in the pastoral play *Hymens Triumph* (1614).

Daniel must meet Florio shortly after his matriculation at Magdalen Hall, Oxford, in the early 1580s; the first record of a connection between the two men is Daniel's Latin tetrastichon *In proverbia Italica Johannis Flori* in the manuscript collection of Italian proverbs *Giardino di Recreatione*, dated November 1582.[2] Their friendship is a lifelong one, as is demonstrated by Daniel's frequent commendatory poems to Florio's works, the latest one printed over thirty years later in the 1613 edition of *The Essayes of Montaigne*, and by their shared status as Grooms of Queen Anne's Privy Chamber until her death in 1619.[3] Florio is almost certainly responsible for the foundations of Daniel's knowledge of both Italian and French, which he probably teaches to his young student simultaneously. Although remembered primarily as an instructor in the Italian tongue, Florio seems to have concentrated initially on improving Daniel's mastery of French. Daniel's first work to be printed in 1585, *The Worthy Tract of Paulus Iovius*, apparently a translation from an Italian text, is in actuality based on a French version of Giovio's treatise, with evidence of some cross-referencing against the Italian original.[4]

Daniel visits France in the early months of 1586, and it is during this stay that he develops an interest in French poetry readily apparent in his earliest printed verse. These poems are all in the form of the sonnet, and the close attention to French models in many of them suggests that they may have their origins in the kind of translation exercises encouraged by Florio and other language teachers. Daniel provides the perfect example for an analysis of the relationship between translation and creative imitation that grows out of the language-learning process, as it is possible to trace the composition and construction of his sonnet sequence *Delia* to two separate phases. Each phase reflects the predominant use of sources from a specific sonnet tradition (French and then Italian), and a comparison of the two helps to elucidate the development of Daniel's imitative methods.

'Toyes of mine owne travell': *Delia* and the assimilation of the Italian sonnet

The first authorised edition of the *Delia* sequence, containing fifty sonnets, is printed early in 1592, but versions of almost half of the poems have already appeared some six months earlier appended to the surreptitious edition of Sidney's *Astrophil and Stella*, published by Thomas Newman.[5] When this edition is printed in September 1591 Daniel is still in Italy with his patron Sir Edward Dymoke, where he has been travelling for eighteen months. However Daniel's poems come to be added to Sidney's sequence, it is likely that the manuscript(s) from which they are printed predate Daniel's departure for the continent in March 1590. These poems probably date from the late 1580s, shortly after Daniel's visit to Paris, and it is evident that the principal impetus for them comes from the French sonnet tradition. Mitchell observes that there are discernible French sources for a quarter of the poems printed in 1591: 'Of the twenty-eight sonnets in Nashe's text, four are probably based on originals by Desportes and three on du Bellay; only one has an Italian source.'[6] Mitchell underestimates Daniel's direct knowledge of Petrarch in these early poems,[7] but it is clear that the authorised edition, entered on the Stationers' Register in February 1592, a few months after the poet's return from Italy, demonstrates a much deeper engagement with the Italian sonnet tradition. There is, then, a distinct shift in the poetic models Daniel uses for his sonnets as a direct result of his visit to Italy.

This pattern for the development of Daniel's use of his European sources challenges a persistent commonplace of twentieth-century criticism, that the Italian sonnet is assimilated into the English vernacular primarily by means of sixteenth-century French translations and imitations, a view first articulated by Sidney Lee:

> The majority of the Elizabethan sonneteers concentrated their attention on contemporary France, and derived their chief knowledge of Petrarch and of his Italian followers from the French adaptations of Italian work by Ronsard and Desportes rather than by more direct approach.[8]

If this does reflect Daniel's practice to an extent for the poems printed in 1591, it completely fails to account for the direct knowledge of Italian sonnets displayed in all the later editions of *Delia*. The preference for French sources in the earliest poems may suggest Daniel's greater facility in that language than in Italian in the late 1580s, but it probably also reflects the poet's greater ease of access to French texts. The most frequently used source for Daniel's early sonnets is the poetry of Desportes, and three of the four sonnets rendered into English from his sequences are first printed in 1583.[9] It is likely that Daniel encounters these new poems for the first time during his stay in France.

Three of Daniel's sources from Desportes are themselves translations of Italian sonnets, and the fourth is an imitation of a familiar Petrarchan structure. It is unclear from Lee's account of how English sonneteers favour French adaptations whether this preference is intentional or related to an apparent ignorance about the Italian origins of specific poems. In Daniel's case it is initially the latter. Two of his renderings from Desportes display no direct knowledge of the Italian models behind the French versions: 'Why doth my mistress credit so her glass' is a close translation of Desportes' eighteenth sonnet in *Les Amours d'Hippolyte* (1573), rather than an adaptation of the Italian source, Antonio Tebaldeo's 'A che presti, superba, a un vetro fede?'. Similarly, 'I once may see when yeeres shall wrecke my wronge' is based on the sixty-third sonnet of *Cléonice* (1583), rather than the Italian original by Tasso. Daniel does, however, later discover Desportes' immediate source in Italy, and adds imitations of the two following sonnets in Tasso's *Rime* to the authorised version of the *Delia* sequence printed in 1592. This indicates that Daniel is willing and able to use *both* Italian originals and later French adaptations as and when they become available to him. Daniel's version of another Desportes' poem, imitated closely from a sonnet by Petrarch, printed among the 1591 sonnets suggests that this dual linguistic focus is, where possible, already his favoured method for sonnet composition.

Lee is the first critic to draw attention to the similarities between Daniel's 'If that a true hart and faith unfained' and the eighth sonnet in the first book of *Les Amours de Diane* (1583) and its original, 'S' una fede amorosa' [224], described by Svensson as 'one of Petrarch's best-known and most frequently imitated sonnets'.[10] Unsurprisingly Lee regards Desportes as the decisive influence, although subsequent criticism has argued strongly for either the French or the Italian sonnet as a direct source.[11] There has been a marked critical reluctance, however, to consider the third alternative, that the poet is working with *both* European sources concurrently to construct his English version of a celebrated Petrarchan model.[12] The fame of Petrarch's original suggests that, in this instance, Daniel is likely to recognise the immediate source for Desportes' translation. Despite the critical desire to focus more closely on the French version, it becomes clear that Daniel does know the Italian sonnet directly. The final line of his first quatrain ('Fed but with smoke, and cherisht but with fire' [4]) vividly recalls a phrase in Petrarch ('in gentil foco accese' [3]), which Desportes chooses not to translate. On a couple of occasions Daniel follows the French in switching the word order of the Italian (in the opening line and the original version of the start of the sestet, 'If I haue wept the day, and sigthd the night' [9]). The most striking phrase in the English poem, however, is derived equally from both of Daniel's models. The 'broken words halfe spoken' [6], which reveal the poet's love to the cruel beloved, recall the interrupted, barely understood words of the Italian ('voci interrote a pena intese' [6]) but also the faltering voice of the French ('voix empeschée' [6]). This poem, which becomes sonnet XV of *Delia* in 1592, is probably the most successful of Daniel's early imitations of foreign models. Daniel modifies the structure from both his sources, and adds the mythological image of the 'Vultur-gnawne hart' [8], indicative to Thomson of the more 'savage' mood of the English poem, which qualifies it as 'an imitation proper' in comparison with the 'paraphrase' of the original in Desportes' version.[13] It is tempting to attribute some of the strengths of this particular rendering to the process of composition from parallel texts. The use of more than one source concurrently allows Daniel to progress beyond the most basic form of imitation, in terms of Greene's model of four distinct types.[14] The creative choices born out of Daniel's careful comparison of the Italian and French sonnets are examples of what Greene describes as eclectic or exploitative imitation.

The relative sophistication of Daniel's imitative method in this sonnet is striking in contrast with his use of sources in many of the other early poems. His renderings of other French poems printed in 1591 tend to be close translations, with only the occasional modification of structure or vocabulary, as in the opening quatrain of sonnet XIV, which is taken almost literally from du Bellay's *L'Olive*:

> Those amber locks, are the same nets my deere,
> Wherewith my libertie thou didst surprize:
> Loue was the flame, that fired me so neere,
> The darte transpearsing, were those Christall eyes.
> [XIV, 1–4]

> Ces cheveux d'or sont les liens, Madame,
> Dont fut premier ma liberté surprise,
> Amour la flamme autour du coeur eprise,
> Ces yeux le traict qui me transperse l'ame.
> [10, 1–4][15]

(These golden tresses are the nets, Madam, in which my freedom was first surprised, love the flame around my enamoured heart, these eyes the arrow that pierced my soul.)

It is questionable whether Greene would consider these sonnets as 'genuine imitations',[16] and, if they are, they certainly display only the simplest form of imitation, the reproductive or sacramental. Daniel's proximity to his French models, which is uncharacteristic of the sonnets printed in 1592 and later, suggests that his early sonnets have their origins in translation exercises. The attempt to reproduce the original as closely as possible in English is a feature of these sonnets that Daniel shares with Drummond and Elizabeth Carey, whose language-learning translations were considered in the previous chapter. Daniel's disavowal of his intention to have the early poems printed in the dedicatory epistle to *Delia* seems to refer primarily to his desire to conceal 'the priuate passions of my youth'.[17] It may, however, be an indication that some of these sonnets are personal in a different sense, stemming from private language exercises, first encouraged by his teacher Florio, which are intended to improve the poet's understanding of French and Italian by means of careful translation into English from poetic sources.

If the early poems, and particularly the close adaptations, are genuinely not intended for print, it becomes necessary to account for the appearance of almost all of them, usually in revised form, in the authorised sequence of 1592.[18] One explanation might lie in the theory and sonnet practice of Joachim du Bellay, Daniel's single most important French model. Daniel's direct source *L'Olive* is first printed in 1549 as a sequence of fifty sonnets, in a volume that also contains *Vers lyriques*, and, more significantly, the highly polemical *La Deffence et illustration de la langue francoyse*. Greene describes this treatise as a 'theoretical statement' of imitative directions for French poetry,[19] which stridently advocates the development of the vernacular language through the adoption and adaptation of both classical and Italian poetic forms into French. Special attention is paid to the Italian sonnet, and many of the sonnets in *L'Olive* are themselves based closely on Italian originals, as a practical illustration of du Bellay's theoretical position. This theory of the development of one's native poetic language through careful imitation of prior models, going as far as direct translation, clearly appeals to Daniel. The English poet's renderings of French sonnets in the *Delia* sequence mirror exactly the technique of both du Bellay and the later Desportes in relation to their voluminous Italian sources.

Greene draws attention to 'the eclecticism of *Olive*, with its refractions of Petrarch and Ariosto and its virtual translations of obscure contemporaneous Italian sonneteers' but he doubts whether the latter can be considered as 'genuine imitations':

> Certain sonnets of the *Olive*, for example, are based on sonnets appearing in contemporary fashionable anthologies. Presumably the intentionality of the subtexts from Francesco Coccio or Bernadino Tomitano has a status different from that of Virgil's in the *Antiquitez*. The question has less to do with du Bellay's private intention than with the claim an allusion could reasonably make upon a knowledgeable contemporary reader.[20]

For Greene, the mark of a true imitation is in the way that 'the relationship to the subtext is deliberately and lucidly written into the poem as a visible and acknowledged construct', so that it can be recognised by a well-versed reader.[21] Daniel advertises his engagement with his numerous subtexts in the authorised *Delia* sequence in a variety of ways. The poet's shift of focus to the Italian sonnet tradition in many of the new poems printed in 1592 is signalled by the direct comparison of his poet-lover and beloved Delia to Petrarch and his Laura in sonnet XXXV. His acknowledgement of du Bellay's theoretical precedent for and direct influence on the poetry in the sequence is carefully written into the dedicatory letter that precedes the sonnets in the first edition of 1592. This allusion is simultaneously a compliment to his informed dedicatee 'Ladie *Mary*, Countesse of Pembroke' and an indication of one of his principal poetic models, which makes twentieth-century accusations of Daniel's plagiarism in these sonnets seem anachronistic and unfounded.[22]

While there are three sonnets in the sequence which are literal renderings of poems from *L'Olive* (numbers XIV, XVIII, and XXII in 1592), it is the framework of du Bellay's collection that is more revealing in relation to how the poet presents *Delia* to the Countess of Pembroke. The French sonnets are dedicated in 1549 to an anonymous lady ('sa dame'). In the prefatory letter to the reader, du Bellay complains that he has been forced to publish his private poems ('je ne pensoy' rien moins qu'à les exposer en lumiere'), because he has heard that they have reached the hands of an unscrupulous printer, who intends to print them in an imperfect form:

> Doutant ou qu'il voulust les publier soubz son nom . . . ou faire tort à ma renommée, les exposant soubz le mien, incorrectz et pleins d'erreurs.[23]

> (Uncertain whether he wanted to publish them in his own name, . . . or to wrong the one whom I am celebrating, by printing them in my name, uncorrected and full of mistakes.)

Daniel's letter to Lady Pembroke at the start of his sequence, which also contains exactly fifty sonnets in its original form, shows some striking similarities:

> Although I rather desired to keep in the priuate passions of my youth, from the multitude, as things vtterd to my selfe, and consecrated to silence: yet seeing I was betraide by the indiscretion of a greedie Printer, and had some of my secrets bewraide to the world, vncorrected: doubting the like of the rest, I am forced to publish that which I neuer ment.[24]

Almost half of Daniel's sonnets have already been printed by this point, and they are printed by the same 'greedie Printer', John Charlewood, responsible for the first authorised edition of *Delia*, an irony not lost on Henry Woudhuysen.[25] Du Bellay's contemporary Barthélemy Aneau is similarly suspicious of the French poet's account of his necessity to publish, a criticism to which du Bellay responds directly in a much expanded version of *L'Olive*, containing one hundred and fifteen sonnets, printed in 1550. In this later edition the anonymous lady and dedicatee of the original sequence has become Marguerite de France, the sister of King Henri II and a noted patron of poets, and of du Bellay in particular. Béné has argued convincingly that the dedicatee in the two editions is one and the same person,[26] which suggests that the Petrarchan model is used here predominantly to describe the relationship between the writer and his female dedicatee, rather than an actual amatory situation.[27] Daniel's letter to the Countess of Pembroke is not an attempt to cover up his complicity in the surreptitious printing of her brother's *Astrophil and Stella* in 1591, but rather the subtlest of literary compliments. The echoes of du Bellay's letter are deliberate, and Daniel's purpose is to associate du Bellay's 'Dame' with his own noble 'Ladie', an anagram for Delia in its most common Elizabethan form. Mary Sidney Herbert, like Marguerite de France, is a famous sister, and by 1592 she is similarly known as a celebrated 'Patronesse of the Muses',[28] as well as an adept translator from various languages. The sonnets in *Delia* are a carefully constructed tissue of Italian and French poems, and they are offered by the poet to his future patron as proof of the possibility of creating a sequence in English verse fit to rival and overgo the achievements of the most illustrious European predecessors.

The close adaptations of French sonnets eventually included in *Delia* can be shown to date originally from the late 1580s, shortly after a visit to France during which the poet strives to improve his knowledge of the language and its literary traditions. Similarly, it is possible to trace the significant shift in impetus towards the Italian language in the early 1590s directly to Daniel's extended stay in Italy, where he certainly encounters many sonnets for the first time and consequently refines his habits of imitation from modern European sources. The consideration of another lyric sequence, Robert Tofte's *Laura, The Toyes of a Traueller* (1597), helps to clarify how Daniel comes to develop his impressive awareness of the Italian sonnet tradition. Tofte's first collection is unique among Elizabethan sequences for its exclusive use of Italian source materials.[29] Petrarch is Tofte's principal model in *Laura*, as the title and the echo of the poet's 'primo giovenile errore', from the opening sonnet of the *Canzoniere*, in the dedicatory epistle to Lucy Percy indicate ('and by the follies of my rechlesse youth, behold plainly the virtues of your flowering age').[30] Tofte's epistle also accounts for the Italian influence in his poems,[31] describing them as 'a few Toyes of mine owne travell, most part conceived in *Italie*, and some of them brought foort in *England*'. This is reinforced by the headings given to twelve of the one hundred and twenty poems, listing the names of the Italian cities in which they are composed.[32] Tofte's *Two Tales, Translated out of Ariosto* (1597) indicate more specifically that he is working on them in Siena in July 1592, and in Naples in March 1593. Williams records that the poet travels in Europe between March 1591 and June 1594, and suggests that during his lengthy stay in Italy he 'acquired a good knowledge of the language and a considerable acquaintance with Italian literature', probably improving each by means of his translation exercises.[33]

It becomes clear that Daniel too is improving his knowledge of *both* the language and the literature simultaneously while he is in Italy, despite the strong likelihood that he starts to learn Italian under Florio's tutelage at Oxford in the 1580s. It is not essential to infer a very profound knowledge of the language when Daniel is working on *The Worthy Tract of Paulus Iovius* in the mid-1580s, as he primarily uses a French translation of Giovio as his source text. The suspicion that his Italian is not perfect before his journey is further aroused when a clear linguistic misunderstanding of one of his sonnet models is noted. Schaar argues that the awkward couplet of sonnet XXXVII derives from a mistake in Daniel's understanding of a line in a sonnet by Bernadino Rota, which is the direct source for various phrases in the English poem:

> Tu dico, in cui bella onestà s'indonna.
> [5]
> (I tell you, in whom beautiful honesty takes the upper hand.)
>> That grace, that vertue, all that seru'd t'in-woman;
>> Dooth her vnto eternitie assommon.
>> [XXXVII, 13–14][34]

Daniel takes the verb *indonnarsi* to mean 'to be personified in a woman' rather than the correct 'to gain the upper hand'; this gives rise to the clumsy neologism *to inwoman*, which Schaar describes as 'a strange rather than a felicitous invention. It does not seem to have been adopted by any other English poet, and Daniel uses it in this particular passage only.'[35]

The model for the genesis of Tofte's collection by means of his copious reading in Italy is instructive for an examination of *Delia*, another sequence that self-consciously advertises its author's connection with Italy. In the expanded version of 1594 two poems are preceded by titles that indicate a journey to the peninsula. Sonnet XLVII, an addition to the sequence for the new edition, is entitled '*At the Author's going into Italie*', while sonnet XLVIII, which has already appeared in both editions of 1592, is given the new heading '*This Sonnet was made at the Author's being in Italie*'. Daniel travels to Italy in the company of his patron Sir Edward Dymoke, and Eccles marks the limits for the date of this visit between March 1590 and November 1591.[36] Significantly, Tofte fondly recalls his meeting with Dymoke while in Italy in a later dedicatory epistle addressed to him:

> This Worke then being but a trifle, my labour therein cannot be much, which, neverthelesse, if it be any, is onely due to your true, courteous, and bountifull Nature; to which not my selfe alone, but diuers other Gentlemen, as well English as Strangers, were beholding for the kinde Entertainment you gaue vs at our being in Italy together.[37]

This meeting must take place some time after March 1591, when Tofte leaves England, and before November 1591, by which time Dymoke has returned home. Williams suggests of Daniel that 'Tofte may have made his acquaintance' while in Italy, presumably in the company of his patron.[38] One of the 'diuers other Gentlemen' to benefit from Dymoke's bounty in Padua is another sonneteer, William Fowler, who leaves Scotland in September 1591 and registers at the university of Padua in 1592.[39]

The likelihood of a meeting between these aspiring poets in Italy is given greater credence by certain similarities in the sequences themselves. Tofte's volume contains numerous echoes of Daniel's sequence,[40] the most conspicuous of which is a poetic 'tribute' to the celebrated opening quatrain of the first *Delia* sonnet:

> Vnto the boundles Ocean of thy beautie
> Runs this poore riuer, charg'd with streames of zeale:
> Returning thee the tribute of my dutie,
> Which heere my loue, my youth, my playnts reueale.
> [I, 1–4]

> Rivers unto the Sea doo tribute pay:
> A most unconstant mooving Sea art thou,
> And I within mine eyes (bedeawed ay)
> A River hold of bitter teares as now.
> Receive then from these moystened cheekes of mine
> Into thy lap the water I foorth powre,
> Of dutie mine of thy Debt a signe,
> And mixt together with my sweet thy sowre:
> So shall the water to the water bee
> More precious, and the Sea more rich to th' Sea.
> [*Laura*, II, xxxiv][41]

Strikingly, one of the poems in Fowler's manuscript sonnet sequence *The Tarantula of Love* also uses the same image:

> Bot thow, fearse damme, of fairnes ful and pryde,
> yea, beautyes sea to quhome the tribute dewe
> of teares, and sighs, of prayers oft denyed,
> I have deburdend from a harte maist trewe,
> dois rease thy stormes, and maks thy wynds more blaw,
> to drone me in lovs sees and overthrawe.
> [XXXVI, 9–14][42]

Fowler's sequence is usually considered to date from the end of the 1580s,[43] when he also translates Petrarch's *Trionfi*, but the echo of Daniel suggests the early 1590s as a likelier period for the composition of the sonnets.[44] It is certainly an interesting coincidence that the three late sixteenth-century poets whose influences are most conspicuously Italian in their lyric sequences are in Padua simultaneously for a brief time in 1591.[45] It is probably more than coincidental that there are discernible similarities between the three sequences, and particularly in how the poets approach their common Italian sources.

An unexceptional sonnet by Tasso, which provides source material for both Daniel and Tofte, is ultimately more revealing than the conscious allusions to Daniel's poems in the other sequences. Schaar has suggested that the third quatrain of sonnet XII of *Delia* is a compressed rendering of an Italian poem that is first printed in a Genoese collection edited by Cristoforo Zabata, *Della Scelta di Rime, Di Diversi Eccellenti autori* (1582):[46]

> For she that can my hart imparadize,
> Holdes in her fairest hand what deerest is:

My fortunes wheele, the circle of her eyes,
Whose rowling grace deigne once a turne of blis.
[XII, 9–12]

> Costei, che su la fronte ha sparsa al vento
> L'errante chioma d'or, Fortuna pare;
> Anzi è vera Fortuna, e può beare
> E più miseri farne in un momento.
> Dispensatrice no d'oro o d'argento,
> O di cose che mandi estraneo mare;
> Ma tesori d'Amor, cose più care
> Fura, dona, e ritoglie a suo talento.
> Ciecà non già, se non quando a i martiri
> Nostri s'infinge tal, ciechi ne rende:
> Con due luci serene e fiammeggianti.
> Chiedi qual fia la rota, ove gli amanti
> Travolve e 'l dubbio lor fato sospende?
> La rota son de' suoi begli occhi i giri.[47]

(This woman, on whose forehead the unkept golden hair is scattered to the wind, appears like Fortune; rather truly she is Fortune, and can cause happiness or create more misery in a moment. She is not a giver of gold or silver, or of things sent from foreign seas; but treasures of Love, objects more valuable she steals, donates and takes back according to her whim. She is not blind, unless when she feigns it to our agonies, but she makes others blind with her two clear and flaming lights. You ask what is the wheel around which the lovers revolve, and the uncertainty that holds their fate in the balance? The motions of her two beautiful eyes are the wheel.)

The same sonnet is also a model for Tofte in the first part of *Laura*, where the opening quatrain of the thirty-first poem is an expanded translation of the first two lines from the Italian:

> Ladie, thou seemst Fortune unto me
> When I most wistly marke, how thou dost go
> With golden tresses loose, (a joy to see)
> Which gentle winde about thy eares doth blow:
> And as thou her resembleth in this sort,
> So doest thou in attire and all thy port.
> Only thou wantest for thy swift right hand
> The rolling wheele, and shadowing vaile to hide
> Those eyes, which like controllers do command:
> But if thou longst of these to be supplide,

> Take me (thy prisoner) for to play this part
> For my Desire's the wheele, the Vaile's my HART.
>
> [*Laura*, I, xxxi]⁴⁸

Both Daniel and Tofte follow Tasso in focusing on the power of the beloved's eyes and Fortune's wheel in the second half of their poems, but there is no suggestion that Tofte's later version is mediated through Daniel's elliptical rendering of the Italian. The two English poets clearly have a direct knowledge of Tasso's sonnet, and it is likely that this is gained in the period of their mutual acquaintance in Italy.

Whether Daniel and Tofte discover Tasso's sonnet together or separately, their independent use of it highlights a similarity in *how* they acquire first-hand access to Italian poetry while in that country, and then assimilate it directly into their own vernacular verse. Sonnet XII is not among the twenty-eight Daniel sonnets included in Newman's surreptitious printing of *Astrophil and Stella* in 1591, appearing only in the first authorised edition of *Delia*, entered on the Stationers' Register in February 1592, after the poet's return from Italy. Mitchell argues plausibly that 'his turning to Italian sources ... at a time just after a trip to Italy that may have included a meeting with Guarini, suggests that Daniel made his first real acquaintance with Italian sonnet literature during the period 1590–1591'.⁴⁹ Daniel's familiarity with Petrarch's sonnets in Italian predates his visit, but his growing awareness of the voluminous sixteenth-century Italian sonnet tradition, and particularly the numerous verse anthologies containing work by various authors, certainly coincides with the period of his sojourn in Italy. A further poem from the Genoese *Scelta di Rime*, in which Daniel and Tofte find their common Italian source, is used as the starting point for another sonnet in the 1592 sequence. Sonnet XLVII, 'Like as the Lute that ioyes or else dislikes', expands the image of the poet-lover as a lute from the sestet of a different sonnet by Tasso in the collection.

Daniel's immediate assimilation of sonnets encountered in verse anthologies in Italy is a habit he shares with both Tofte and William Fowler. The Scottish poet uses poems from at least five different collections in the process of composition of his sonnets in *The Tarantula of Love*.⁵⁰ Daniel evidently becomes acquainted with a similar number of anthologies, and there is some common ground between the two poets, in terms of both the collections and specific authors used.⁵¹ Probably the most influential collection is *I fiori delle Rime de' Poeti illustri*, edited by Girolamo Ruscelli, first printed in 1558, and then again in expanded form in 1569 and 1579. The sources for four Daniel sonnets, and three by Fowler, can all be found in the enlarged edition of this anthology, including poems by Luigi Tansillo and Giovanni Mozzarello, whose work both poets choose to imitate.[52] The same edition of Ruscelli's collection is also one of Desportes' most frequently used sources for his French adaptations of Italian sonnets, and it is noteworthy that two of the sonnets Daniel imitates have already been translated into French.[53] In each case it is apparent that Daniel makes use of both the Italian and the French versions to construct his own sonnet, confirming that his preferred method of composition focuses on the use of parallel multilingual sources when they are available to him. Another new sonnet for the 1592 sequence, the celebrated 'Care-charmer sleepe' [XLV], is constructed similarly from an Italian original and its French adaptation,[54] but Daniel ultimately transcends both sources in his creation of a sombre, independent poem that builds on a familiar sonnet theme:

> Care-charmer sleepe, sonne of the Sable night,
> Brother to death, in silent darknes borne:
> Relieue my languish, and restore the light,
> With darke forgetting of my cares returne.
>   [XLV, 1–4][55]

Daniel's increasing linguistic facility and rapidly expanding acquaintance with the sixteenth-century Italian sonnet through the verse anthologies he reads in Italy have a significant, direct impact on his processes of sonnet composition. His new familiarity with the original versions of poems that he has already encountered in Desportes' translations allows him to approach these sources as parallel texts, in the manner recommended by Florio's tuition. The greater range of creative choices stemming from the regular comparison of multiple sources encourages Daniel to develop more thoroughly a technique of eclectic imitation that is glimpsed only rarely in the sonnets printed in 1591.

Daniel's deepening knowledge of contemporary Italian sonnet writing and his increasingly sophisticated imitative techniques are best illustrated by a detailed analysis of the genesis of 'the magnificent series of sonnets promising Delia poetic immortality' for the 1592 *Delia* sequence (sonnets XXX to XXXIIII).[56] Only the first of these five sonnets ('I once may see when yeeres shall wrecke my wronge') appears among Daniel's poems in the 1591 *Astrophil and Stella*, and

Lee has traced its source to Desportes.⁵⁷ He was unaware, however, that Desportes' sonnet is itself a direct translation from Tasso, and that there are thus two potential sources for the English version. Subsequent criticism has considered both possible models, and found the debt to the French poet the more pervasive, particularly in the octave:

> I once may see when yeeres shall wrecke my wronge,
> When golden haires shall chaunge to siluer wyer:
> And those bright rayes, that kindle all this fyer
> Shall faile in force, their working not so stronge.
> Then beautie, now the burthen of my song,
> Whose glorious blaze the world dooth so admire;
> Must yeelde vp all to tyrant Times desire:
> Then fade those flowres which deckt her pride so long.
> [XXX, 1–8]

> Je verray par les ans vangeurs de mon martyre
> Que l'or de vos cheveux argenté deviendra,
> Que de vos deux Soleils la splendeur s'esteindra,
> Et qu'il faudra qu' Amour tout confus s'en retire.
> La beauté qui si douce à present vous inspire,
> Cedant aux lois du Temps, ses faveurs reprendra:
> L'hyver, de vostre teint les fleurettes perdra,
> Et ne laissera rien des thresors que j'admire.⁵⁸

(I will see by means of the vengeful years of my agony that your golden hair will turn silver, that the splendour of your two Suns will be dimmed, and that Love will have to withdraw in confusion. The delicate beauty which now inspires you, giving way to the laws of Time, will take back her favours: winter will take away the buds from your complexion, and will leave nothing of the treasures that I marvel at.)

Daniel follows Desportes' structure and vocabulary closely, and ignores only the final line of the first quatrain of the French sonnet in his rendering. Uniquely in the *Delia* sequence, Daniel employs a variation of the Italian form for the sonnet (*abbaabbacdcdcd*), and, although he intensifies certain expressions (the seventh line is much stronger than the equivalent 'cedant aux lois du Temps' in French), and tones down others (Lever notes how he uses 'wronge' in place of Desportes' 'martyre' in the opening line),⁵⁹ it is clear that the French poem is a direct model. The same cannot be said for Tasso's original, and it seems that Daniel is unaware of the Italian poem when he first works on his imitation of Desportes:

> Vedrò da gli anni in mia vendetta ancora
> far di queste bellezze alte rapine;
> vedrò starsi negletto il bianco crine,
> ch'ora l'arte e l'etate increspa e 'ndora;
> e 'n su le rose, ond'ella il viso infiora,
> sparger il verno poi nevi e pruine:
> così 'l fasto e l'orgoglio avrà pur fine
> di costei, ch'odia più chi più l'onora.
> Sol rimarrano allor di sua bellezza
> penitenza e dolor, mirando sparsi
> suoi pregi, e farne il Tempo a sé trofei.
> E forse fia ch'ov'or mi sdegna e sprezza,
> poi brami accolta dentro a' versi miei
> quasi in rogo Fenice rinovarsi.
> [XVII][60]

(I will see noble robbery committed on these beauties by the years as my vengeance; I will see the white hair lie neglected, which now art and age curl and make golden; and winter will spread snow and frost on the roses, the flowers with which she decks her face: thus the pomp and pride of this lady, who hates most those who honour her most, will have their end. Then only penitence and grief will remain of her beauty, wondering at her lost charms, which Time will make his trophies. And perhaps it will be that, whereas now she scorns and disdains me, then she will yearn to be reborn in my accepted verse, like the Phoenix on the pyre.)

It is apparent, however, that Daniel *has* become familiar with Tasso's sonnet by the time that he is preparing the first authorised edition of *Delia*, where he uses the two sonnets that immediately follow Desportes' model in Tasso's *Rime* as direct sources. Leishman tries to account for his use of Desportes rather than Tasso in the first sonnet by suggesting that Daniel finds the French version more congenial:

> Since Daniel has also imitated this second sonnet, and since the first immediately precedes it in the editions of Tasso's *Rime*, there is no reason why Daniel should have here preferred to follow Desportes except perhaps that he found something in Tasso's first sonnet that repelled him, something he felt alien to the *cor gentil*.[61]

The chronology of Daniel's sonnets offers a far simpler explanation, however. Sonnets XXXIII and XXXIIII, which imitate the second and third Tasso poems, do not appear in print until 1592, after the poet's return from Italy, while sonnet XXX, modelled on Desportes, is surreptitiously printed in 1591, when Daniel is almost certainly still abroad. The manuscript, from which these twenty-eight early sonnets are published, is likely to predate his departure. It is probable, therefore, that Daniel first encounters Tasso's three thematically linked sonnets when he is in Italy. The sonnets are printed consecutively in all the unauthorised editions of the first part of the *Rime del signor Torquato Tasso* in the 1580s,[62] although they first appear in this sequence as early as 1567, in the *Rime degli academici eterei*, to which Tasso contributes forty-two poems. This anthology of works by members of the Paduan academy is edited by Luigi Gradenigo and Battista Guarini, whom Daniel meets with Dymoke in Italy.[63] Woudhuysen suggests that Guarini may have presented a copy of his recently printed play *Il pastor fido* to his two English visitors on this occasion,[64] and it is equally plausible that he offers them a copy of the earlier collection of verse. In the Bodleian Library copy, the dedicatory epistle to Margherita di Vallois, Duchessa di Savoia,[65] written by Gradenigo and Guarini under the pseudonyms *L'Occulto Principe* and *Il Costante Secretario*, is autographed 'Battista Guarino'. Without implying that this is the very copy given to Dymoke (and Daniel), it does at least suggest that the poet offers copies of his works as gifts.

Whether or not Daniel discovers Tasso's sonnets as a consequence of Guarini's generosity, the impact that they have on him is instant. This is particularly true of the first Italian sonnet, from which he has already unwittingly fashioned an English version through Desportes' French translation. Daniel responds directly to Tasso's short sequence offering the beloved poetic immortality by creating his own series of sonnets on the same theme. The new poems in the 1592 edition (sonnets XXXI to XXXV) are all linked by the *corona* technique, which immediately suggests the importance of reading them cumulatively as a group. Daniel's use of his source materials for the immortality sonnets is the most highly developed and complex in the *Delia* sequence, 'an art of eclectic assimilation' drawing from Italian and French models simultaneously,[66] which reveals the exceptional associative faculty of his poetic mind.

Ronsard has long been considered a source for Daniel's most celebrated sonnets, sometimes alongside Tasso (and Desportes) but more frequently as the decisive influence,[67] and yet it is only Leishman who has attempted to demonstrate that the English poet consciously alludes to *both* his Italian and French predecessors. He suggests that sonnet XXXIII, while principally modelled on Tasso's second immortality sonnet, also alludes to a specific poem by Ronsard, which may itself be indebted to Tasso:

> It seems not impossible (for poetry written on the other side of the Alps seems to have reached him with surprising rapidity) that they [Tasso's three sonnets] may have contributed, together with much else, to the inspiration of Ronsard's most famous sonnet, 'Quant vous serez bien vieille'.[68]

Ronsard's sonnet does not appear in print until 1578 in the second book of *Les sonnets pour Helene*, over ten years after the first printing of Tasso's poems, so it is conceivable that Ronsard knows them. Legend certainly has it that Tasso reads Ronsard extracts from his epic *Gerusalemme liberata* during his stay in Paris from November 1570 to March 1571.[69] Daniel clearly registers this similarity between Ronsard and the Italian sonnets, and thus combines elements from both in this poem, and in the immortality sequence as a whole. Leishman argues for Ronsard as the principal influence at the start of sonnet XXXIII, stating that the opening quatrain 'contains no more than a general sense of Tasso's first four lines':[70]

> When men shall finde thy flowre, thy glory passe,
> And thou with carefull brow sitting alone:
> Receiued hast this message from thy glasse,
> That tells thee trueth, and saies that all is gone.
> [XXXIII, 1–4]

> Quand vous serez bien vieille, au soir à la chandelle,
> Assise aupres du feu, devidant et filant,
> Direz, chantant mes vers, en vous esmerveillant,
> Ronsard me celebroit du temps que j'estois belle.
> [*Helene*, II, 24, 1–4][71]

(When you are very old, winding and spinning by candlelight in the evening, sitting close to the fire, you will say, reciting my poems and marvelling to yourself, 'Ronsard celebrated me at a time when I was beautiful'.)

He also suggests that two lines in Daniel's third quatrain, which have no direct source in Tasso, are modelled on a line from Ronsard's second tercet ('Regrettant mon amour, et vostre fier desdain' [12]):

> Then what my faith hath beene thy selfe shalt see,
> And that thou wast vnkinde thou maiest repent.
>   [11–12]

Neither Leishman nor Kau, however, makes anything of the *collige rosam* motif in the final lines of the French sonnet, particularly with reference to its reappearance as the central theme of *Delia* XXXI. Daniel evidently associates Ronsard's use of the motif with Tasso's celebrated *canto della rosa* from *Gerusalemme liberata* (1581), which he chooses to imitate earlier in the immortality sequence. Kastner argues that sonnet XXXI ('Looke *Delia* how wee steeme the half-blowne Rose') is a condensed version of the two stanzas of Tasso's song:

> – Deh mira – egli cantò – spuntar la rosa
> dal verde suo modesta e verginella,
> che mezzo aperta ancora e mezzo ascosa,
> quanto si mostra men, tanto è piú bella.
> Ecco poi nudo il sen già baldanzosa
> dispiega; ecco poi langue e non par quella,
> quella non par che desiata inanti
> fu da mille donzelle e mille amanti.
>
> Cosí trapassa al trapassar d'un giorno
> de la vita mortale il fiore e 'l verde;
> né perché faccia indietro april ritorno,
> si rinfiora ella mai, né si rinverde.
> Cogliam la rosa in su 'l mattino adorno
> di questo dí, che tosto il seren perde;
> cogliam d'amor la rosa: amiamo or quando
> esser si puote riamato amando.
>   [XVI, xiv–xv][72]

(He sang, 'You must see how the shy, virginal rose peeps from out of her green, which is half open and still half closed, and how much more beautiful she is, the less she shows. Later, already self-confident, she displays her naked bosom, and then she languishes, and does not look like something that was just desired by a thousand maidens and a thousand lovers.

'So in the course of a single day does the budding and flowering of a mortal life pass away. It can never sprout or flower again, because it cannot reverse and make April return. Gather the rose whilst she is adorned with the morning of the day, which will soon lose its serenity, gather the rose of love: let us love now, when we can still be loved in return whilst loving'.)

It is the urgency of the *carpe diem* theme in the conclusion of Ronsard's sonnet ('Vivez, si m'en croyez, n'attendez à demain: / Cueillez dés aujourd'huy les roses de la vie'), completely absent from Tasso's immortality sonnets, which prompts Daniel to include a rendering in sonnet form of Tasso's song of persuasion in his sequence.[73] Where the three Italian sonnets consider only an unspecified time in the future, both Ronsard and Daniel combine a bleak vision of the beloved's future with pressing claims on her in the present:

> But loue whilst that thou maist be lou'd againe,
> Now whilst thy May hath fill'd thy lappe with flowers;
> Now whilst thy beautie beares without a staine;
> Now vse thy Summer smiles ere winter lowres.
> [XXXII, 1–4][74]

The urgent repetitions at the start of Daniel's original sonnet XXXII, written as a companion piece to intensify the themes of the previous rose sonnet, demonstrate the importance of the persuasive aspect of the immortality trope. Klein suggests that Daniel here characteristically 'drains the implicit erotic content from the sonneteer's plea for reciprocity': 'Even in the poems that sound the carpe diem theme, the poet-lover's aim is not seduction but a gentle reminder of mortality appropriate for the devout reader.'[75] Daniel, however, devotes two entire sonnets to the theme of persuasion in his sequence. Even in Ronsard's sonnet it is only the turn in the final two lines that refers to the present, whereas Daniel places his direct appeal to the beloved (XXXI and XXXII) at the heart of the immortality sonnets,[76] between the three poems modelled on Tasso's vision of the beloved and her poet-lover in the future.

The placement and ordering of the sonnets becomes the prime consideration in the poet's construction of the sequence. After making the initial offer of poetic immortality to the beloved through his version of Desportes' translation of Tasso's first sonnet, Daniel immediately switches to the present for the two *carpe diem* sonnets. The final quatrain and couplet of sonnet XXXII, however, again move to a consideration of the future, and prefigure Daniel's return to the themes and imagery of Tasso's second sonnet in the following poem. Significant elements of quatrains two and three of sonnet XXXIII are translated directly from Tasso (lines 5 and 6 render the equivalent lines in the Italian, and lines 9 and 10 derive from the second tercet), but it is necessary to consider the Italian sonnet in its entirety to appreciate fully the use that Daniel makes of it:

> Quando avran questi luci e queste chiome
> perduto l'oro e le faville ardenti,
> e di tua beltà l'arme or sì pungenti
> saran dal tempo rintuzzate e dome;
> fresche vedrai le piaghe mie, né come
> in te le fiamme, in me gli ardori spenti,
> e rinovando gli amorosi accenti
> rischiarerò la voce al tuo bel nome;
> e quasi in specchio, che 'l difetto emende
> de gli anni, ti fian mostre entro a' miei carmi
> le tue bellezze in nulla parte offese.
> Fia noto allor ch'a lo spuntar de l'armi
> piaga non sana, e ch'esca un foco apprende
> che vive quando spento è chi l'accese.
>
> [XVIII][77]

(When these beams have lost their blazing sparks and this hair its gold, and the weapons of your beauty, now so sharp, will be tempered and blunted by time; then will you see anew my wounds, not diminished like the flames in you, and the heat in me, and, reviving my passionate tones, I will clear my voice for your beautiful name; and like a mirror, that corrects the flaws of age, I will reflect in my verse your attractions to you in no way damaged. Then it will be recognised that a wound inflicted by the point of a weapon does not heal, and you will learn that a flame exists which lives on even when she who ignites it is spent.)

It is the image of Tasso's verse as a corrective mirror, in the first tercet of the sonnet, that becomes central to Daniel's conception of his own immortality sequence.[78] The mirror in the first quatrain of sonnet XXXIII is a literal one, which accurately reflects the beloved's ageing, but in the sestet of sonnet XXX Daniel has already developed the conceit of his poetry as a substitute mirror, independently from either Desportes or Tasso:

> When if she grieue to gaze her in her glas,
> Which then presents her winter-withered hew;
> Goe you my verse, goe tell her what she was;
> For what she was she best shall finde in you.
>
> [XXX, 9–12][79]

Mitchell makes reference to the preceding sonnet, which he describes as transitional, to draw attention to the continuity of imagery that Daniel achieves in this part of the sequence: 'In hinting by reference to the Narcissus myth of the lady's possible likeness to a flower, Daniel prefigures the main subject and the central image of the following group of sonnets.'[80] While it is true that the image of the beloved as a flower appears throughout the immortality sonnets, it is the image of the false mirror, another aspect of the Narcissus story, that Daniel makes the controlling conceit at this point in the sequence. Sonnet XXIX, another poem modelled on Desportes,[81] is first printed in the 1591 Newman collection: it appears in a slightly different form from the revised version in the authorised edition of 1592, and, most significantly, does not immediately precede sonnet XXX.[82] Daniel's decision to place his warning to the beloved against excessive vanity in a position that serves as an introduction to the immortality sonnets, where the trope of poetry as a true mirror emerges so strongly, demonstrates the care with which the poet is ordering the sequence, before its authorised printing. Svensson notes, referring to sonnet XXIX, that 'the next poem contains a reference to a mirror too', and it is clear that Daniel intends the association of flower and mirror in the Narcissus allusion to resonate throughout the poems that follow:[83]

> Then leaue your glasse, and gaze your selfe on mee,
> That Mirrour shewes what powre in in your face:
> To viewe your forme too much, may daunger bee,
> *Narcissus* chang'd t'a flowre in such a case.
>
> [XXIX, 9–12]

Svensson also suggests a further parallel in the *Gerusalemme liberata* for the idea of the lover as the best mirror of the beloved's beauty. Rinaldo's plea to Armida to pay more attention to him than to her glass, which occurs directly after the *canto della rosa*, is conveyed in very similar terms.[84] There is, however, an essential difference in both the tone and the nature of the situations. Rinaldo's self-pitying passivity in Armida's garden contrasts strongly with the active stance of Daniel's poet-lover in the immortality sonnets. He articulates the bird's song of persuasion from Tasso, and develops what Williamson describes as a 'triumphant confidence' in the power of his poetry to construct a 'lasting monument' [XXXIIII, 9] of, and for, the beloved.[85]

The sense of rivalry between the lover and the beloved's mirror in sonnet XXIX derives from Desportes, the immediate model for the English poem,[86] but it recalls another Italian literary context, which is the final part of the elaborate allusive web that Daniel weaves in his immortality sequence. Guggenheim, unaware of Daniel's knowledge of the French sonnet tradition, refers to sonnets 45 and 46 of Petrarch's *Canzoniere* as potential sources for the image of the lover as a substitute mirror.[87] The well-known sonnet 45, with its explicit rivalry between lover and mirror ('Il mio adversario in cui veder solete / gli occhi vostri') and its Narcissus allusion in the final tercet, *is* Daniel's ultimate (if indirect) source, through the adaptations and translations by Tebaldeo and Desportes. It is, however, the example of Petrarch's consecutive mirror sonnets that is most relevant for an understanding of the arrangement of Daniel's sequence: Petrarch's sonnet 46 continues the images of both flowers ('i fior vermigli e i bianchi' [1]) and mirrors from the preceding poem:

> Però i dì mien fien lagrimosi et manchi,
> ché gran duol rade volte aven che 'nvecchi;
> ma più ne colpo i micidiali specchi
> che 'n vagheggiar voi stessa avete stanchi.
>
> [46, 5–8]

(Therefore my days will be tearful and cut short, for it is rare that a great sorrow grows old, but most I blame those murderous mirrors which you have tired out with love of yourself.)[88]

The two images are similarly made the keynote of Daniel's series of immortality sonnets, although there is not the same sense of despair that characterises Petrarch's poet-lover in the conception of his rivalry with Laura's mirror. Daniel's poet-lover responds to the threat posed by the beloved's mirror by emphasising Petrarch's tropes in a different, more positive way. The fading flowers are used as a reminder of Delia's transient beauty,[89] and a means of persuasion to love. The literal mirror is transformed into a metaphor for the power of (his own) poetry to reflect and preserve an image of the beloved's beauty that is not subject to inevitable decay. This confident challenge to the Petrarchan originals in Daniel's carefully constructed immortality sequence constitutes an act of heuristic imitation. The distinguishing feature of this more advanced, third level of imitation in Greene's model is a conscious effort by the poet to distance his work from the acknowledged subtexts, as 'a declaration of conditional independence' from his poetic models.[90]

Daniel's Petrarchan precedent is alluded to directly in sonnet XXXV, the final poem in the run connected by the *corona* technique. The apparent humility of the English poet-lover with regard to the most celebrated Italian sonneteer ('Though thou a *Laura* hast no *Petrarch* founde, / In base attire, yet cleerely Beautie shines' [3-4]) is slightly disingenuous. Even if the poet-lover seems to be admitting his own poetic inferiority, the very comparison between Delia and Laura indicates a keen literary rivalry with his Italian master. Daniel's sense of intense competition with the Italian sonneteers is fully recognised in Iudicio's judgement on the poet in the first act of the satirical Cambridge play *The Second Part of the Return from Parnassus*, performed in 1601:

> Sweete hony dropping *Daniell* may wage
> Warre with the proudest big Italian
> That meets his heart in sugred sonetting.
> [235-237][91]

There is a further hint of irreverence in the potential pun on 'rime' and the Italian *rime* in the second quatrain of sonnet XXXV. Petrarch may have written more poems, but his amorous faith was no greater for that, is one possible reading of the seventh line ('He neuer had more faith, although more rime' [7]). There is a similar ambiguity at the end of the third quatrain. The word 'stile' can mean either 'a literary composition' (*OED*, 12a) or 'a manner of expression characteristic of a particular writer, . . . or of a literary group of period' (*OED*, 13), with another possible pun on the Italian *stile*, particularly the *dolce stil nuovo*, that characterises the linguistic register of Petrarch's sonnets:

> And if my penne could more enlarge thy name,
> Then shouldst thou liue in an immortall stile.
> But though that *Laura* better limned bee,
> Suffice, thou shalt be lou'd as well as shee.
> [XXXV, 11-14][92]

The recurrence of the word 'limned' in the couplet, referring to Laura in this instance, recalls the picture of the beloved 'Limned with a Pensill not all vnworthy' in the preceding sonnet (XXXIIII, 6). Even with the litotes, the image is designed to emphasise the force of his 'lasting monument' to Delia in *English* verse, which Daniel has so skilfully created from many different strands of the European sonnet tradition. The reference to Daniel in the Cambridge *Parnassus* play immediately goes on to suggest that his borrowings from earlier sonnets are perhaps rather too plentiful:

> Onely let him more sparingly make vse
> Of others wit, and vse his owne the more,
> That well may scorne base imitation.
>
> [238–240]

In this instance, Daniel's conspicuous allusions to Petrarch and the other European sonneteers are not considered as acts of plagiarism, as they often have been in twentieth-century criticism, but rather examples of 'base' or simple imitation. This detailed analysis of the development of Daniel's imitative strategies, however, is intended to illustrate how the poet gradually progresses towards a consistent level of complex imitation in his sonnet writing. Daniel's best sonnets fully acknowledge their European subtexts, but they also expand upon and challenge many of the inherited tropes in them, in order to demonstrate the possibility of naturalising the sonnet form successfully into English vernacular poetry through this process of creative imitation.

The mask of humility that the poet-lover assumes in relation to Petrarch in sonnet XXXV returns towards the end of the *Delia* sequence, when Daniel again makes the offer of poetic immortality:

> None other fame myne vnambitious Muse,
> Affected euer but t'eternize thee:
>
> [XLVIII, 1–2]

The ambitions in this sonnet are expressed in a narrowly English context, and their limits are conveyed through the juxtaposition of the Thames with a river from Daniel's native West country (and one close to the Countess of Pembroke's residence at Wilton):

> No no my verse respects nor Thames nor Theaters,
> Nor seekes it to be knowne vnto the Great:
> But *Auon* rich in fame, though poore in waters,
> Shall haue my song, where *Delia* hath her seate.
> *Auon* shall be my Thames, and she my Song;
> Ile sound her name the Ryuer all along.
>
> [9–14][93]

The reference to the rivers here, as the sequence draws to its close, clearly recalls the opening conceit from the first sonnet: the poetic 'tribute' to Delia is reconveyed specifically through the eternising trope in this sonnet. However, the significance of the insistent puns on 'tribute' in the sequence, which also recurs in the 'tributary plaints' [5] of the final sonnet, becomes fully apparent only when considered in the context of Daniel's wider use of the conceit in his poetry of the 1590s.

In 1594 *Delia* and *The Complaint of Rosamond*, both substantially revised, are reprinted in a volume that also contains *The Tragedie of Cleopatra*, a new play written as a companion piece to the Countess of Pembroke's *Antonie*. The edition is again dedicated to Mary Herbert, and the prefatory letter from the 1592 volume is replaced by a sonnet ('Wonder of these, glory of other times'), which addresses the dedicatee in much more familiar terms as the 'Great patroness of these my humble rhymes' [3]. In the long dedicatory poem to *Cleopatra*, 'To the right Honourable, the Lady Mary, Countess of Pembrooke', Daniel makes explicit the almost missionary zeal which he shares with his patron for promoting both the possibilities and the achievements of English poetry in relation to a prior European vernacular tradition. Daniel longs for the day when the recently printed works of Sidney and Spenser will be recognised as 'With those *Po*-singers being equalled' [90], and he develops the river allusion further to confirm his own rising confidence in the power of English verse:

> But that the melodie of our sweete Ile,
> Might now be heard to *Tyber*, *Arne*, and *Po*:
> That they might know how far Thames doth out-go
> The Musike of declined Italie:
> And listening to our songs another while,
> Might learne of thee their notes to purifie.
> [75–80][94]

The juxtaposition of the rivers of England and the rivers of Italy, with specific reference to poetic achievement, is a feature of Daniel's work throughout the 1590s. It is a trope that he uses repeatedly to privilege the status of English poetry, although its very origin in the Italian verse that it attempts to supersede demonstrates a simultaneous sense of indebtedness and continuity, which complicates the relationship between the two vernacular traditions. The metaphorical connection between a national river and a national poetry is not unique to Daniel in English poetry of the 1590s, although it is certainly most fully realised in his writing. In his verse the river Po comes to assume a centrality and significance that distinguishes it from other contemporary uses of the image:

> When myrth-lesse Thames shall haue no Swanne to sing,
> All Musique silent, and the Muses dombe.

> And yet euen then it must be knowne to some,
> That once they florisht, though not cherisht so,
> And Thames had Swannes as well as euer Po.
>
> [723–727][95]

Spenser later uses the same image of the swan as poet in *Colin Clouts Come Home Againe* (1595) to celebrate the achievements of recent English poetry:[96]

> Nor *Po* nor *Tyburs* swans so much renowned,
> Nor all the brood of *Greece* so highly praised,
> Can match that *Muse* when it with bayes is crowned,
> And to the pitch of her perfection raised.
>
> [412–415][97]

Spenser, however, brings the achievements of Classical Greece and Rome, in addition to those of modern Italy, into the comparison. For Daniel the emphasis falls on Italy, with particular attention to the achievements of the vernacular poets. While in 'To the right Honourable, the Lady Mary, Countess of Pembrooke' he does allude to the river Tiber, suggesting the poetic achievements of ancient Rome, the two other rivers, the Arno and the Po, are associated with the triumphs of modern Italian poetry. The Arno brings to mind the initial flowering of Florentine verse in the works of Dante, Boccaccio, and especially Petrarch. The Po is frequently associated poetically with the city of Ferrara,[98] and here it represents the triumph of vernacular poetry at the Ferrarese court in the sixteenth century, from Boiardo to Ariosto, and eventually to Tasso.

It is Tasso's verse in particular which gives poetic impetus to Daniel, both as the origin of his persistent use of the river image, and more widely as an example of vernacular literary achievement. The two reveal themselves to be intimately linked. The analogy of the river's source corresponding to a source of poetry has been amply demonstrated by Quint, who traces the trope from Virgil through sixteenth-century adaptations of it.[99] Both Tasso and Daniel use the image in their epic poems to focus on the increasing power of the river as it flows from its source towards the sea. Daniel's repeated use of this device in *The Civil Warres* has been remarked upon, but usually as a complex metaphor for the nature of political power, and without any consideration of his immediate source in Tasso:

> The equation of the monarchy with the ocean, and the nobility with the rivers, is a figure that Daniel uses frequently... The figure con-

flates the idea of feudal tribute with the image of a tributary river, wishfully implying that tribute might be withheld, at least for a time.[100]

Daniel twice uses an extended simile to refer to the amassing of forces of rebellion. In Book II, stanza vii, first printed in 1595, the growing support for Bullingbrook is compared to the increasingly powerful Thames, while in Book V, printed in 1599, York's uprising is seen in relation to the growth of the Severn from its modest origins:

> Like as proude *Seuerne* from a priuat head,
> With humble streames at first, doth gently glide,
> Till other Riuers haue contributed
> The springing riches of their store beside,
> Wherewith at length high swelling, shee doth spread
> Her broad distended waters layde so wide,
> That comming to the Sea, she seemes from farre,
> Not to haue tribute brought, but rather warre.
> [V, cxi, 1–8][101]

The play on the double sense of 'tribute' as offering and tributary stream, already familiar from the opening *Delia* sonnet, is common to both examples, and reveals the specific Italian origin of Daniel's image. In canto IX of *Gerusalemme liberata* Tasso describes how the Christian army flocks to its leader Godfrey, like the river Po flowing to the sea. In Book V Daniel offers a close paraphrase of Tasso's stanza, with the final line a direct translation. Again the rivers of England are substituted for an Italian river, but the very use of the trope pays a subtle tribute to its own source:

> Così scendendo dal natio suo monte
> non empie umile il Po l'angusta sponde,
> ma sempre più, quanto è più lunge al fonte,
> di nove forze insuperbito abbonda:
> sovra i rotti confini alza la fronte
> di tauro, e vincitor d'intorno inonda:
> e con più corna Adria respinge e pare
> che guerra porti e non tributo al mare.
> [IX, xlvi, 1–8][102]

Tasso's use of the image is intended equally to reveal its own source. The only part of Tasso's stanza that Daniel does not incorporate into his version is the image of the Po as a horned bull. Fairfax's translation faithfully renders the comparison, although in his version, of course, it still refers directly to the Po:

> And horned like a bull his forehead bold
> He liftes, and ore his broken banks doth floe,
> And with his horne to pearce the sea assaies,
> To which he profreth war, not tribute paies.
> [IX, xlvi, 5–8]¹⁰³

Daniel, however, understands the image to be appropriate exclusively to the Po, and so does not transfer it to the Severn in his poem. Scipione Gentili's commentary on the *Gerusalemme liberata*, printed in 1586, identifies the same source for the image on which Quint focuses four hundred years later.¹⁰⁴ Virgil's *Georgics* are a direct precedent for the privileging of the river Po in both Ariosto and Tasso. The description of the Po in the first *Georgic* as 'fluuiorum rex Eridanus' [I, 482] inspires Ariosto's 're de' fiumi', while Tasso's source is in the fourth *Georgic*:

> et gemina auratus taurino cornua uultu
> Eridanus, quo non alius per pinguia culta
> in mare purpureum uiolentior effluit amnis.
> [IV, 371–373]¹⁰⁵

Quint describes Virgil's passage on the location of the source as 'a myth about poetic origins and an opposition between rival forms of poetry'.¹⁰⁶ Ariosto and Tasso allude to the Virgilian subtext to declare both a continuity with, and an independence from, one of their great Classical epic predecessors. Daniel's repeated use of the river image in his work of the 1590s, particularly in connection with the poetry of Tasso, achieves a similar effect. It registers a simultaneous indebtedness to the example of modern Italian poetry as a means of promoting vernacular poetic achievement over that of the Classical past, while also stressing the importance of developing a distinctive, autonomous English voice from an imposing European source:

> Even more important than the nostalgic yearnings toward classicism, however, especially for a people whose own national literature was still in the first speculative stirring of its youth, was the example in Italy of a modern language with a vigorous and highly imaginative literature of its own, a bold challenger to the supremacy of Greece and Rome.¹⁰⁷

One final example from the 1590s clarifies the implicit connection in Daniel's poetry between the growth of the English rivers from their humble sources and the growth of the English language through recent poetic endeavour. In *Musophilus* (1599), printed in the same year as Book V of *The Civil Warres*, Daniel returns for one final time to Tasso's image of the river bursting its banks ('i rotti confini' [IX, xlvi, 5]), through its own growing impetus. On this occasion, however, he does not use the image to describe the rise of a political faction, but rather to voice Musophilus' firm belief in the expansion of the English language itself. He charts its rise from the confines of Philocosmus' 'little Point, this scarce discerned Ile' [427] out into a mainstream of European culture:

> And do not thou contemne this swelling tide
> And streame of words that now doth rise so hie
> Aboue the vsuall banks, and spreads so wide
> Ouer the borders of antiquitie.
>
> [927–930][108]

'The whole complection of *Arcadia* chang'd': Daniel and Italian pastoral drama

Daniel continues to revise his sonnet sequence up until its final appearance in the *Works* folio, printed in 1601. His major addition to *Delia* for this edition is the new poem 'A Pastorall', placed at the end of the sequence and indeed the volume as a whole. This poem is a highly accomplished translation of the well-known first chorus of Tasso's pastoral play *Aminta* ('O bella età de l'oro'), as Sidney Lee recognised at the start of the twentieth century.[109] Lee is characteristically suspicious of the fact that the poet again never explicitly reveals his source: 'Although Daniel gave no hint that he owed the verse to any outside suggestion, he was translating, as literally as the two languages admitted, the pensive words of Tasso.'[110] John Pitcher, however, suggests that the title and placement of 'A Pastorall' at the end of the 1601 folio are a deliberate acknowledgement of the new direction in which Daniel's poetry is moving in the early seventeenth century.[111] Daniel's close attention to Tasso's chorus in 1601 is not a thinly veiled act of plagiarism, but rather the first indication of the poet's growing interest in the language and forms of Italian pastoral drama. Daniel's sonnets demonstrate most clearly his engagement with Italian lyric poetry in the 1590s, but during the next dozen years he repeatedly turns his attention instead to Italian pastoral plays, from which clear structural and linguistic echoes are discernible in both *The Queenes Arcadia* (1605) and *Hymens Triumph* (1614).

The critical argument over the addition of Daniel's version of the Tasso chorus to his sonnet sequence has been conducted largely on the grounds of thematic content.[112] It is more important, however, to consider another aspect of Daniel's poem, focusing rather on its form and linguistic register, in order to illustrate the poet's larger purpose in attempting to find a suitable English idiom to render faithfully Tasso's lyrical Italian. A consideration of the date and context of its first appearance in 1601 is vital in revealing the larger picture that surrounds the poem. Grosart in his Victorian edition of Daniel mistakenly suggests that 'A Pastorall' was part of the sequence from 1592 onwards, like the preceding 'Ode', and, although both Svensson and Roche, following Sprague's edition, correct the error, neither makes anything of the timing of the addition. It is an intriguing coincidence that Thomas Campion's version of the *carpe diem* motif that concludes Daniel's poem, from Catullus via Tasso,[113] appears as the first song in his *Book of Ayres* in the same year. Campion's name becomes closely associated with Daniel in the following two years. The argument over the propriety of imposing classical quantitative meter on native English verse reaches its climax in 1602 with the printing of Campion's *Observations in the Art of English Poesy* and Daniel's response in *A Defence of Ryme*, composed in the same year. Davis suggests in his edition of Campion, however, that the former tract dates from as early as 1591, and that when it finally came to the press in 1602 the 'debate had been dead for a decade'.[114] While it is not possible to detect where the impetus for reviving the argument originates, it is instructive to consider Daniel's version of the Tasso chorus as a direct expression of his position in this controversy.

Daniel's choice of title for the translation recalls the only English version of Tasso's chorus to precede his, that of Abraham Fraunce in *The Countesse of Pembrokes Yvychurch*, printed in 1591. The two versions, however, could hardly be more different, with the exception of the idle–idol pun that both poets use to render Tasso's repeated 'idolo' at the start of the second stanza. Daniel's is the more faithful of the two in both form and language, following 'the stanzaic pattern and rhyme scheme of the Italian as best he can in English', whereas Fraunce uses considerable verbal amplification and alliteration to expand Tasso's *settenari* into ponderous, unrhymed hexameters.[115] It is not only his successful attempt to render Tasso's complex form into English verse that distinguishes Daniel's translation from Fraunce's; he strives also to capture in his diction a feeling for the delicate sensuality of the Italian, an aspect of the poem that is completely lacking in Fraunce's version. This can be illustrated by examining how the poets variously handle Tasso's description of the lovers in the central stanza of the chorus. Daniel seeks to convey the amorous languor of the original by employing a similar combination of sibilance and assonance:

> sedean pastori e ninfe
> meschiando a le parole
> vezzi e susurri, ed a i susurri i baci
> strettamente tenaci;
>> [685–688]

> And Nymphs and shepheards sings,
> Mixing in wanton sort
> Whisp'rings with Songs, then kisses with the same
> Which from affection came:
>> [30–33][116]

Fraunce's characteristic alliteration, on the other hand, fails to capture any sense of Tasso's alluring charm:

> Lou's yong wanton waggs were always woont to be singing,
> And had noe light lampes, and had no dangerous arrowes.
> Then braue iolly Shepheards and Nymphs sate sweetly togeather,
> Tempring woords with smyles, and euery smyle with a kissing.

It is possible that Fraunce is deliberately eschewing the sensuality of Tasso's Italian in his rendering. The dedication of the *Aminta* translation to his patron Mary Herbert, Countess of Pembroke, may partially account for the very different linguistic register of the first English version:

> Some even attributed a specific morality to her. In translating Tasso's *Aminta*, for example, Abraham Fraunce changed a love scene in a pastoral dialogue to conform to what he thought would be a tribute to the Countess. Unlike Tasso's heroine, Fraunce's Phillis refuses to let Aminta kiss her because without marriage this kind of love is not 'Discrete and sober'.[117]

Yet Daniel is another poet intimately connected with the Countess of Pembroke's patronage, from his dedication of the first authorised printing of the *Delia* sequence to her in 1592. It is clear that Mary

Herbert's name is fundamentally associated with the genesis and development of Daniel's sonnet sequence. The addition of Daniel's pastoral poem at the end of the collection is intended to be a final compliment to her. It simultaneously revives some of the poetic concerns of the Countess's literary circle, where he was nurtured in the 1590s, 'receiuing the first notion of the formall ordering of those compositions at *Wilton*, which I must euer acknowledge to haue beene my best Schoole' [23–25].[118]

In his translation of the *Aminta* chorus Daniel is consciously trying to supersede both linguistically and formally the earlier English version by another member of the Wilton circle. Daniel's formal dexterity in assimilating the complex Italian rhyme pattern into English prosody is in itself a strong declaration of intent in the renewed debate with Campion over rhyme and meter. Equally pertinent is his choice of linguistic register, which, by attempting to naturalise Tasso's Italian diction, reflects Daniel's pan-European concern with the status of vernacular verse, fostered in his time at Wilton. The poet's interest in encouraging a wider appreciation of modern European literary achievement is repeatedly demonstrated in his work in the early years of the seventeenth century. In the following year Daniel cites the greatest examples of Italian vernacular poetry to support his position in *A Defence of Ryme*:

> *Franciscus Petrarcha* (who then no doubt likewise found whom to imitate) shewed all the best notions of learning, in that degree of excellencie, both in Latin, Prose and Verse, and in the vulgare Italian, as all the wittes of posteritie haue not yet much ouer-matched him in all kindes to this day: . . . All which notwithstanding wrought him not that glory & fame with his owne Nation, as did his Poems in Italian, which they esteeme aboue al whatsoeuer wit could haue inuented in any other forme then wherein it is: which questionles they wil not change with the best measures, Greeks or Latins can shew them; howsoeuer our Adversary imagines. Nor could this very same innouation in Verse, begun amongst them by *C. Tolomei*, but die in the attempt, and was buried as soone as it came borne, neglected as a prodigious & vnnaturall issue amongst them: nor could it neuer induce *Tasso* the wonder of *Italy*, to write that admirable Poem of *Ierusalem*, comparable to the best of the ancients, in any other forme then the accustomed verse. [414–419 /427–441][119]

The poet is simultaneously active in the dissemination of one of the most popular of contemporary Italian works by sponsoring the first

English translation of Guarini's *Il pastor fido*.[120] The text is published by Daniel's regular publisher Simon Waterson, and contains a revealing introductory sonnet by Daniel, addressed 'To the right worthy and learned Knight, Sir Edward Dymoke'. Biographically it informs us that the poet and his patron Dymoke met Guarini while travelling in Italy,[121] prompting a sincere expression of Daniel's desire to raise the international status of his native language to counter claims of linguistic barbarity:

> Though I remember he hath oft imbas'd
> Unto us both, the vertues of the North,
> Saying, our costes were with no measures grac'd,
> Nor barbarous tongues could any verse bring forth.
> I would he saw his owne, or knew our store,
> Whose spirits can yeeld as much, and if not more.
>
> [9–14]

The sonnet also contains an endorsement of the translator's achievement, a standard feature of the commendatory poem, but which here gains added resonance from Daniel's own Tasso translation of the previous year. The insistence on matching the English idiom to that of the original in translation is characteristic of Daniel's own work in this field:

> That by the hand of thy kinde Country-man
> (This painfull and industrious Gentleman)
> Thy deare esteem'd *Guarini* comes to light:
> Who in thy loue I knowe tooke great delight
> As thou in his, who now in England can
> Speake as good English as Italian,
> And here enioyes the grace of his owne right.
>
> [2–8][122]

Pitcher suggests with regard to Daniel's commendatory verse that 'every time he commends a close personal friend on a translation, he is advertising his own reputation and judgment in that same public market'.[123] This is particularly true of his sponsorship of the Guarini translation. The close relationship between Guarini's play and Tasso's *Aminta*, especially in their versions of the Golden Age chorus, is emphasised by the later Italian playwright;[124] the chronological proximity of Daniel's version of the Tasso chorus to the Guarini translation draws similar attention to the respective English versions. In the *Annotationi* to the 1602 edition of *Il pastor fido*, Guarini encourages his readers to pass critical judgement on the respective literary merits of the two choruses:

> Non aspetti il Lettore, ch' io dica qual di loro mi paia più bella; percioche non conuiene à me di dar vna tal sentenza; ma dico bene, che questa è di maggior fatica, di maggior arte, e 'n conseguenza, degna di maggior lode.[125]

(The reader should not expect me to comment on which of the two appears the more beautiful, because it is not advisable for me to give such a judgment; but I will say this, that this one is constructed with greater labour, with greater skill, and is consequently worthy of greater praise.)

Daniel's involvement in translations of both choruses at the start of the seventeenth century suggests that he is anticipating a similarly positive comparative judgement from his own readers. Guarini's translator follows Daniel's lead in retaining the original rhyme pattern for the choruses of the play, although, unlike Daniel, he does not attempt to convey the varied *endecasillibi* and *settenari* of the Italian verse, choosing instead a uniform metrical pattern. The translation is largely faithful, although, in comparison with Daniel's poem, it often lacks felicity in rendering the Italian succinctly:

> Whilst Wily-craft found always showers,
> Showers of sharpe will, and wills annoy:
> Were it in Woodes or Caves for quiet rest,
> The name of Husband still was likéd best.
> [36–39]

> furtivo amante ascose
> le trovò sempre, ed aspre voglie e crude
> o in antro o in selva o in lago;
> ed era un nome sol marito e vago.
> [IV, 1429–1432][126]

The impact of Daniel's translation of the Tasso chorus is revealed by placing it in a context that stresses its relationship to the other English versions of the Golden Age choruses. It is the expression of a poetic agenda very different from, and written in deliberate contrast to, Fraunce's earlier translation. The poem is also a more complete practical example of this technique of close adaptation than the contemporary Guarini translation that Daniel sponsors, displaying a level of virtuosity worthy of that which Guarini dubiously claims distinguishes his own chorus from Tasso's original poem. Daniel's success in conveying to posterity his agenda for literary translation is demonstrated by looking at the next, Caroline version of the chorus. Henry Reynolds's translation of the play is printed in 1628, and its first chorus clearly owes much to Daniel. Reynolds retains Tasso's rhyme scheme and varied line lengths, strives for a diction to match the mellifluous Italian, and occasionally recalls Daniel's own word choice, in the 'ydle–Idoll' pun, and most notably in the final line of the first stanza, which Roche considers the best part of the whole translation:

> Nor that the wandring Pine of yore
> Brought neither warres, nor wares from forraine shore;
> [*Aminta Englisht*, 12–13]

> Not for no ship had brought
> From forraine shores, or warres or wares ill sought.
> [*A Pastorall*, 12–13][127]

Daniel translates Tasso's chorus some ten years after his stay in Italy, so clearly this skilful translation is not a direct product of his language-learning exercises, as are some of the early sonnets based on French and Italian sources. It is striking, however, that Daniel's attempts to naturalise the language of Italian dramatic pastoral into English verse in the seventeenth century follow a similar pattern to his earlier assimilation of the European sonnet, which does have its origins in the poet's language-learning habits. Daniel again begins with close translation from specific sources, before progressing on to an eclectic conflation of material from a wider range of Italian pastoral plays, which gradually allows the poet to develop a greater independence from these models in his later pastoral work. Daniel's sources for his two pastoral plays are, of course, dramatic as well as lyrical, and he consequently displays a growing interest in the structure of Italian plays, particularly the elaborate theory and practice of pastoral tragicomedy in Guarini's *Il pastor fido*. This is most readily apparent in the earlier of his experiments with pastoral drama.

The Queenes Arcadia, written for performance during the visit of the royal family to Oxford university in August 1605,[128] is noteworthy as the earliest vernacular version of an Italianate pastoral play for the English stage, albeit an academic one. It is also the first university play to draw characters and incidents eclectically from the *corpus* of Italian pastoral drama rather than translating a single work.[129] Daniel's first pastoral, however, does contain passages that are trans-

lated directly from his Italian models. For example, he returns to
Tasso's *Aminta*, the source of the Golden Age chorus, for the memorable image of the suicidal lover as a bee, which finally pierces the
heart of the cruel beloved as it dies:

> And poore *Amyntas*, if thou now be gone,
> Thou hast (like to the Bee that stinging dyes,
> And in anothers wound leaft his owne life),
> Transpiercéd by thy death, that marble heart,
> Which, liuing, thou couldst touch by no desert.
> [IV, iv, 86–90]

> Tu, in guisa d'ape che ferendo muore
> e ne le piaghe altrui lascia la vita,
> con la tua morte hai pur trafitto al fine
> quel duro cor che non potesti mai
> punger vivendo.
> [IV, i, 1615–1619][130]

Daniel also translates extensively from a now forgotten pastoral
drama, Luigi Groto's *Il pentimento amoroso* (1576). The entire argument between Amyntas and Carinus about whom the nymph Cloris
favours in the second scene of *The Queenes Arcadia* is taken from the
opening scene in Groto's play (where the equivalent characters are
Nicogino and Ergasto), with forty lines amounting to direct translation. The first modern critic to detect this borrowing praises Daniel's
rendering over the original Italian, suggesting that 'his flowing and
musical lines seem even more graceful when placed side by side with
the harshness and stiff monotony of Groto's *endecasillibi sdrucciolo*'.[131]
Despite his proximity to the Italian, Daniel compresses and modifies
slightly Groto's scene, and elaborates certain images, such as the
mythological reference to Diana and Actaeon, where he introduces an
allusion to his own earlier *Delia* sonnet on the same theme ('Castes
water-cold disdaine vpon my face' [V, 8]):

> AMY: Whilst at a Chrystall spring the other day,
>   She washt her louely face, and seeing me come,
>   She takes vp water with her daintie hand,
>   And with a downe-cast looke besprinkles me.
> CAR: That shew that she would gladly quench in thee
>   The fire of loue, or else like loue doth beare,
>   As did the *Delian* Goddesse, when she cast
>   Disdainefull water on Actaeons face.
> [I, ii, 49–56]

> NIC: Da poi s'avien, ch'ella si lavi gli' homeri
> Ad un fonte, o il viso, o il crin, mirandomi
> Quivi, e fingendo di non farlo dedita
> Opra, mi spruzza di quelle acque.
> ERG: Spengere
> Vuole il tuo fuoco: o mostrarti, che simile
> È l'amor, che ti porta, a quel che Delia
> Portava ad Attheon.
>
>   [I, i, 76–82][132]

Daniel uses both *Aminta* and *Il pentimento amoroso* as sources for larger plot structures, as well as for specific images and short passages of dramatic dialogue. Joan Rees describes *The Queenes Arcadia* as little more than 'a reshuffling of themes and incidents from Italian pastoral drama',[133] with the majority of these taken from Guarini's celebrated *Il pastor fido* (1590). This is the most immediately recognisable of the 'few *Italian* herbs' with which Jonson accuses Daniel of seasoning his slight work, in a sly reference to Daniel's pastoral in 1606.[134] It has become a critical commonplace to suggest that Lady Would-be's opinions on Guarini in *Volpone* contain a barely concealed allusion to Daniel's play;[135] however, no one has fully appreciated the depth of Jonson's attack. Jonson deliberately uses Lady Would-be's parade of Italian authors to expose systematically the wide range of sources that Daniel has drawn on in *The Queenes Arcadia*:

> Which o' your Poets? PETRARCH? or TASSO? or DANTE?
> GUERRINI? ARIOSTO? ARETINE?
> CIECO *di Hadria*? I haue read them all.
>   [III, iv, 79–81][136]

The list corresponds closely with that in the *Epistle Dedicatorie* of the first edition of Florio's Italian dictionary, which Jonson uses to add local linguistic colour to his Venetian setting in the play. The only anomaly is Jonson's inclusion of 'Cieco di Hadria' alongside Tasso and Guarini, ahead of Boccaccio, Guazzo, and Castiglione.[137] The blind poet of Adria is Luigi Groto, who enjoys a brief spell of popularity in England at the start of the seventeenth century. This is most notable in Daniel's substantial translation from *Il pentimento amoroso* in the second scene of his pastoral play. The suspicion that Jonson notices this, some three hundred years before it is detected by a modern critic,[138] and also that he wants Daniel to know it, is confirmed when, immediately after, he has Lady Would-be mention the other two most conspicuous sources of *The Queenes Arcadia* side by side:

> Here's *PASTOR FIDO* – ... All our *English* writers,
> I mean such as are happy in th' *Italian*,
> Will deigne to steale out of this author, mainely;
> Almost as much as from MONTAIGNIE;
> He has so moderne, and facile a veine,
> Fitting the time, and catching the court-eare.
> [III, iv, 86–92]

The seemingly anomalous reference to the French essayist Montaigne is explained by Butrick's identification of the Florio translation of Montaigne's essay 'Of the Resemblance between Children and Fathers' as the 'principal source' for the satirical central act of Daniel's play.[139] Philip Stringer suggests shortly after the royal visit that Daniel's play is 'drawn out of Fidus Pastor, which was sometimes acted by the King's College men in Cambridge',[140] referring to a prior Latin translation of Guarini's play, indicating that Jonson scores palpable satiric hits on all three fronts. This concerted effort to expose the sources of a successful university play by means of another play performed at, and dedicated to, both universities clearly demonstrates Jonson's strong disapproval of both the methods and extent of his rival's eclectic borrowing in the process of dramatic composition.

Daniel's choice of sources, though, is entirely consistent with the vogue for Italian drama that characterises Cambridge university plays at the start of the seventeenth century, where the Italian pastoral is fast gaining currency by means of Latin translations.[141] It is helpful to consider Daniel's play as a response to this expanding rival tradition. Stringer's observation that *The Queenes Arcadia* is based on a Latin translation that he has already seen performed at Cambridge does so, with the barbed implication that Oxford is still some way behind in terms of its theatrical models. Ristine explicitly states what Stringer has only implied, when he describes *The Queenes Arcadia* as 'an obvious attempt to imitate Guarini's dramatic innovation on the English academic stage, further inspired perhaps by the fact that the rival university had already several times presented the original in Latin'.[142]

Daniel's play, however, marks a significant advance as the first university pastoral to be performed in English and also to draw from a range of models rather than adapting a single source closely. Story Donno describes Daniel's awareness of pastoral as a 'developing dramatic form',[143] which is manifest in *The Queenes Arcadia* in his method of interweaving various types of plot from the Italian tradition. The structural simplicity of Tasso's *Aminta*, which is echoed in Daniel's final bringing together of the despairing Amyntas and scornful Cloris after his attempted suicide, is superseded by a more complex multiple plot, which derives from *Il pastor fido*. Amyntas' suspicion of Cloris is aroused by the false interference of an outsider, Techne, who is secretly in love with the shepherd, exactly as Corisca tries to convince Mirtillo, whom she loves, of Amarilli's faithlessness in Guarini's play. The secondary relationship between the scornful hunter Silvio and the fawning Dorinda in *Il pastor fido* is recalled in Daniel's Carinus and Amarillis, who are united when Carinus, like his other model Ergasto in *Il pentimento amoroso*, accepts that his pursuit of his friend's beloved (Cloris) is futile. Daniel expands structurally on these inherited dramatic situations by adding two more sets of troubled young lovers. The Dorinda–Mirtillo relationship is a further variation on the Silvia–Aminta type in Tasso's play, while the mutual suspicion between the betrothed Silvia and Palaemon, fostered by Colax's lies, is based on Ergasto's attempt to turn Dieronima against his rival by falsely suggesting that Nicogino favours Panurgia in Groto's play. Daniel resolves the problems in each strand of the plot with a grand sweep in the final scene, when the old shepherds Melibaus and Ergastus come forward to reveal that it is the machinations of the intruders Colax and Techne that are responsible for unsettling the dramatic world of Arcadia. The scene is the longest in the play, with all eighteen named characters on stage, and the complexity of the denouement is clearly inspired by the elaborate last act of *Il pastor fido*.

The structural eclecticism of *The Queenes Arcadia*, described by Jeffery as 'a jumble of borrowed episodes',[144] may ultimately be counterproductive, though, as it seems to prevent Daniel from successfully integrating the language of his various source materials into a convincing English pastoral voice. Daniel consciously eschews both the sensual lyricism of Tasso and the elevated pastoral style of Guarini's Italian in his play, as he explains in the dedicatory poem 'To the Queenes most excellent Maiestie':

> And though it be in th' humblest ranke of words,
> And in the lowest region of our speach,
> Yet it is in that kinde, as best accords
> With rurall passions.
>
> [9–12][145]

His decision, however, repeatedly creates an uncomfortable disjunction in the play between the romantic passions inherited from the Italian pastoral situations and the deliberately understated English verse in which the characters express them. For example, when Daniel borrows episodes directly from Tasso's play, he is unable to achieve the same lyrical delicacy as he does in his earlier translation of the Golden Age chorus. Greg is utterly disparaging about Daniel's renderings of two scenes from *Aminta* in the play. The softening of Cloris' scorn for the despairing Amyntas in IV, iv, based closely on Silvia's change of heart in IV, i, is described as 'little better than a parody of the scene in his model'.[146] Rees is troubled by a discrepancy between Daniel's simple linguistic register and the emotional pitch that the action seems to require in this scene, particularly in the brutal common sense with which Cloris responds to Amyntas' apparent death:[147]

> If it be done, my help will come too late
> And I may stay, and saue that labour here.
> [IV, iv, 24-25]

Greg is equally dismissive of Daniel's prolonged narration of the shepherd's attempted suicide, and the subsequent bringing together of the lovers in the final act:

> In spite of the identity of the situations and even of the close similarity of the language, the tone and atmosphere of the two passages are essentially different; for if Daniel's treatment of the scene, which is typical of a good deal of his work, has the power to call a tear to the eye of sensibility, his sentiment, divested as it is of the Italian's subtle sensuousness, appears perfectly innocuous and at times not a little ridiculous.[148]

Greg's criticisms of the uneven poetry of *The Queenes Arcadia*, particularly in the scenes based on Tasso, are pertinent, as it is an issue that Daniel himself seeks to address, and redress, in his second pastoral play. For *Hymens Triumph*, performed to celebrate a royally sponsored wedding in February 1614, the poet turns again to *Aminta*, but on this occasion he strives to create a greater sense of imitative distance from his principal structural model.[149] Where Tasso centres his pastoral on the initially unrequited love of Aminta for the scornful Silvia, Daniel focuses instead on the mutual but thwarted love between Thirsis and his apparently lost Silvia, and the eventual attainment of their happiness after two years of intense suffering:

Thirsis is Daniel's Aminta, at times quite deliberately echoing his original... Echoing, but not simply reproducing his original. Thirsis is of a different cast of temperament; not passionately impulsive, but still loving deeply;... Tasso is the poet of the feeling heart, Daniel of the thinking heart.[150]

Daniel's most significant alteration is in the reciprocated love of the protagonists, and the great constancy that each maintains towards the other during the period of their separation. Silvia eventually returns to Arcadia disguised as the serving-boy Clarindo, unwilling to reveal her true identity to Thirsis until her father's choice of husband, Alexis, is married to the nymph Galatea. Aspects of his plot suggest Daniel's knowledge of earlier English dramatic examples of the disguised female character.[151] The direct source for Silvia's concealed return, however, is another Italian pastoral play, Carlo Noci's *La Cinthia* (1594), where the eponymous heroine visits her beloved Silvano as the 'boy' Tirsi after an absence of four years. Cinthia's return is motivated by the news that Silvano has found a new love, whereas Silvia discovers that Thirsis' apparent affection for Amarillis is only an unfounded rumour. Daniel takes great care to alter any aspects of his Italian models that might detract from the purity and constancy of the love between Thirsis and Silvia in his play.

The simplicity of *Hymens Triumph*, thematically, structurally, and linguistically, allows Daniel to achieve a more consistently realised naturalisation of the Italian pastoral idiom than in *The Queenes Arcadia*. By rejecting the Guarinian complex structure of his first pastoral in favour of a single plot, echoing Tasso's *Aminta*, Daniel is able to focus more fully on the poetic register of the play. There is a consistency to the pastoral voice in *Hymens Triumph* that the poet was unable to achieve convincingly in the earlier play:

> He deliberately avoids extremes. His language is restrained, and his pastoral 'low' style lacking in rich ornament; there is no sensuous, passionate, let alone erotic writing, as Daniel seeks the purest language to evoke a state of complete simplicity.[152]

The purity of both the plot and the poetry is fully appropriate for a play that is commissioned by Queen Anne for performance at the wedding of her chief lady-in-waiting.[153] It is also indicative of Daniel's greater confidence in attempting to naturalise, and sustain, the form and the language of Italian pastoral over the length of an entire play. Greg is moved to praise Daniel's verse in *Hymens Triumph*, even in comparison with the lyricism of Tasso. He finds Aminta's account of his childhood friendship with Silvia full of 'artificial conceits', but suggests that the equivalent scene in Daniel's play, where Thirsis relates the story of his developing love for Silvia to Palaemon, is 'instinct with a delicacy and freshness that even Tasso might have envied':[154]

> A poco a poco nacque nel mio petto,
> non so da qual radice,
> com' erba suol che per se stessa germini,
> un incognito affetto
> che mi fea desiare
> d'esser sempre presente
> a la mia bella Silvia;
> e bevea da' suoi lumi
> un estranea dolcezza,
> che lasciava nel fine
> un non so che d'amaro;
> sospirava sovente, e non sapeva
> la cagion de' sospiri.
> Cosí fui prima amante ch'intendessi
> che cosa fosse Amore.
> [I, ii, 424–438][155]

(Little by little, and I don't know from what root, like grass that germinates of its own accord, an unknown emotion, which made me always want to be in the presence of my beautiful Silvia, was conceived in my breast; and I drank an unusual sweetness from her eyes which finally left me with an indescribably bitter taste; I sighed frequently, and did not know the reason for my sighs. Thus I became a lover before I understood what Love was.)

> Ah I remember well, (and how can I
> But euermore remember well?) when first
> Our flame began, when scarse we knew what was
> The flame we felt, when as we sate, and sigh'd
> And look'd vppon Each other and conciu'd
> not what we ayld, yet something we did ayle,
> And yet were well, and yet we were not well.
> And what was o^r disease we could not tell;
> Then would we kiss, then sight, then looke: and thus
> In that first garden of o^r simplenes
> Wee spent o^r childhood:
> [I, i, 81–91][156]

Daniel takes up the hint of the Petrarchan register in Aminta's account of his unrequited love, but, in contrast to Tasso, he uses the oxymoron as a powerful means of expressing the awakening mutual affection between Thirsis and Silvia. The former conceives of his grief for the apparent loss of Silvia in specifically Petrarchan terms, but in a resigned manner that suggests his suffering has taken him beyond the range of experience of the typical sonnet or indeed pastoral lover:

> Thinke but what cause I haue, when hauing passd
> The heates, the Coldes the trembling Agonies
> of feares, and hopes, and all the strange assalts
> of passion that a tender heart could feale
> In the attempt, and pursuite of his love,
> And then to be vndon when all was donne
> To perish in the hauen after all
> Those Ocean sufferings, and euen then to haue
> My hopefull nuptiall bed, turnd to a graue.
> [I, i, 10–18][157]

It is revealed later in the play that Thirsis used to write love sonnets. The theme and tone of his poems are evidently rather different from the characteristic laments for an unrequited love, as they originate in the period of his romantic contentment:

> For yo^w were wont, I doe remember well,
> To sing me Sonnets, wch in passion I
> Compos'd in my happier dayes, when as
> Her beames inflam'd my spirits, wch now ar set.
> [IV, ii, 17–20][158]

Thirsis' language in the play is frequently evocative of the voice of Daniel's poet-lover from his own *Delia* sonnet sequence. The 'sad memorials' (I, i, 31) of the seemingly dead Silvia echo the 'sad memorials of my loues despaire' (IX, 4), the imploring invocation to sleep ('Come then, refresher of all liuing things, / Soft sleepe' [IV, i, 30–31]) recalls sonnet XLV ('Care-charmer sleepe'). Most tellingly, Thirsis' private obsequies to Silvia on the anniversary of her disappearance are expressed by means of the same image that memorably opens the sonnet sequence:

> This day doth clayme
> Th' especiall tribuite of my sighes and teares,
> Though euery day I duely pay my teares
> Vnto that soule which this day left the world.
> [III, iii, 6–9][159]

Thirsis' verse in *Hymens Triumph*, the last poetry to be printed before Daniel's death in 1619, consciously invokes the starting point of the poet's own earliest work in order to stress how far each has progressed in writing about the experience of a deeply felt romantic love.

Thirsis is not the only character to adopt and modify the Petrarchan register in the play. Daniel reverses a familiar sonnet motif when he has Silvia, in her disguise as Clarindo, figure Thirsis, the male beloved, as an injured deer, in the report of her encounter with him to the infatuated Cloris:

> I found him all alone like a hurt deare
> Gott vnder Cover in a shadie grove,
> Hard by a litle Christall purling spring
> wch but one sullen note of murmer held
> And where no sun could see him. where no eye
> Might ouerlooke his lovely priuacie.
> [II, iv, 20–25][160]

Silvia's image combines a sense of the purity and intangibility of the celebrated Petrarchan deer, with the frequently used pastoral technique of conveying human emotion through the natural surroundings (the 'sullen note' of the spring).[161]

It is in the poetry of *Hymens Triumph* that Daniel finally achieves a consistent fusion of the Petrarchan and Italianate pastoral registers, which he had first hinted at so brilliantly by adding his rendering of the Tasso chorus to the *Delia* sequence in 1601. In the early nineteenth century both Charles Lamb and Coleridge praise very highly Daniel's verse in *Hymens Triumph*, which the latter describes as 'a continued series of first-rate beauties'. Coleridge suggests that the language of the play 'may without extravagance be declared to be imperishable English'.[162] In the last verse to be printed in his lifetime, Daniel succeeds in creating a pastoral poetry that posterity has defined as quintessentially English. The final irony is that this distinctive poetic voice is the culmination of more than ten years experimenting with Italian pastoral drama, and a full quarter of a century carefully assimilating the forms and language of Italian lyrical poetry into English vernacular verse.

Notes

1 See the dialogue, 'Should a language be learnt in the country itself?', in Torriano, *Italian Tutor*, sig. F4.

2 In the letter 'To the curteous Reader' printed in his translation of *The Essayes of Montaigne* (1603) Florio recalls that he and Daniel, along with 'N. W.', watched Giordano Bruno dispute at the University of Oxford in June 1583.
3 Daniel writes poems for both the 1603 and 1613 editions of Florio's translation of Montaigne, as well as for the 1611 edition of his dictionary, *Queen Anna's New World of Words*. Daniel refers to Florio as his 'brother' (as well as 'friend') in the titles of two of these poems, which gives rise to the widespread belief that the Italian marries the poet's sister, first recorded by Anthony Wood in the mid-seventeenth century.
4 See Kau, 'Renaissance *Impresa*-makers'.
5 The edition is often referred to as Thomas Nashe's edition, as he writes the introductory epistle.
6 Mitchell, 'Daniel's *Delia*', p. 41.
7 The one 1591 poem for which Mitchell acknowledges an Italian source is 'Happie in sleepe, waking content to languish' (sonnet XVI in the first edition of 1592), based on Petrarch's sonnet 212. He is, however, entirely dependent on Janet G. Scott, *Les sonnets élisabéthains* (Honoré Champion, Paris, 1929) for Daniel's sources. There is evidence of borrowings from Petrarch in at least three other early sonnets: Scott cites sonnet 224 alongside Desportes as a source for sonnet XV, and there are also direct traces in sonnets IX and XVIII. Sonnet XXVII is unique amongst the 1591 poems for its use of a non-Petrarchan Italian source: the original version of the second quatrain is indebted to two sonnets by Luigi Tansillo on the theme of Icarus, which are first printed in the *Rime di diversi illustri signori napoletani* (1552).
8 Lee, *Elizabethan Sonnets*, p. xxxiv.
9 Two of Daniel's poems are based on sonnets in the first book of *Les Amours de Diane*, and another imitates a sonnet in *Cléonice, Dernières Amours*.
10 Lee, *Elizabethan Sonnets*, pp. lv–lvii; Svensson, *Silent Art*, p. 157.
11 See, for example, Joan Rees, *Samuel Daniel: A Critical and Biographical Study* (Liverpool University Press, Liverpool, 1964), p. 25, and Pierre Spriet, *Samuel Daniel: sa vie, son oeuvre* (Didier, Paris, 1968), p. 229, who favour Desportes, and Patricia Thomson, 'Sonnet 15 of Samuel Daniel's *Delia*: a Petrarchan imitation', *Comparative Literature* 17 (1965), 151–7, and Svensson, *Silent Art*, pp. 157–63, who favour Petrarch.
12 Only LaBranche gives equal weight to Daniel's two sources for the sonnet: Anthony LaBranche, 'Imitation: getting in touch', *MLQ* 31 (1970), 308–29; p. 317.
13 Thomson, 'Sonnet 15', p. 155. See also Rees, *Samuel Daniel*, p. 25, for a positive evaluation of Daniel's sonnet in relation to the French poem.
14 See Greene, *Light in Troy*, pp. 38–46. The four levels of imitation that Greene describes are the reproductive or sacramental, the eclectic or exploitative, the heuristic, and the dialectical.
15 Sprague, *Poems and a Defence of Ryme*, p. 17; Ernesta Caldarini, ed., *Joachim du Bellay: L'Olive* (Droz, Geneva, 1974), p. 64. Scott, *Les sonnets*

élisabéthains, p. 124, classifies the sonnets from French sources as 'traductions presque littérales'. Daniel's practice is similar for his first version of Petrarch's sonnet 212, the only early sonnet to be derived solely from an Italian source. The previous chapter demonstrates how Daniel moves away from his Petrarchan model through a series of revisions in subsequent editions of *Delia*.

16 Greene, *Light in Troy*, p. 220. He is referring to du Bellay's practice in *L'Olive*, one of Daniel's favoured French sonnet sources, to conclude that his 'virtual translations of obscure contemporaneous Italian sonneteers' are 'not genuine imitations at all in our sense'.

17 Sprague, *Poems and a Defence of Ryme*, p. 9.

18 Twenty-two of the twenty-eight 1591 sonnets are included in the 1592 sequence. The four poems adapted from Desportes are sonnets IX, XV, XXIX, and XXX in the 1592 edition. Two of the 1591 poems taken from du Bellay's *L'Olive* appear as sonnets XIV and XVIII; a third, 'The only bird alone that nature frames' is not printed in 1592, but sonnet XXII is an equally close rendering of a poem in *L'Olive* printed for the first time.

19 Greene, *Light in Troy*, p. 197.

20 *Ibid.*, p. 220 and p. 49.

21 *Ibid.*, p. 31.

22 Lee, *Elizabethan Sonnets*, p. lv, suggests that Daniel's versions of Desportes in particular exhibit 'a servility that a nice literary morality could hardly justify'. Kastner makes the accusation explicit in his suggestion that 'Daniel has so boldly plagiarised du Bellay': L. E. Kastner, 'The Elizabethan sonneteers and the French poets', *MLR* 3 (1908), 268–77; p. 271.

23 Caldarini, *L'Olive*, p. 168.

24 Sprague, *Poems and a Defence of Ryme*, p. 9.

25 See Henry R. Woudhuysen, *Sir Philip Sidney and the Circulation of Manuscripts, 1558–1640* (Clarendon Press, Oxford, 1996), pp. 374–8. Woudhuysen does not mention the possibility of Florio's involvement in the surreptitious edition of *Astrophil and Stella*. His work with Greville on the 1590 edition of Sidney's *Arcadia*, and his subsequent falling out with the Countess of Pembroke, give him both a possible opportunity, and motive, for having the manuscript sonnet sequence printed. His knowledge of Daniel's manuscript poems is demonstrated by an allusion in the *Second Frutes* (1591) to an unpublished sonnet, and thus their appearance in the 1591 edition, whether with or without the poet's prior consent, at least suggests Florio's involvement.

26 Charles Béné, 'Marguerite de France et l'oeuvre de Du Bellay' in Louis Terreaux, ed., *Culture et pouvoir au temps de l'humanisme et de la Renaissance* (M. Slatkine and Honoré Champion, Geneva and Paris, 1978), pp. 223–41.

27 See Arthur F. Marotti, '"Love is not love": Elizabethan sonnet sequences and the social order', *ELH* 49 (1982), 396–425.

28 Sprague, *Poems and a Defence of Ryme*, p. 9.

29 Grosart, referring to the Dantean epigraph on the title page of the sequence (*Poca favilla gran fiamma seconda*), suggests that 'Tofte's style is formed not

on Dante, but on writers of his own day, with frequent turnings and returnings to Serafino. I suspect that both in *Laura* and *Alba* several of the pieces are translations from the Italian': Rev. A. B. Grosart, ed., *Alba* (Manchester, 1880), p. xliii.

30 Jeffrey N. Nelson, ed., *The Poetry of Robert Tofte, 1597–1620* (Garland, New York and London, 1994), p. 3.

31 The poems cannot strictly be called 'sonnets' as they are written in two alternating metrical patterns, neither of which has the fourteen lines of the Italian form. The first pattern has twelve lines, consisting of two six-line stanzas (rhyming *ababccdedeff*), and the second ten lines, made up of two quatrains and a concluding couplet (*ababcdcdee*).

32 The ten cities, as Tofte designates them, are: Padua, Venice, Mantoa, Siena, Pisa, Fiorenza, Roma, Napoli, Pesaro, and Fano, which precedes three poems.

33 Franklin B. Williams, 'Robert Tofte', *RES* 13 (1937), 282–96 and 405–24; p. 289. After the 'original' poems in both *Laura* and *Alba* (1598) Tofte confines his literary endeavours to translations from Italian. His *Two Tales* are translated from canto XLIII of Ariosto's *Orlando furioso*. He also translates three cantos of the first book of Boiardo's *Orlando inamorato*, printed in 1598; a dialogue by Tasso, *Dell' amogliarsi* (1594), printed as *Of Mariage and Wiving* (1599); *Ariosto's Satyres*, printed in 1608 and again in 1611, and *The Blazon of Iealousie*, translated from Benedetto Varchi, and printed in 1615.

34 Sprague, *Poems and a Defence of Ryme*, p. 29.

35 Claes Schaar, 'A textual puzzle in Daniel's *Delia*', *English Studies* 40 (1959), 382–5. Daniel does improve the couplet for the final 1601 version of the poem, but he retains the verb. Schaar, p. 385, suggests that the poet discovers Rota's poem in an anthology of Italian sonnets, and that 'it is not improbable that Daniel read the Neapolitan's poem during his travels in Italy', especially as it does not appear among the poems printed in 1591. An equivalent linguistic misunderstanding occurs in Fowler's translation of Petrarch's *Trionfi*: the word 'drappelletto', meaning 'small group' is rendered as 'clothe of stait', which is actually a translation of the Italian 'drappellone'. See Jack, *Italian Influence*, p. 80.

36 Mark Eccles, 'Samuel Daniel in France and Italy', *Studies in Philology* 34 (1937), 148–67; p. 165.

37 'To My Honourable Friend, Sir Edward Dimmock Knight' in *The Blazon of Iealousie* (London, 1615), sig. A2v.

38 Williams, 'Tofte', p. 287.

39 A Latin poem in praise of Fowler's virtues written by Dymoke is preserved in the Hawthornden manuscripts.

40 In the first part of *Laura*, poem viii has the image of the vulture gnawing at the poet-lover's heart, as in *Delia* XV; poem xxii alludes to the story of Mucius Scaevola, as does *Delia* LI (1594); poem xxxix alludes to a mirror and Medusa, like *Delia* XXIX, which also contains the image of the poet-lover as the beloved's mirror, which recurs in Tofte's poem xvii of part III; poem xxxii in part III refers to the sacrifice of the poet-lover's heart, as does *Delia* VIII.

41 Sprague, *Poems and a Defence of Ryme*, p. 11. Nelson, *Poetry of Tofte*, p. 45. The earliest reference to Daniel's image ('And as each riuer to the sea, so do I run to offer my selfe vnto you') is in Florio's *Second Frutes*, printed in April 1591, which is almost a year before its appearance in the first edition of *Delia*. Clearly Florio is familiar with his friend Daniel's poems before they are printed. As well as Tofte's and Fowler's allusions to the image, there are further references to it in the draft version of the Countess of Pembroke's 'To the Angell Spirit of Sir Philip Sidney' ('And that my thoughts (like smallest streames that flow, / Pay to their sea, their tributary fee)' [46–7]); the prologue to the anonymous play *The Maydes Metamorphosis*, printed in 1600; and, most memorably, in Ben Jonson's *Every Man in His Humour*, performed in 1598 and printed in 1601. In the quarto version of the play the opening quatrain is quoted almost verbatim, but in the revision for the 1616 *Workes* folio, Jonson scorns his rival poet through the absurd 'parodie' of it attributed to the poetaster Matthew: 'Vnto the boundless Ocean of thy face, / Runs this poor riuer charged with streams of eyes' [V, v, 23–24].

42 Meikle, *Works of Fowler*, i, p. 174.

43 See Meikle, *Works of Fowler*, iii, p. 25.

44 Jack, *Italian Influence*, p. 83, suggests that 'as a sonneteer, Fowler is primarily indebted to Italian writers in general and to Petrarch in particular although the voices of Sidney and Daniel are also strong'.

45 Jack, *Italian Influence*, p. 89, describes Fowler as 'the first Scottish poet fully to profit from the wealth of Italian literature'.

46 Claes Schaar, *An Elizabethan Sonnet Problem* (Gleerup, Lund, 1960), p. 38.

47 Sprague, *Poems and a Defence of Ryme*, p. 16; Cristoforo Zabata, ed., *Della Scelta di Rime* ii (Genoa, 1582), p. 277.

48 Nelson, *Poetry of Tofte*, p. 22.

49 Mitchell, 'Daniel's *Delia*', p. 42.

50 See Scott, *Sonnets élisabéthains*, pp. 327–9. Eight of Fowler's seventy-five sonnets are indebted to Italian sources, and a further six to French models.

51 Fowler uses the *Rime diversi di molti eccelenti autori* (1545), *I fiori delle Rime de' Poeti illustri* (1558), *Il primo* and *Il secondo volume delle Rime scelte* (both 1563), and *De le rime di diversi nobili poeti Toscani* (1565). Daniel knows the first two collections, plus the *Rime di diversi illustri signori napoletani* (1552), *Rime degli academici eterei* (1567), the Genoan *Scelta di Rime* (1579–1582), and *Rime di diversi Celebri poeti dell' èta nostra* (1587).

52 Daniel's sonnets are XXVII, which uses twinned poems by Luigi Tansillo, XXXVII (Bernadino Rota), XXXIX (Giovanni Mozzarello), and XLIX (Angelo di Costanzo). The new poems tend to appear in the second half of the 1592 sequence, whereas the majority of the twenty-two sonnets already printed in 1591 are placed in the first half.

53 Desportes' version of Mozzarello's poem is sonnet 30 in *Les Amours d'Hippolyte*, and his version of di Costanzo is sonnet 58 of *Cléonice*.

54 The Italian poem is by Giovanni della Casa, adapted by Desportes as sonnet 75 of *Les Amours d'Hippolyte*.

55 Sprague, *Poems and a Defence of Ryme*, p. 33.
56 Svensson, *Silent Art*, p. 316. Roche credits Daniel with the invention of the 'immortality trope' in an English sequence in these sonnets: Thomas P. Roche, *Petrarch and the English Sonnet Sequences* (AMS Press, New York, 1989), p. 362.
57 Lee, *Elizabethan Sonnets*, p. lvii, suggests that Daniel is imitating sonnet LXIII of Desportes' *Cléonice, Dernières Amours* (1583).
58 Sprague, *Poems and a Defence of Ryme*, p. 25; Victor E. Graham, ed., *Cléonice* (Droz, Geneva and Paris, 1962), p. 88. See Scott, *Sonnets élisabéthains*, p. 120, and Schaar, *Sonnet Problem*, p. 43, for Daniel's use of his French source.
59 J. W. Lever, *The Elizabethan Love Sonnet* (Methuen, London, 1956), p. 151.
60 Tasso's sonnet first appears in the anthology of *Rime degli academici eterei* (Padua, 1567), sig. 65r.
61 J. B. Leishman, *Themes and Variations in Shakespeare's Sonnets* (Hutchinson, London, 1961), p. 80.
62 The sonnets appear only in an authorised, and revised, form in the Osanna edition, printed in Mantua in November, 1591. The date is important, as Daniel is very unlikely to have seen Tasso's revised poems while still in Italy. This raises some problems, as critics have uniformly cited the altered versions when considering Daniel's use of Tasso as a source for his sonnets.
63 See Daniel's dedicatory sonnet, 'To the right worthy and learned Knight, Sir Edward Dymoke', which precedes the anonymous 1602 English translation of *Il pastor fido*.
64 Woudhuysen, *Circulation of Manuscripts*, p. 360.
65 By an interesting coincidence, the dedicatee of the Paduan volume is the same woman to whom du Bellay dedicates *L'Olive* in 1550. Marguerite de France becomes the Duchess of Savoie after her marriage to Emmanuel-Philibert in June 1559.
66 Greene, *Light in Troy*, p. 158. Greene's phrase describes Poliziano's technique in his *Stanze*.
67 See Lee, *Elizabethan Sonnets*, p. liv, and Lever, *Love Sonnet*, p. 152. Even more recent considerations of Daniel's sonnets fail to take into sufficient account the Italian influences on these poems: see Lisa M. Klein, *The Exemplary Sidney and the Elizabethan Sonneteer* (University of Delaware Press, Newark, 1998), pp. 149–51 and p. 267.
68 Leishman, *Themes and Variations*, p. 54.
69 See Solerti, *Torquato Tasso*, i, pp. 144–5.
70 Leishman, *Themes and Variations*, p. 81. Kau also claims that 'it is quite likely that Daniel knew Ronsard's poem and imitated it in his first quatrain': Joseph Kau, *'Delia*'s gentle lover and the eternizing conceit in Elizabethan sonnets', *Anglia* 92 (1974), 334–48; p. 340.
71 Sprague, *Poems and a Defence of Ryme*, p. 27; Georges Margolin, ed., *Pierre de Ronsard: Les Amours* (Delmas, Paris, 1954), p. 161.
72 L. E. Kastner, 'The Italian sources of Daniel's *Delia*', *MLR* 7 (1912), 153–6; p. 155; Lanfranco Caretti, ed., *Torquato Tasso: Gerusalemme liberata* (Einaudi,

Turin, 1971), p. 478. There is a precedent in the French sonnet for the compression of two stanzas of *ottava rima* from Italian epic into the fourteen lines of the sonnet form. Ten poems in du Bellay's *L'Olive* (1550) derive from passages in Ariosto's *Orlando furioso* (1532). Du Bellay's sonnet 97 ('Qui a peut voir la matinale rose') is based on Ariosto's own rose *stanze* ('La verginella è simile alla rosa', I, xlii–xliii), which is the model for Tasso's later song.

73 This is not to suggest that Ronsard himself is alluding to the *Gerusalemme liberata* passage at the end of his sonnet: Tasso's epic is not printed until 1581, three years after *Les sonnets pour Helene*. The conclusion to the French sonnet, however, clearly brings to Daniel's mind the most famous contemporary treatment of the rose motif, a version of which Spenser has already included in the Bowre of Blisse episode in *The Faerie Queene* (1590) [II, xii, 74–75].

74 Sprague, *Poems and a Defence of Ryme*, p. 26.

75 Klein, *Exemplary Sidney*, pp. 148–9.

76 There is a striking switch from addressing the beloved in the third person, in sonnet XXX, to the second person at the start of sonnet XXXI.

77 *Rime degli academici eterei*, sig. 65v.

78 The reference to the mirror is replaced by the image of a painter in Tasso's revised sonnet, printed in November 1591: 'E'n guisa di pittor che il vizio emende / del tempo, mostrerò ne gli alti carmi / le tue bellezze in nulla parte offese' [9–11]. Although this is almost certainly not the version that Daniel uses for the 1592 *Delia*, critics have consistently followed Guggenheim's suggestion that the picture 'Limned with a Pensill not all vnworthy' [6] in sonnet XXXIIII derives from the image in Tasso's revised tercet. See Leishman, *Themes and Variations*, p. 81, Svensson, *Silent Art*, p. 262, and Josef Guggenheim, *Quellenstudien zu Samuel Daniels Sonnettencyclus 'Delia'* (Berlin, 1898), p. 50.

79 Sprague, *Poems and a Defence of Ryme*, p. 25.

80 Mitchell, 'Daniel's *Delia*', p. 77.

81 Lee, *Elizabethan Sonnets*, p. lvi, first detects Daniel's debt to sonnet XVIII of *Les Amours d'Hippolyte* (1573).

82 Sonnet XXIX appears as the sixth of the twenty-eight Daniel sonnets in 1591, and sonnet XXX is the twenty-seventh.

83 Svensson, *Silent Art*, p. 243.

84 Sprague, *Poems and a Defence of Ryme*, p. 25. Svensson, *Silent Art*, pp. 252–3, draws attention to stanzas xx–xxii in canto XVI, and to the following lines in particular: '– Volgi, – dicea – deh volgi – il cavaliero / – a me quegli occhi onde beata bèi, / ché son, se tu no 'l sai, ritratto vero / de le bellezze tue gli incendi miei; / la forma lor, la meraviglia a pieno / piú che il cristallo tuo mostra il mio seno' [XVI, xxi, 3–8]. Caretti, *Gerusalemme liberata*, p. 480. ('The knight said, "Turn, blessed, you must turn to me these eyes, which have the power to bless, that gain, even if you do not realise it, a true reflection of your beauties in my ardour; my heart shows their shape and wonder to the full, far more than your mirror does".')

85 C. F. Williamson, 'The design of Daniel's *Delia*', RES 19 (1968), 251–60; p. 254.
86 'Pourquoy si folement croyez-vous à un verre, / Voulant voir les beautez que vous avez des cieux? / Mirez-vous dessus moy pour les connoistre mieux' [XVIII, 1–3]. Victor E. Graham, ed., *Les Amours d'Hippolyte* (Droz, Geneva and Paris, 1960), p. 29. ('Why do you trust so foolishly in a mirror, wishing to see the charms that you have from heaven? Gaze on me to appreciate them better.') Kastner, 'Elizabethan Sonneteers', p. 272, unconvincingly suggests that Daniel's sonnet is closer to Desportes' Italian source, Antonio Tebaldeo's 'A che presti, superba, a un vetro fede?', than to the French version.
87 Guggenheim, *Quellenstudien*, p. 31.
88 Durling, *Petrarch's Lyric Poems*, pp. 111–12.
89 In Tasso's third immortality sonnet the poet-lover refers to his own old age in the first quatrain. Daniel, however, refers to the beloved's ageing at the start of sonnet XXXIIII, in what is otherwise a close translation from the Italian: 'Quando vedrò nel verno il crine sparso / aver di neve e di pruine algenti, / e 'l seren de' miei dì lieti e ridenti / col fior de gli anni miei fuggito e sparso' [XIX, 1–4]. 'When Winter snowes vpon thy golden heares, / And frost of age hath nipt thy flowers neere: / When darke shall seeme thy day that neuer cleares, / And all lyes withred that was held so deere' [XXXIIII, 1–4]. *Rime degli academici eterei*, sig. 65v; Sprague, *Poems and a Defence of Ryme*, p. 27.
90 Greene, *Light in Troy*, p. 41.
91 J. B. Leishman, ed., *The Three Parnassus Plays (1598–1601)* (Ivor Nicholson and Watson Ltd, London, 1949), pp. 238–9. Iudicio shares his opinions with Ingenioso on the English poets included in the anthology *Bel-vedere, or the Garden of the Muses* (1600).
92 Sprague, *Poems and a Defence of Ryme*, p. 28.
93 *Ibid.*, p. 34.
94 Samuel Daniel, *Delia and Rosamond Augmented. Cleopatra* (London, 1594), sig. H6v.
95 *The Complaint of Rosamond* (1592): Sprague, *Poems and A Defence of Ryme*, p. 62.
96 The most celebrated source for the image of the poet as a swan is St John the Evangelist's description to Astolfo in Ariosto's *Orlando furioso*: 'Ma come i cigni che cantando lieti / rendeno salve le medaglie al tempio, / cosí gli uomini degni da' poeti / son tolti da l'oblio, piú che morte empio' [XXXV, xxii, 1–4]. Lanfranco Caretti, ed., *Orlando furioso* (Einaudi, Turin, 1966), p. 1054. ('But as the swans with their glad song convey the plaques safely to the shrine, so it is that men of worth are rescued from oblivion – crueller than death – by poets' (translation Guido Waldman, *Orlando Furioso* (Oxford University Press, Oxford, 1983), p. 424).)
97 *Colin Clouts Come Home Againe*, in William Oram et al., eds, *The Yale Edition of the Shorter Poems of Edmund Spenser* (Yale University Press, New Haven, 1989), p. 541.
98 St John the Evangelist foretells the growth of Ferrara to political and cultural prominence in *Orlando furioso*: 'Del re de' fiumi tra l'altiere corna /

or siede umil (diceagli) e piccol borgo: / dinanzi il Po, di dietro gli soggiorna / d'alta palude un nebuloso gorgo; / che, volgendosi gli anni, la piú adorna / di tutte le città d'Italia scorgo, / non pur di mura e d'ampli tetti regi, / ma di bei studi e di costumi egregi' [XXXV, vi, 1-8]. Caretti, *Orlando furioso*, p. 1049. ('"Between the mighty branches of the king of rivers", he continued, "there now nestles a humble village; before it flows the Po; behind it spreads a misty vortex of deep marsh. I see it becoming, with the passage of time, the fairest of all the cities of Italy, not only for its walls and great regal piles, but also for the quality of its learning and manners"' (Waldman, *Orlando Furioso*, p. 422).)

99 See David Quint, *Origin and Originality in Renaissance Literature: Versions of the Source* (Yale University Press, New Haven, 1983), pp. 23-30.

100 Richard C. McCoy, *The Rites of Knighthood: The Literature and Politics of Elizabethan Chivalry* (University of California Press, Berkeley, 1989), p. 117. Michel offers a similar interpretation: 'The image of a river, springing obscurely but strengthened with tributaries until it becomes mighty and powerful, destined to lose its sovereignty in the ocean but sometimes giving battle before submitting, is a favorite one of Daniel's in describing the rise of rebellious factions.' Laurence Michel, ed., *The Civil Wars by Samuel Daniel* (Yale University Press, New Haven, 1958), p. 33.

101 Samuel Daniel, *Works* (London, 1601), sig. 81r.

102 Caretti, *Gerusalemme liberata*, p. 279.

103 K. M. Lea and T. M. Gang, eds, *Godfrey of Bulloigne* (Clarendon Press, Oxford, 1981), p. 305. Fairfax's translation is printed in 1600, the year after the appearance of Daniel's Book V.

104 Scipione Gentili, *Annotationi di Scipio Gentili sopra la Gerusalemme liberata di T. Tasso* (Leida, 1586), p. 35: 'Gli antichi poeti finsero i fiumi con la faccia e con la corna di Toro, per significare la forza e l'impeto dell'aque' ('The ancient poets figured rivers with the face and horns of a Bull, to indicate the force and impetus of the water').

105 R. A. B. Mynors, ed., *Virgil's Georgics* (Clarendon Press, Oxford, 1990), p. xxxiv and p. lxxxv.

106 Quint, *Origin and Originality*, p. 42.

107 John L. Lievsay, *The Elizabethan Image of Italy* (Cornell University Press, Ithaca, 1964), p. 16.

108 Sprague, *Poems and a Defence of Ryme*, p. 95.

109 Lee, *Elizabethan Sonnets*, pp. liii-liv.

110 Sidney Lee, 'Shakespeare and the Italian Renaissance' in F. S. Boas, ed., *Elizabethan and Other Essays* (Clarendon Press, Oxford, 1929), pp. 140-68; p. 155. The essay is originally printed in 1915.

111 John Pitcher, 'Essays, works and small poems: divulging, publishing, and augmenting the Elizabethan poet, Samuel Daniel' in Andrew Murphy, ed., *The Renaissance Text* (Manchester University Press, Manchester, 2000), pp. 8-29; p. 16.

112 This is illustrated in the radically different readings of the poem offered by Roche and Svensson. The latter reads Daniel's translation of Tasso literally, regarding the *carpe diem* theme in the final lines as the climax to the poet's

exhortations to love throughout the sequence: 'This programme constitutes a powerful antithesis to Delia's Diana-like disdain and provides a patent contrast to the main conflict in the sequence proper. This impression is further strengthened by the final injunction to love while it is not yet too late.' Daniel's ability to capture the lyrical sensuality of Tasso's Italian in English prompts Svensson to stress how in this invocation to love freely the 'balance is restored between chastity and passion' in the sequence: Svensson, *Silent Art*, p. 342. Roche's interpretation of Daniel's ironic intent in translating the chorus is entirely different: 'Daniel appends Tasso's version of this poem to his own sonnet sequence because Tasso's irony is precisely what he needs to complement the inadequate complaints of his Rosamond, and his own inadequacy in his pleas to Delia.' Roche, *English Sonnet Sequences*, p. 377.

113 See Gordon Braden, '"*Vivamus mea Lesbia*" in the English Renaissance', *ELR* 9 (1979), 199–224.

114 Walter R. Davis, ed., *The Works of Thomas Campion* (Faber, London, 1969), p. xix.

115 Roche, *English Sonnet Sequences*, p. 378. A good example of Fraunce's technique is his expansion of the original 'gli angui errâr senz'ira o tosco' [661], which Daniel leaves out of his version altogether, into two complete lines: 'Nor that stingles snakes and harmeles slippery serpents/Slyded abroad by the fields and neuer breathed any poyson' [5–6]. Abraham Fraunce, *The Countess of Pembrokes Ivychurch* (London, 1591), sig. C2r.

116 B. T. Sozzi, ed., *Aminta* (Liviana Editrice, Padua, 1957), p. 42; Daniel, *Works*: *To Delia*, p. 29.

117 Tina Krontiris, *Oppositional Voices: Women as Writers and Translators of Literature in the English Renaissance* (Routledge, London, 1992), p. 68.

118 Sprague, *Poems and a Defence or Ryme*, p. 129; Daniel's nostalgia for the Golden Age of the Wilton circle at this particular moment may have been inspired by the knowledge that it has come to an end with the death of the second Earl of Pembroke in January 1601.

119 Sprague, *Poems and a Defence of Ryme*, pp. 140–1.

120 Story Donno persuasively argues that Tailboys Dymoke is responsible for the translation: Elizabeth Story Donno, ed., *Three Renaissance Pastorals* (Medieval and Renaissance Texts and Studies, Binghamton, 1993), pp. xxiii–xxiv.

121 See Eccles, 'Daniel in France and Italy', p. 165, for the dates of the trip.

122 Story Donno, *Renaissance Pastorals*, p. 55.

123 John Pitcher, 'Samuel Daniel's occasional and dedicatory verse: a critical edition' (Oxford DPhil thesis, 1978), i, p. 7.

124 'Il Poeta nostro habbia fatta questa Canzona à concorrenza del primo Choro, che è nell'Aminta, il qual comincia anch'egli. O bella età dell' oro; (i concetti della quale son presi in gran parte dalla quarta Egloga di Virgilio) hauendo egli prese tutte le rime di quella; & con esse, non solo fabbricata la sua, ma detto tutto 'l contrario di quello, che disse il Tasso: biasimando quella l'honore, & questa lodandolo.' ('Our poet has written this Canzone to rival the first chorus of the *Aminta*, which also begins 'O bella età dell' oro'

(whose images are derived largely from the fourth Eclogue of Virgil), having taken all the rhymes from it; and with them, he has not only constructed his own poem, but has expressed the exact opposite of what Tasso wrote, censuring that notion of honour, and praising this.') Battista Guarini, *Il pastor fido* (Venice, 1602), p. 349.

125 Guarini, *Pastor fido*, p. 349.
126 Story Donno, *Renaissance Pastorals*, p. 143; Luigi Fassò, ed., *Il pastor fido* (Einaudi, Turin, 1976), p. 172.
127 Story Donno, *Renaissance Pastorals*, p. 16; Daniel, *Works: To Delia*, p. 30.
128 For the circumstances surrounding the commissioning of Daniel to write a play for this occasion see Jason Lawrence, '"The whole complection of *Arcadia* chang'd": Samuel Daniel and Italian lyric drama', *Medieval and Renaissance Drama in England* 11 (1999), 143–71; pp. 154–7.
129 Latin versions of Guarini's *Il pastor fido* and Groto's *Il pentimento amoroso*, two of Daniel's direct sources, are performed at Cambridge in the early years of the seventeenth century. Scott suggests a date of around 1603 for *Parthenia*, the anonymous Latin version of Groto's play: Mary A. Scott, *Elizabethan Translations from the Italian* (Houghton Mifflin, Boston, 1916). W. W. Greg, *Pastoral Poetry and Pastoral Drama: A Literary Inquiry* (A. H. Bullen, London, 1905), p. 251, cites 1602 as the date for the performance of *Pastor fidus* at King's College.
130 Story Donno, *Renaissance Pastorals*, p. 230; Sozzi, *Aminta*, p. 106.
131 Violet M. Jeffery, 'Italian and English pastoral drama of the Renaissance, III: sources of Daniel's *Queen's Arcadia* and Randolph's *Amyntas*', *MLR* 19 (1924), 435–44; p. 438.
132 Story Donno, *Renaissance Pastorals*, p. 187; Giorgio Brunello and Antonio Lodo, eds, *Luigi Groto: Opere* (Minelliana, Rovigo, 1987), ii, p. 212.
133 Rees, *Samuel Daniel*, p. 116.
134 See Jonson's preface to *Hymenaei*, printed in 1606, in C. H. Herford and Percy Simpson, eds, *Ben Jonson*, vii (Clarendon Press, Oxford, 1941), pp. 209–10. Donaldson argues that *Volpone* is first performed at the Globe in the early months of 1606, and is also successfully performed at both Oxford and Cambridge before its first printing, with a dedication to the two universities, in 1607: Ian Donaldson, ed., *Ben Jonson* (Oxford University Press, Oxford, 1985), p. 617.
135 See, for example, Rees, *Samuel Daniel*, p. 112.
136 Herford and Simpson, *Ben Jonson*, v, p. 73.
137 Florio, *Worlde of Wordes*, sig. A4r.
138 See Jeffery, 'Italian and English pastoral drama'. Daniel's borrowings from Groto continue to elude the attention of some critics. Orr mentions a Latin translation of Groto's play, called *Parthenia*, found in manuscript at Cambridge, but claims that *Il pentimento amoroso* 'apparently had no other influence in England': David Orr, *Italian Renaissance Drama in England before 1625* (University of North Carolina Press, Chapel Hill, 1970), p. 90.
139 Lyle H. Butrick, '*The Queenes Arcadia* by Samuel Daniel, edited, with introduction and notes' (unpublished PhD thesis, SUNY: Buffalo, 1968), p. 149.

140 See Stringer's report of the royal visit to Oxford, quoted in John Nichols, *The Progresses, Processions, and Magnificent Festivities, of King James the First* (London, 1828), i, pp. 530–60; p. 553.
141 See F. S. Boas, *University Drama in the Tudor Age* (Clarendon Press, Oxford, 1914), and 'University Plays' in Ward and Waller, eds, *The Cambridge History of English Literature*, vi (Cambridge University Press, Cambridge, 1910), pp. 293–327, and Orr, *Italian Renaissance Drama*, pp. 3–5.
142 Frank H. Ristine, *English Tragicomedy: Its Origin and History* (Russell and Russell, New York, 1910), p. 105.
143 Story Donno, *Renaissance Pastorals*, p. xxxi.
144 Jeffery, 'Italian and English pastoral drama', p. 435.
145 Samuel Daniel, *The Queenes Arcadia* (London, 1606), sig.A2r.
146 Greg, *Pastoral Poetry*, p. 254.
147 Rees, *Samuel Daniel*, p. 118, draws attention to 'the confusion of Latin fervour in matter and Anglo-Saxon phlegm in manner' in the play. Story Donno, *Renaissance Pastorals*, p. 228.
148 Greg, *Pastoral Poetry*, p. 254.
149 Proctor argues that *Hymens Triumph* is 'more independent of its models' than the earlier pastoral: Johanna Proctor, 'The Queen's Arcadia and Hymen's Triumph: Samuel Daniel's court pastoral plays' in J. Salmons and W. Moretti, eds, *The Renaissance in Ferrara and its European Horizons* (University of Wales Press, Cardiff, 1984), pp. 83–109; p. 87.
150 Proctor, 'Daniel's court pastoral plays', pp. 104–5.
151 Phillis' hopeless love for Clarindo recalls Olivia's love for Cesario in *Twelfth Night*, and Montanus' wounding of the disguised Silvia echoes Philaster's stabbing of Bellario, the disguised Euphrasia, in Beaumont and Fletcher's tragicomedy.
152 Proctor, 'Daniel's court pastoral plays', p. 106.
153 The play is performed on 3 February, 1614, at the newly renovated Somerset House to celebrate the marriage of Robert Ker, first Lord Roxborough, and Jean Drummond.
154 Greg, *Pastoral Poetry*, p. 259.
155 Sozzi, *Aminta*, pp. 29–30.
156 Pitcher, *Hymen's Triumph*, p. 7.
157 *Ibid.*, p. 5.
158 *Ibid.*, p. 50.
159 *Ibid.*, p. 40.
160 *Ibid.*, p. 30. See Petrarch's sonnet 190 ('Una candida cerva sopra l'erba'), where Laura is figured as the elusive white doe.
161 Silvia addresses the inanimate landscape and its inhabitants directly in IV, iii, when she discovers Thirsis resting.
162 'Note on Chalmer's life of Daniel' in H. N. Coleridge, ed., *The Literary Remains of Samuel Taylor Coleridge* (London, 1836–39), iii, p. 360. Coleridge also refers to *Hymens Triumph* on another occasion, when he says that 'the style and language are such as any very pure and manly writer of the present day ... would use': *Table Talk* 6 (1834), p. 505.

3

'Give me the ocular proof': Shakespeare's Italian language-learning habits

THE MATTER and extent of Shakespeare's knowledge of the Italian language is one that continues to provoke much critical scepticism. No critic has ever seriously denied Shakespeare's use of Italian materials in composing several of his plays, but for some two hundred and fifty years the question of in which language Shakespeare read these sources has been a highly contentious one.[1] Even the most recent consideration of 'Shakespeare's knowledge of Italian' is unable to provide any conclusive answers: 'Did Shakespeare read these sources in Italian, or did he have to rely on English and French translations of these works? Nothing certain is known.'[2] This quest for absolute certainty is probably impossible to fulfil, but it has arisen in response to the strong critical desire to disprove Shakespeare's knowledge of other languages. The favoured method of negative proof for Italian has its origins in Richard Farmer's notorious *An Essay on the Learning of Shakespeare* of 1767, where 'again and again he shows that passages which had been urged as convincing proof of knowledge of Latin or Greek are either borrowed from contemporary translations or illustrated by contemporary usage'.[3] For all his invaluable rigour in demonstrating Shakespeare's indebtedness to North's version of Plutarch and Golding's version of *Metamorphoses*, there are serious flaws in Farmer's approach which need to be explored, as they have continued to have a pervasive negative impact on considerations of Shakespeare's language acquisition. Farmer's rigour has not always been matched in the 'craze for translation-hunting' with regard to Shakespeare's use of sources in modern languages, particularly Italian, where the mere existence of a contemporary English translation (or, failing that, a French one) is deemed sufficient to cast doubt on the playwright's ability to read the original:[4]

> One meets with difficulty in the study of his sources because where the original of a drama or comedy is clearly an Italian *novella*, Shakespeare seems often to have had access to it through an earlier English play or poem, or through a French or English translation.[5]

Lytton Sells's remark is characteristic of two widely adopted critical weaknesses in approaching the question of Shakespeare's knowledge of Italian. Firstly, there is the privileging of available translations at the expense of the original text, and secondly there is an almost unwitting emphasis on the means by which Shakespeare might have had access to his Italian materials, rather than any attempt to explore the method by which he might have acquired a working knowledge of the language itself. Farmer's contention that Shakespeare's plays display no direct Classical learning was convincingly rebutted only by Baldwin's meticulous investigations into the playwright's apparent references to Latin literature in relation to the typical educational methods and grammar-school syllabus of the 1570s.[6] There has been no equivalent inquiry into Shakespeare's borrowings from Italian literature in the light of late sixteenth-century modern language-learning habits; this chapter will provide such an exploration, arguing that Shakespeare approaches the matter of learning a new language in exactly the manner of his contemporaries. This will demonstrate that the critical desire always to choose decisively between versions of a text in different languages is fundamentally flawed. From the 1570s onwards, the language-learning process is clearly predicated on the sustained use of parallel texts.

As there is no evidence to suggest that Shakespeare ever visited Italy, his putative knowledge of the Italian language must have been acquired in England either by means of a professional language teacher or from his own self-study of the language-learning manuals so popular in the late Elizabethan period. These two options are not mutually exclusive, and the name of one prominent Italian teacher is frequently given in connection with Shakespeare in both fields. Since the 1930s critics have been seeking parallels between the plays and John Florio's two Italian–English dialogue books, *Florio his First Fruites* (1578) and the *Second Frutes* (1591), though often to reinforce the possibility of a direct connection between the two men.[7] Certainly no acquaintance is necessary to explain Shakespeare's apparent familiarity with Florio's manuals, yet it still seems critically preferable to hypothesise about personal instruction than to accept the equally likely method of private book learning.

The latest attempt to link the two figures depends on the presence of both Florio and Shakespeare in the household of the Earl of Southampton at the time when the latter dedicates his poems *Venus and Adonis* and *Lucrece* to Henry Wriothesley, that is between April 1593 and May 1594. Florio himself reveals that the Earl was one of his pupils for Italian in the dedicatory epistle to Southampton, the Earl of Rutland and the Countess of Bedford printed with the 1598 edition of his dictionary, *A Worlde of Wordes*, and Yates has shown that the teacher was certainly a member of the Earl's household in October 1594.[8] Bate encourages the reader to accept an acquaintance between teacher and playwright at this time primarily to make the playful suggestion that Florio's wife might be a biographical candidate for the Dark Lady of *Shakespeare's Sonnets*. Additionally, however, he almost casually credits Florio with a striking impact on Shakespeare's future dramatic progression:

> His presence in the household seems to have been of considerable importance for the development of Shakespeare's career – it accounts for much of the dramatist's broad, though very patchy, acquaintance with Italian literature and his slight knowledge of the Italian language. It seems to have been immediately after the period of Southampton's patronage during the closure of the theatres that Shakespeare began to make extensive and ambitious use of Italian settings and plots in his plays. Florio was the obvious person to introduce him to his sources for these. In the same period, phrases from Florio's Italian language manual, *First Fruits*, start appearing in Shakespeare's works; it is even possible that the Italian's affected language is parodied in the character of Don Armado and his pedantry in the character of Holofernes in *Love's Labour's Lost*, Shakespeare's sonnet-ridden play of circa 1595. That play's title and subject matter, its merry demolition of stale courtly love-language, are strongly suggested by a passage in *First Fruits*: 'We need not speak so much of love, all books are full of love, with so many authors, that it were labour lost to speak of Love'.[9]

For Bate, then, it is the meeting between Shakespeare and Florio that gives the playwright the impetus to turn to Italian sources, and it is the teacher who provides him with both a rudimentary knowledge of the language and guided access to a collection of Italian books. The apparently simultaneous appearance of phrases from the *First Fruites* in Shakespeare's work certainly demonstrates his knowledge of Florio's manual, but it does not depend on an actual acquaintance with its author. Is Bate suggesting that Shakespeare acquires 'his slight knowledge of the Italian language' from Florio's private instruction, from his printed works, or possibly both? It is perhaps unfair to expect too much detail in such a fleeting reference, but it is indicative of a wider critical practice, which neglects any analysis of the specific method of language acquisition. There is a strong likelihood that Florio taught his pupils by working through the dialogues printed in his manuals,[10] but in this instance it seems to be enough merely to suggest personal contact between the two men to account for Shakespeare's language-learning habits.

It is essential to probe Shakespeare's borrowings from Florio's manuals to determine what they might reveal about the playwright's attempts to acquire some knowledge of Italian. For the past two hundred and fifty years, following Warburton's observation that Florio was the model for Holofernes, critics have tended to look towards *Love's Labour's Lost* most frequently in connection with the dialogue books. Bate points out the similarity between the title and an English phrase from chapter thirty-one of the *First Fruites*; the only other borrowing in this play, however, appears to be the badly mangled proverb about Venice given by Holofernes in Act IV. The version printed in both the quarto and first Folio ('*Vemchie vencha, que non le unde, que non te perreche*') is presumably based on the proverb '*Venetia, chi non ti vede, non ti pretia, ma chi ti vede, ben gli costa*',[11] found in both the *First* and *Second Frutes*, but also in James Sandford's *The Garden of Recreation* (1573), one of Florio's own sources.

It is Shakespeare's allusion to another proverb, which also appears in both Florio's collections, in *The Taming of the Shrew* that points towards an earlier engagement with the Italian manuals. After the Induction scenes, the play opens with Lucentio's observation that he is 'arriv'd fore Lombardy,/The pleasant garden of great Italy'. While these lines may suggest that Shakespeare's knowledge of Italian geography is not much improved from *The Two Gentlemen of Verona* (Lucentio has just arrived in Padua in the Veneto), they do demonstrably recall the proverb 'Lombardie is the garden of the world'.[12] Again the proverb is not unique to Florio, but the use of occasional Italian phrases in the opening act of the play confirms Shakespeare's acquaintance with the *First Fruites*. The second scene contains the most sustained Italian dialogue in any of Shakespeare's plays:

> PET: Signior Hortensio, come you to part the fray?
> *Con tutto il cuore ben trovato*, may I say.
> HOR: *Alla nostra casa ben venuto, molto honorato signior mio Petruccio.*
>
> [I, ii, 23–26][13]

The use of the Italian language is uncharacteristic of Shakespeare, however, even in the numerous plays with Italian settings. Hoenselaars suggests that here uniquely 'the use of Italian serves to establish the locale shortly following the transition from the Cotswolds of the Induction to the Padua location of the inset comedy', providing a kind of 'local colour' through the language.[14] This linguistic detail derives almost entirely from the opening chapters of the *First Fruites*, which are full of these polite greetings in the *'Parlar familiare'*, including the expression which Shakespeare partially translates in the final line of the scene: 'Petruccio, I shall be your *ben venuto*' [I, ii, 282].[15] Ironically, the longest single passage of Italian in Shakespeare's work may not be an indication of his mastery of the language but rather of his apprenticeship in it. Shaheen doubtfully argues that 'the manual itself presupposes that the reader has some knowledge of Italian since the first chapter includes not only everyday greetings, but also advanced conversation'.[16] This apparently advanced conversation extends only to a series of simple questions and expressions of likes and dislikes, and it is clear that there is intended to be a gradual increase in complexity, in terms of both grammar and vocabulary, throughout the dialogues in the first seventeen chapters. A beginner in the language would, like Shakespeare, be expected to begin at the beginning, and it is possible that the bemused response to this exchange given to the ostensibly Italian servant Grumio is a sly reference to the playwright's own inability, until very recently, to distinguish between Latin and Italian: 'Nay, 'tis no matter, sir, what he 'leges in Latin' [I, ii, 28].[17]

If an analysis of the opening scenes of *The Taming of the Shrew* helps to uncover Shakespeare's earliest attempt to engage with the Italian language, it is clearly necessary to consider when this might have occurred. The play is not printed before the Folio in 1623, but it is now generally thought to precede by at least a year or two *The Taming of a Shrew*, printed in 1594.[18] It is probably not the first comedy for which Shakespeare uses an Italian setting (that is *The Two Gentlemen of Verona*), but it does seem to be the first to combine the setting with a discernible interest in Italian source materials. The love intrigues in the Bianca plot derive from Gascoigne's *Supposes* (printed in 1573), a translation of Ariosto's comedy *I Suppositi*. Even if Shakespeare's language skills are insufficiently advanced to permit a direct knowledge of Ariosto's play at this point, it is *The Taming of the Shrew*, rather than the later *Love's Labour's Lost*, which decisively marks the playwright's deepening engagement with the Italian language and literary traditions.

Shakespeare's earliest borrowings from Florio's manuals seem also to predate the period of Southampton's patronage, which suggests that the impetus for the playwright to start learning Italian in his late twenties may not have come directly from a meeting with the language teacher. Speculation about what triggers Shakespeare's interest is probably futile, but the printing of the *Second Frutes* in 1591 might have been a catalyst. If the appearance of Florio's second manual creates a revived interest in his methods of instruction for Italian, then it would make sense for the uninitiated language learner to seek out the first manual, and begin by studying its opening dialogues before progressing through that book, and on to the more advanced material in the *Second Frutes*. The evidence that can be gathered from Shakespeare's relatively frequent allusions to the manuals fits exactly this hypothesis. In around 1592 Shakespeare uses expressions from the early chapters of the *First Fruites* in *The Taming of the Shrew*, and also displays a nascent interest in Italian proverbs. His growing knowledge of Italian proverbial material can be traced in *Richard III* (1592–93), *Love's Labour's Lost* (1594–95), *The Merchant of Venice* (1596–97) and *Henry V* (1599).[19] Florio cites many proverbs in both manuals, but the source for Shylock's expression 'Fast bind, fast find' [II, v, 53] is found only in the first chapter of the later one, which implies that Shakespeare has advanced on to the *Second Frutes* during the course of his studies.

The pattern of verbal echoes from Florio in Shakespeare's plays suggests a similar progression. The most celebrated line from Shakespeare's early works, certainly written before September 1592 when it is parodied in the attack on the upstart playwright attributed to Robert Greene,[20] recalls a phrase from Florio's first manual. In chapter fourteen, '*Parlar amoroso*', one of the speakers vividly describes a disdainful woman with 'her hart of Tiger', which is clearly suggestive for the Duke of York's description of the viciously cruel Queen Margaret in *3 Henry VI*: 'O tiger's heart wrapped in a woman's hide!' [I, iv, 138].²¹ The nurse's response to Friar Laurence's wise advice to Romeo in *Romeo and Juliet* (1594–95) echoes the listener's impressed response to the 'Sentences divine and profane' recounted in chapter eighteen of the *First Fruites*:

> O Lord, I could have stayed here all the night
> To hear good counsel! O, what learning is!
> [III, iii, 158–159]

> Certis if you wyl beleeue me, I coulde staye night and daye, to heare such sentences, you have much reioced my hart. [sig. 28r]²²

In addition to his use of proverbs from both of Florio's manuals in *The Merchant of Venice*, Shakespeare seems to allude to the teacher's repeated complaint about the typically monolingual Englishman in Portia's description of her potential suitors to Nerissa:

> You know I say nothing to him, for he understands not me, nor I him. He hath neither Latin, French, nor Italian, and you will come into the court and swear that I have a poor pennyworth in the English. He is a proper man's picture, but alas, who can converse with a dumb show? [I, ii, 57–61]

> When I arriued first in London, I coulde not speake Englishe, and I met aboue fiue hundred persons, afore I coulde find one, that could tel me in Italian, or French, where the Post dwelt. [*First Fruites*, sig. 51r]²³

This play is the first to demonstrate a simultaneous acquaintance with both the Italian manuals, suggesting that Shakespeare has progressed on to the *Second Frutes* by the middle of the 1590s. The Bastard's description of 'your traveller' in *King John* (1595–96) confirms Shakespeare's knowledge of one of the most frequently cited chapters of Florio's second manual.²⁴ Yates suggests that the passage displays Shakespeare's familiarity with what is a popular topos in language-learning manuals,²⁵ but the allusion is more specific. The parodic over-politeness of the exchange, clearly learnt from a primer, and in particular the verbally redundant triple phrases (a useful means of offering synonyms in Italian in the manual itself), are entirely characteristic of Florio's sixth chapter 'concerning many familiar and cerimonius complements, among sixe gentlemen, . . . who talke of many pleasant matters, but especially of diuers necessarie, profitable, ciuill, and prouerbiall precepts for a trauailour':[26]

> He and his toothpick at my worship's mess;
> And when my knightly stomach is sufficed,
> Why then I suck my teeth and catechize
> My pickèd man of countries. 'My dear sir,'
> Thus leaning on mine elbow I begin,
> 'I shall beseech you-'. That is Question now;
> And then comes Answer like an Absey book.
> 'O sir,' says Answer, 'at your best command,
> At your employment, at your service, sir.'
> 'No, sir', says Question, 'I, sweet sir, at yours.'
> And so, ere Answer knows what Question would,
> Saving in dialogue of compliment,
> And talking of the Alps and Apennines,
> The Pyrenean and the River Po,
> It draws toward supper in conclusion so.
> [I, i, 190-204]

Florio's 'precepts' for a traveller may also be recalled later in Polonius' advice to Laertes before his return to France in *Hamlet* (1600-1).[27] It is striking that, after the composition of *The Merchant of Venice*, which is the first play with an Italian source for which no contemporay translation exists, most of Shakespeare's echoes of Florio are from the more advanced manual. This strongly suggests the playwright's increased linguistic competence by the latter years of the 1590s. The latest borrowing from Florio is Iago's proverb-laden description of women to Desdemona in *Othello* (1603-4), which, according to Simonini, derives directly from an equivalent passage in the long debate between Silvestro and Pandulfo in the final chapter of the *Second Frutes*:

> Come on, come on, you are pictures out of door,
> Bells in your parlours, wildcats in your kitchens,
> Saints in your injuries; devils being offended,
> Players in your housewifery, and hussies in your beds.
> [II, i, 112-115]

> Women are in churches, Saints: abroad, Angels: at home deuills: at windowes Syrens: at doores, pyes: and in gardens, Goates. [p. 175][28]

The evidence indicates that, in the ten or more years between *The Taming of the Shrew* and *Othello*, Shakespeare has carefully worked his way from the opening dialogues of the *First Fruites* through to the concluding dialogue of the *Second Frutes*. It is important to stress this sense of progress in the language-learning process; as the dialogues increase in complexity in terms of both grammar and vocabulary, the student's reading skills in Italian are expected to improve accordingly. Even if Shakespeare is unable to read an Italian source directly when writing *The Taming of the Shrew*, his close study of Florio's manuals should certainly enable him to read the original Italian prose source for *Othello* by the early years of the seventeenth century. Indeed, there is evidence to suggest that Shakespeare succeeds in acquiring a competent reading ability in Italian rather more quickly than this. By the second half of the 1590s Shakespeare makes frequent use of Italian settings and stories, particularly in his comedies, and at least one of these direct sources exists only in Italian; there is no available translation in either English or French. Shakespeare, then, evidently has the ability to read Italian prose unaided by the latter 1590s, but by what means does he acquire his knowledge of specific Italian books?

The principal advantage in advocating a direct relationship between Florio and Shakespeare is to offer a plausible explanation for how the playwright might have gained access to his Italian materials. Although this emphasises means rather than methods of reading, it is a significant issue to address in any investigation of sources. Florio strives to develop a substantial library of Italian books in England, which he bequeaths in his will to William Herbert, the third Earl of Pembroke. It is possible to trace the development of his library closely by means of the lists of 'the names of the Bookes and Auctors, that haue bin read of purpose, for the accomplishing of this Dictionarie' which precede both *A Worlde of Wordes*, printed in 1598, and *Queen Anna's New World of Words*, printed in 1611. The dictionary is first entered on the Stationers' Register in March 1596, and the expanded version is probably completed by 1609. In the intervening years Florio's collection of Italian books more than trebles, from around seventy texts for the first edition to over two hundred and fifty for the second, including many of 'the wordes of some twenty good Italian auctors, that I could neuer obtaine the sight of, and hope shortly to enioy', while working on the first version.[29] Florio's letter 'To the Reader' indicates the difficulty of acquiring Italian books in England, certainly in the mid-1590s when he is first compiling the dictionary and when, according to Bate, he would also be guiding Shakespeare in his Italian reading. Of Shakespeare's putative Italian sources only

Boccaccio's *Decamerone* is consulted by Florio for the first edition of the dictionary.[30]

If it is Florio who introduces Shakespeare directly to his Italian materials, then theirs must be a continuing association stretching beyond the immediate period of Southampton's patronage. This can be argued quite plausibly by cross-referencing Shakespeare's probable Italian sources in plays from the late 1590s onwards with Florio's expanded list of books consulted for the second edition of the dictionary. There are four texts with which Shakespeare seems to have been familiar that are referred to only in Florio's second dictionary, and which were presumably acquired after the completion of the first (by March 1596). Matteo Bandello's two-volume *Novelle* (1554) provide the main plot and certain names for *Much Ado about Nothing*, probably composed in late 1598,[31] as well as a version of the story used in *Twelfth Night*, probably written in 1601. Giambattista Giraldi Cinthio's *Gli Hecatommithi* (1565) provides the original stories for both *Measure for Measure* and *Othello*, possibly written simultaneously in 1603–4. Stories from both of these collections are already available in French translations, by Belleforest and Chappuys respectively, perhaps offering further sources for plot details, but there is no way of tracing whether Florio, a professional teacher of French as well as Italian, possessed these volumes alongside the Italian originals.

The one anomalous Italian prose source used by Shakespeare is Ser Giovanni Fiorentino's *Il Pecorone*, written in the fourteenth century but not printed until 1558. This is the only volume not to have been consulted by Florio for either edition of the dictionary; perhaps more significantly, it is the one collection not to have been translated into either French or English during the sixteenth century. The insistent parallels between one of Fiorentino's stories and *The Merchant of Venice* thus complicate the arguments that Florio was the principal source for all of Shakespeare's Italian materials, and also that the playwright needed to depend on a translation in order to understand an Italian prose text by 1596–97.[32]

Although Shakespeare is drawn predominantly towards prose sources for his dramatisations, his knowledge of Italian materials seems to have extended to certain plays as well. Indeed, the only contemporary reference to the playwright's use of a modern European source alludes specifically to Italian drama. After witnessing a performance of *Twelfth Night* at the Middle Temple in February 1602, the law student John Manningham records his observations on the play in his diary: 'At our feast we had a play called "Twelve night, or what you will", much like the *Comedy of Errors*, or *Menaechmi* in Plautus, but most like and near to that in Italian called *Inganni*.'³³ Manningham notes a similarity between this play and an earlier Shakespeare comedy as well as a Roman one, but he observes that the closest analogue can be found in an Italian comedy. There are two sixteenth-century plays entitled *Gl' Inganni* ('The Deceptions'), the first by Niccolò Secchi, printed in 1562, and the other by Curzio Gonzaga, printed in 1592. Florio refers to an 'Inganni, Comedia' in his 1611 book list, but unfortunately he does not specify its author. The later play includes a cross-dressing girl who uniquely disguises herself as Cesare, which is clearly suggestive for Viola's disguise as Cesario. Both of these plays derive, as does the version in Bandello's *Novelle*, from an earlier prose comedy *Gl' Ingannati* ('The Deceived'), first performed in 1531 and then printed in 1538 with another interlude *Il Sacrificio*, which is given first on the title page of all eight editions printed by 1595. Bullough argues that this, rather than *Gl' Inganni*, is the play 'with a story nearest to Shakespeare's account of Viola, Orsino and Olivia',³⁴ and it is thus noteworthy that 'Sacrificio, Comedia' is another play consulted by Florio for the expanded version of the dictionary.³⁵ Any lingering uncertainty about the likelihood of Shakespeare's access to more than one Italian dramatic version of this story at the start of the seventeenth century can, then, be accounted for with reference to the playwright's continuing association with Florio.

Does a connection with Florio provide the only possible explanation for Shakespeare's access to Italian books? Answers to the question of how and where Shakespeare may have conducted his voluminous reading must remain largely conjectural, but one recent theory posits a connection between the playwright and the printer Richard Field, a fellow Warwickshire man. In 1579 Field is apprenticed to the immigrant French printer Thomas Vautrollier, who eventually becomes his father-in-law. Field succeeds Vautrollier in 1590, and Duncan-Jones twice suggests that his London printing house may have been used as a 'working library' by Shakespeare.³⁶ She points out that Field is responsible for a reprinting in 1595 of Sir Thomas North's translation of Plutarch's *Lives*, a book that Shakespeare uses repeatedly as a source from the late 1590s. Field maintains Vautrollier's interest in printing materials in French, and also expands into printing in Italian in the early 1590s. Between 1592 and 1599 Field prints six works by the immigrant writer Petruccio Ubaldini, who turns to him immediately after the sudden cessation of Italian editions from the presses of John Wolfe in 1591. If Field's printing house does provide a haven for Shakespeare's reading, then it is certainly one in which he could encounter materials in French and Italian, as well as English.

Duncan-Jones goes on to develop an alternative hypothesis about Shakespeare's access to Italian materials in the early years of the seventeenth century, although it is one which again fails fully to consider his knowledge of the language itself by focusing instead on the playwright's personal connections. Manningham's recognition of an Italian source for *Twelfth Night* is taken as the point of departure:

> Manningham's identification of the comedy's chief source as 'that in Italian called *Inganni*'... has not been taken as seriously as it should, perhaps because of the difficulty of working out quite how Shakespeare could have gained access to an untranslated Italian play. It is true that Shakespeare seems also to have drawn on Barnabe Riche's prose tale of 'Apolonius and Silla', contained in his *Riche his Farewell to Militarie Profession* (1581). But with the half-Italian Marston as his friend and almost his collaborator, neither access to a recent Italian book, nor a good grasp of its narrative contents, seems at all problematic.[37]

There are, however, a number of assumptions behind this neat solution which do prove more problematic. The central argument, that Shakespeare and John Marston share a close working relationship between 1600 and 1602, is persuasive and could even be extended by a year or two, but this suggestion that Marston becomes Shakespeare's principal conduit for Italian materials does not stand up to sustained scrutiny. Firstly, Duncan-Jones is careful to avoid implying that Shakespeare necessarily knows any Italian with the formulation that he could have obtained 'a good grasp' of the narrative contents of the play from Marston. Did the younger playwright merely outline the details of the plot to Shakespeare, rather than use his apparently superior Italian skills to help him actually read the text? There is a similar ambivalence applied to the later *Othello*, which is described as 'a play perhaps written while Shakespeare was still closely associated with Marston, for its Italian source in Cinthio's *Hecatommithi* had not been translated', at least not into English.[38] Marston's influence on Shakespeare at the start of the seventeenth century becomes, in this reading, largely a means to explain away the difficulty of accounting for Shakespeare's untranslated Italian sources without confronting the thorny question of his knowledge of Italian. The principal limitation is that the reading focuses only on the early years of the seventeenth century, despite the fact that Shakespeare has already used Fiorentino's untranslated *Il Pecorone* some four or five years prior to this.

The second problematic area concerns Marston's own acquisition of the Italian language. Duncan-Jones stresses that he is 'half-Italian', creating a direct parallel with Florio, born in England to an Italian father and an English mother. Marston's parents are English (his father) and second-generation Italian (his mother), though it is not certain that his maternal grandparents are both Italian.[39] The assumption that the son inherits an innate familiarity with his mother's *madre lingua* is, then, perhaps unfounded, even if the Page's aside to the audience seems to allude knowingly to the playwright's family background ('some private respect') to explain the sudden switch into melodious Italian in Act IV of *Antonio and Mellida*:

> I think confusion of Babel is fallen upon these lovers that they change their language; ... But howsoever, if I should sit in judgement, 'tis an error easier to be pardoned by the auditors than excused by the authors; and yet some private respect may rebate the edge of the keener censure. [IV, i, 209–216][40]

An examination of Marston's substantial use of Italian in this play, usually given to his characters in moments of heightened emotion, clearly shows a good working knowledge of the language by the turn of the sixteenth century. He is the only contemporary playwright who, instead of using merely the odd word or phrase, composes verse dialogue in the language, perhaps even parodying some of the familiar exaggerations of Italian love poetry in the lyrical exchange between Antonio and Mellida:[41]

> ANT: *Dammi un bacio da quella bocca beata.*
> *Lasciami coglier l'aura odorata*
> *Che in sù aleggia, in quelle dolci labbra.*
> MEL: *Dammi l'impero del tuo gradit' amore,*
> *Che bea me, con sempiterno onore,*
> *Così così, mi converrà morir.*
> [IV, i, 193–198]
>
> (ANT: Give me a kiss from that blessed mouth. Let me gather the perfumed air that hovers there on those sweet lips.
> MEL: Give me the empire of your pleasing love which blesses me with eternal honour, for thus is it fitting for me to die.)[42]

'GIVE ME THE OCULAR PROOF'

If Marston's greater facility in the language sets him apart, it is equally important to stress that his method of using Italian materials in his plays is entirely consistent with that of his contemporaries. Most noteworthy are some significant parallels in his works of the early seventeenth century with Shakespeare's treatment of Italian sources. Any connection between *Twelfth Night, or What You Will* and Marston's *What You Will*, performed in 1601 and printed in 1607, can be extended to their simultaneous use of untranslated Italian plays. Marston is indebted to Sforza degli Oddi's comedy *I morti vivi* ('The Living Dead'), printed in 1576, for key elements of his plot. While this would seem to confirm both Marston's familiarity with the language and his access to relatively obscure Italian texts, there are other practices shared with Shakespeare which would be used, in the latter's case, to argue for a limited or indeed non-existent knowledge of Italian. Marston is evidently as familiar with Florio's Italian dialogue books, or at least his *First Fruites*, as Shakespeare. Mendoza's diatribe against women in the opening act of *The Malcontent*, written between 1602 and 1604, closely echoes Florio's English renditions of 'Certaine fine briefe sayings, and fine sentences' culled from Antonio Guevara in chapter thirty-nine:

> Women? Nay, Furies! Nay, worse, for they torment only the bad, but women good and bad ... O that I could rail against these monsters in nature, models of hell, curse of the earth, women that dare attempt anything, and what they attempt they care not how they accomplish; without all premeditation or prevention, rash in asking, desperate in working, impatient in suffering, extreme in desiring, slaves unto appetite, mistresses in dissembling, only constant in inconstancy, only perfect in counterfeiting; their words are feigned, their eyes forged, their sighs dissembled, their looks counterfeit, their hair false, their given hopes deceitful, their very breath artificial. [I, ii, 78-90]

> The husband that hath a naughty wife, let hym account to haue hel in his house. I say moreouer, that yll women are woorse, then the infernall Furies, for in Hell the badde are onely tormented, but the vnruly women, doo tormente both good and bade ...
> Women are hastye in askyng, determined in woorkynge, impacient in sufferynge, extreme in desirynge: for I see certayne women that wyl set them selues to desyre such thynges as were neuer seene of the dead, neyther heard of the liuyng.[43]

As Marston certainly knows Italian by 1602, it is possible, as Shaheen suggests with reference to Shakespeare's use of Florio's manuals, that 'his main interest in them was not to learn Italian but to tap them for the many English proverbs and quotations they contain'.[44] It is more likely, however, that the playwright is recalling in this dramatic context a striking description that he had first encountered when studying the *First Fruites* in order to improve his Italian language skills.

The other major source for Mendoza's speech, and indeed *The Malcontent* as a whole, is a recent Italian play, Battista Guarini's *Il pastor fido* (1590), which is printed in a definitive edition with the author's *Annotationi* and theoretical *Compendio della Poesia Tragicomica* in 1602. Marston's direct source, however, is the anonymous English translation of the play printed in the same year, as a considerable number of verbal parallels demonstrate:

> What is it that they use which is not counterfeit?
> Ope they their mouths? They lie. Moove they their eyes?
> They counterfeit their lookes. If so they sigh,
> Their sighes dissembled are. In summe, each act,
> Each looke, each gesture, is a verie lie.
> [I, v, 52–56][45]

Why, then, does a playwright capable of writing in Italian allude repeatedly to a new translation of an influential Italian play? If this were Shakespeare, any knowledge of the translation would be taken as a strong indication that he does not know the original, and by extension its language too; similarly Finkelpearl argues that this demonstrable use of the 1602 translation casts doubt on Marston's apparent 'mastery' of Italian.[46] There may be a higher degree of difficulty in understanding Guarini's polished verse than in reading the prose plays and tales more frequently used as sources for English plays, but it is unlikely that this would be beyond a writer who has already composed his own Italian lyrical verse. It seems that Marston's use of the translation, then, is a conscious choice rather than a decision made of linguistic necessity. It may also be indicative of a wider practice in approaching works in other languages, encouraged directly by the parallel-text format of the language-learning manuals. The close comparative attention to original and translation, in terms both of reading and writing, is one of the fundamental contemporary techniques for acquiring and mastering another language; it is also one which develops into a consistent habit of reading beyond the immediate process of language learning itself.

Marston's sustained attention to Guarini's *Il pastor fido* when composing his own tragicomedy *The Malcontent* provides another possible connection with Shakespeare in the early years of the seventeenth century. Hunter argues that both *All's Well That Ends Well* and *Measure for Measure* demonstrate Shakespeare's dramatic engagement with the new form of tragicomedy and display his knowledge of Guarini's play, drawing attention to specific verbal parallels in the case of *All's Well*:

> The evidence suggests that Shakespeare read the original rather than the 1602 translation of *Il Pastor Fido* but it is not substantial. It is commonly supposed, of course, that Shakespeare in the years around 1603 read the *Othello* story in Italian (it was not translated into English). A detailed response to the stylistic qualities of *Il Pastor Fido* implies a better reading ability than any made necessary by a capacity to get the gist of Cinthio's story of the Moor of Venice, but this is where the existence of the 1602 translation may be important. It is certainly an interesting coincidence that Shakespeare was writing *All's Well* in the year of the translation or the year after. The existence of the crib may have made it possible for him to work fruitfully with the Italian as well as the English.[47]

Hunter envisages Shakespeare reading Guarini's play in Italian with the assistance of the recently printed English translation, which is open in front of him simultaneously. This is exactly the kind of close parallel reading encouraged by the language teachers and practised by linguistically adept poets such as Drummond and Daniel. Whether Shakespeare needs to refer to the translation through necessity or through choice (Hunter suggests that Shakespeare's borrowings are closer to the Italian, where the fluent Marston clearly quotes from the English version), this scenario highlights the major weakness of the principal argument against Shakespeare's knowledge of other languages. In a judicious appraisal of Farmer's *An Essay on the Learning of Shakespeare* Martindale focuses on his 'one incorrect assumption', a shortcoming that has had a remarkably persistent influence on later considerations of Shakespeare's language skills:

> He established the principle – still too often ignored – that it is not enough to point to an apparent similarity between a passage in Shakespeare and one in a classical writer. It is necessary to know about Elizabethan and Jacobean literature, . . . possible intermediate vernacular sources, the availability of translations and so forth. Farmer made one incorrect assumption; that if Shakespeare used a translation he cannot also have known the original.[48]

Martindale refers specifically to Shakespeare's knowledge of Classical writers, particularly in Latin. To counter Farmer's argument that his demonstrable proof of Shakespeare's knowledge of Golding's *Metamorphosis* disproves any acquaintance with the Latin,[49] it is possible to illustrate the playwright's simultaneous engagement with both the original and the translation. The particular example used by Farmer is Prospero's renunciation of magic in the final act of *The Tempest*, derived from Medea's similar speech in Ovid's Book VII. Farmer demonstrates that Shakespeare takes the phrases 'Ye elves of hills' and 'standing lakes' (V, i, 33) directly from Golding, and so concludes that 'it is unnecessary to pursue this any further'.[50] Baldwin, however, does pursue the matter further to provide the 'ample evidence' that Shakespeare 'knew the poet in Latin as well as in Golding's translation'.[51] He favours the argument that any similarities between Shakespeare and Golding's versions can be accounted for 'in view of standard instruction in the art of translation in schools', though Kermode concludes rather that 'Shakespeare was adapting Ovid from the Latin, with a glance at Golding here and there'.[52] The example from *The Tempest* is a particularly pertinent one as it suggests that, even late in his career,[53] Shakespeare's approach to his sources maintains the kind of synchronic, bilingual engagement with different versions of a passage encouraged both at grammar school and in contemporary modern-language teaching.

Farmer is equally dismissive of the playwright's putative knowledge of modern European languages.[54] The central flaw in Farmer's argument impacts on considerations of both ancient and modern language learning, and gives rise to the question of whether Shakespeare would have approached his reading and use of these newer sources in a fundamentally different way. Recent accounts of Shakespeare's reading have focused on the habits that he shares with contemporary readers. Miola details the Elizabethan impulse to move 'rapidly, eclectically, and associatively from text to text looking for connections' and suggests that Shakespeare 'often used several sources simultaneously, collecting varying accounts of a character or incident'. With reference to the popular book-wheel, described as 'a metaphor for a kind of reading that subsists on the cross-reference', Miola argues that 'the impulse to read analogically and collect parallels everywhere shows itself in Shakespeare's work'.[55] Everywhere, it would seem, except in the case of the numerous sources in languages other than English. The kind of broad, syncretic reading characteristic of Shakespeare and his contemporaries is perversely denied when the 'varying accounts' of a story exist in more than one language. For example, in discussing the prose sources of *Twelfth Night*, Lothian focuses on the tale of Apolonius and Silla from *Riche his Farewell to Militarie Profession* (1581). He also considers earlier versions of the story in Italian and French, by Bandello (1554) and Belleforest (1570) respectively, even citing plausible parallels from each with Shakespeare's play, only to conclude that 'no clear indebtedness either to Bandello or Belleforest can be established'.[56] This is the legacy, some two hundred years on, of Farmer's approach, which prioritises the direct use of an English source at the expense of all others, even when the evidence seems to argue for a simultaneous acquaintance with accounts in various languages of the same story. It is a method that becomes even more perverse when considered in relation to the language-learning techniques of the time, which actively promote just this kind of comparative parallel reading.

It should not be a surprise either that Shakespeare's sources of Italian origin exist in multiple forms, or that it is possible to make a convincing case for his knowledge of more than one version of them. The fact that the playwright is familiar with a translation certainly does not prove that he must, therefore, be unfamiliar with the original, owing to a perceived lack of linguistic proficiency. Ironically, it may actually lend greater weight to the argument that his knowledge of Italian is sufficiently advanced to read comparatively in that language, given the favoured methods of language instruction. Shakespeare's use of a single Italian prose source for which no translation exists, Fiorentino's *Il Pecorone*, may indicate his ability to read Italian unaided as early as 1596–97, but it is anomalous in another more significant way. It is the only occasion that he does not have recourse to more than one account of an Italian story. Shakespeare's Italianate romantic comedies after *The Merchant of Venice* frequently demonstrate a developing awareness of multiple versions of the same story and, given his evident competence in reading Italian, this must be as a result of conscious choice rather than linguistic necessity. It is not clear whether Shakespeare would always distinguish between original and translation, necessarily privileging the former over the latter, as it seems that he is willing to treat each equally as potential sources. Bandello's *novella* is the principal source for *Much Ado About Nothing*, possibly supplemented with Belleforest's expanded version in French, but Shakespeare also seems to know in Italian the episode from

Ariosto's *Orlando furioso* (canto V), which is the original for the later prose renderings.[57] Shakespeare reads various prose accounts of the main story for *Twelfth Night* and, according to Manningham, he seems also to use at least one Italian play.

If Shakespeare's earliest Italian sources for romantic comedy derive from the prose *novelle*, then by the turn of the century the playwright's reading apparently extends as far as Italian verse: both epic (*Orlando furioso*) and dramatic (*Il pastor fido* and Cinthio's *Epitia*). The rest of this chapter will focus on Shakespeare's use of Italian materials between the years 1602 and 1604, demonstrating his continued adaptation of prose stories, but which is now combined with an additional interest in other generic forms. His apparent awareness of recent theoretical and practical dramatic innovations in Italy such as tragicomedy and Cinthio's *tragedia di fin lieto* ('tragedy with a happy ending') leads to a new experimentalism in Shakespeare's own dramaturgy in the early years of the seventeenth century. This is evident particularly in the so-called 'problem' plays (*All's Well That Ends Well* and *Measure for Measure*), which will be considered together with his friend Marston's simultaneous exploration of the tragicomedic form in *The Malcontent*. This formal experimentation may also be indicative of Shakespeare's increasing ability to assimilate Italian sources fully, as it marks a distinct shift away from using Italian stories principally as repositories of plot and character towards a deepening engagement with matters of genre in his dramatisations. This does not, however, lead Shakespeare to disregard English versions of his new Italian models, where they are available to him. On the contrary, the chapter will emphasise his consistent creative interweaving of details from the Italian originals and from vernacular renderings of these sources in the composition of both *Measure for Measure* and *Othello*.

'The story is extant and written in very choice Italian': Shakespeare's tragicomedic dramatisations of Italian *novelle*

All's Well That Ends Well and *Measure for Measure* derive ultimately from *novelle* by Boccaccio and Giambattista Giraldi Cinthio respectively, although Hunter's argument that he detects the influence of Guarini's *Il pastor fido* in Shakespeare's dramaturgy in the two plays suggests that the playwright approached both stories with a firm idea of dramatic tragicomedy already in his mind.[58] It seems to be Shakespeare's discovery of the works and theatrical practice of Cinthio, alongside Guarini's model for tragicomedy, which inspire his explorations in a new dramatic form, at the same time as Marston's generic experiment with *The Malcontent*. Cinthio's conception of *tragedia di fin lieto* should not to be confused with Guarini's precise definition of tragicomedy in *Il Compendio della Poesia Tragicomica*, but it is clear that the two forms are similar in the dramatic effects that they produce in the denouement. The other aspect of Cinthio's tragedic dramaturgy most relevant to Shakespeare's practice in these plays is the Italian's adaptation of prose sources for dramatic purposes; of the nine plays printed in the posthumous 1583 edition of *Le tragedie di M. Gio. Battista Giraldi Cinthio*, seven share their plots with tales from Cinthio's own prose collection, *Gli Hecatommithi*, first printed in 1565. It is not always clear whether the *novelle* predate the dramatic versions,[59] but, given the respective dates of the two editions, Shakespeare is likely to have approached the plays as dramatisations from an earlier prose source.

This raises the question of how, and when, Shakespeare becomes acquainted with Cinthio's works, and just how extensive his knowledge of them is. Patey suggests that 'if Shakespeare was not directly familiar with Giraldi's critical works, he knew, and this is plain axiomatic fact, his tragedies and "novelle"', although the evidence is certainly not as uncontested as this would imply.[60] The problem arises with identifying the precise Italian sources for *Measure for Measure*, where Cinthio's tale exists in both a prose version (*Hecatommithi*, VIII, 5) and a dramatic version (*Epitia*). Shakespeare's play does have many points of contact with the alterations made to the story for Cinthio's final *tragedia di fin lieto*, but Lascelles still doubts whether he could have had access to a play printed in a solitary Italian edition.[61] There is no such uncertainty in the case of Cinthio's *novelle*. Stories from his prose collection start to find their way into English anthologies almost immediately after their first printing,[62] and by the early years of the seventeenth century *Gli Hecatommithi* is one of the many Italian books to which Florio refers in compiling his Italian–English dictionary.[63] Among the earliest renditions from Cinthio into English prose are the three tales in *Riche his Farewell to Militarie Profession*, first printed in 1581,[64] and it may be by means of this collection that Shakespeare first comes to read Cinthio's stories. Shakespeare reads Riche alongside Bandello, and possibly Belleforest, at the start of the seventeenth century as a source for *Twelfth Night*, and Cinthio may even be an indirect source for that play. The shipwreck which separates Silla from her servant Pedro in Riche's version of the story, and which is not in Bandello, probably derives from Cinthio's account of the same story in *Gli Hecatommithi* (V, 8). Muir argues that 'Shakespeare was presumably scanning Cinthio's book in his search for plots in the early years of the seventeenth century',[65] which suggests that he turns directly to the Italian collection, which provides him with the raw materials for *Othello* and *Measure for Measure*, soon after encountering Cinthio's 'Italian Histories' through Riche's adaptations.[66]

It is more difficult to speculate on how Shakespeare would gain access to Cinthio's dramatic work, but his evident knowledge of both versions of the Epitia story suggests that he reads at least that play, and thus plausibly the entire tragic canon, printed in the single edition of 1583. If this premise is accepted, then a comparison of Cinthio's dramatic practice with that of Shakespeare in the period 1602-4 can be quite revealing. Horne demonstrates that Cinthio's earliest tragedy, the Senecan *Orbecche*, performed in 1541 and printed in 1543, has a plot which parallels a story from the second decade of his own *novelle*, but which also has an analogue in Boccaccio's *Decameron*.[67] The stories of both Orbecche (II, 2) and Altile (II, 3), from which the plot of Cinthio's earliest *tragedia di fin lieto* derives, are indebted to Boccaccio's celebrated tale of Tancredi and Ghismonda (*Decameron* IV, 1). Horne suggests that

> by basing his first tragedy on a romantic theme inspired without a doubt by Boccaccio's story, Giraldi . . . turned to account the essentially dramatic nature of the *novella*. In later plays he continued to exploit the close relationship which he saw existed between the element of the unexpected in the *novella* and the combination of *anagnorisis* and *peripeteia* required by Aristotle as the basis of a good dramatic denouement.[68]

This might almost be a description of Shakespeare's technique in the 'problem' plays, and in *All's Well That Ends Well* in particular. Like *Orbecche* and *Altile*, Shakespeare's play has its origin in a tale from Boccaccio, possibly mediated through the faithful version in William Painter's *The Palace of Pleasure* (1566). In the first tome of Painter's collection the story of Giletta of Narbon appears immediately before that of Tancred and Gismonda.[69] If Shakespeare is perusing this volume for plots at the same time that he is studying Cinthio's works, then he could certainly detect the Italian's double experiment in dramatising Boccaccio's story.

In constructing his first *tragedia di fin lieto*, *Altile*, Cinthio has to rework completely the unhappy ending of Boccaccio's tale, and of his own earlier tragedy *Orbecche*, to reveal Norrino's noble birth, and thus legitimise his marriage to Altile, in anticipation of the happy conclusion. Shakespeare bypasses the problem of having to create a fortunate recognition and reversal for his dramatisation of Boccaccio by choosing instead a story from the third day of the *Decameron*, which tells tales 'di chi alcuna cosa molto da lui desiderata con industria acquistasse o la perduta ricoverasse'.[70] In Boccaccio's tale it is the resourcefulness of the heroine Giletta that enables her finally to recover her scornful husband Beltramo, by proving to him that she has met his seemingly impossible demands. Shakespeare complicates the denouement of the story considerably; Herrick has suggested that Bertram's letter to Helena at the centre of the play is the equivalent to the misunderstood oracle in Guarini's *Il pastor fido*, which prevents resolution of the dramatic action until it has been satisfactorily fulfilled:[71] 'When thou canst get the ring upon my finger, which never shall come off, and show me a child begotten of thy body that I am father to, then call me husband; but in such a "then" I write a "never".' [III, ii, 56–59][72]

Shakespeare slightly adapts the business of the ring and the child from his source; in Boccaccio and Painter, there are two sons and one ring, whereas in *All's Well That Ends Well* there is only one child, but *two* rings. The doubling of the rings is the central element in the creation of what Bullough describes as 'a much more complicated discovery' in the play.[73] Helena, like Giletta, receives Bertram's ring through the intercessions of a chaste Florentine maiden, but she also passes on to her husband another ring, which she has received as a reward for the cure of the King of France. It is the second ring that becomes crucial to the unravelling of the plot. Diana's cryptic explanation in the final scene that this ring, which has been recognised by both the King and Lafew, is both hers and not hers recalls the equivocation of Carino concerning the nature of his relationship to his supposed son Mirtillo in the final act of *Il pastor fido* [V, v]. For Hunter, this similarity suggests a direct connection between the technique of Shakespeare's denouement and the dramaturgy of Guarini's tragicomedy, where the prevarication maintains a tension between the modes of tragedy and comedy until the final resolution into the 'ordine comico'.[74] Many of his other additions to the prose source indicate Shakespeare's direct knowledge of Guarini's play,[75] and he conceives his adaptation of Boccaccio's tale as an experiment in an Italianate dramatic form that responds to the practical precedents of both Guarini and Cinthio. The complex and unexpected denouement is an integral part of both tragicomedy and *tragedia di fin lieto*,[76] yet the final impact is quite distinct in each case. Where Guarini's definition of tragicomedy ultimately requires a complete submission to the comic order, which includes the repentance and forgiveness of any wrongdoers,[77] Cinthio's play concludes generically in a more mixed mode. Alongside the joy of Altile and Norrino at their royally sanctioned marriage, there is the suicide of the villainous Astano. In the final scene of *All's Well That Ends Well* the prolonged discomfiture of both Parolles and especially Bertram, who behaves very differently from Beltramo at the conclusion of the *novella*, suggests that Shakespeare fully appreciates the dramatic viability of this mixed mode.

The twin components of surprise and discomfort also inform the final act of *Measure for Measure*. Bullough has suggested that the intricate denouement of this play is a deliberate development from that of *All's Well That Ends Well*,[78] but it also marks a development in the mode of Cinthian dramaturgy. In the long final scene Shakespeare concentrates variously on the anxieties of Isabella, Angelo, Mariana and Lucio, which take the play beyond both versions of Cinthio's original story. At the conclusion of the Italian *novella* the focus is exclusively on the reactions of Epitia and Iuriste, who correspond to Isabella and Angelo respectively, while in *Epitia* there is the additional figure of Angela, who intercedes on her brother Iuriste's behalf and who, according to Ball, may have suggested the character of Mariana to Shakespeare.[79] The revelation that Epitia's brother Vico has, in fact, been preserved comes only in the dramatic version, where it provides the final reversal of fortune in the concluding scene. Shakespeare adds an onstage recognition to this reversal by having the muffled Claudio actually appear in *Measure for Measure*, albeit silently. The sense of wonder onstage is, however, held in constant check by the levels of unease to which the characters are subjected in the denouement. Shakespeare's decision to withhold knowledge of her brother's survival from Isabella until his belated appearance leads to a significant change of emphasis at the end of the play.[80] In *Epitia* it is only when the heroine learns that Vico is still alive that she will speak out for Iuriste, whereas Shakespeare requires Isabella, at Mariana's behest, to speak in defence of Angelo *before* Claudio's reappearance. The sense of genuine emotional and moral turmoil that permeates the final act

'GIVE ME THE OCULAR PROOF'

of *Measure for Measure* prevents any easy acceptance of the comic pattern that the multiple marriages seem ultimately to suggest.

The precedent for the brother's survival in Cinthio's own dramatisation of his story seems to be the decisive factor in assessing Shakespeare's indebtedness to *Epitia*; as with Cinthio's play, the denouement in *Measure for Measure* builds up to this revelation at the climax of the play. There is, however, a similar precedent in an English source, also existing in both a prose and a dramatic version, which further complicates the issue. Both versions of George Whetstone's adaptation of Cinthio's story predate the printing of *Epitia*, and yet they too contain the unexpected reappearance of the heroine's brother, in this case Andrugio, who returns disguised as a friar at the story's conclusion.[81] Lever has demonstrated Shakespeare's knowledge of Whetstone's two-part play *The Right Excellent and Famous Historye of Promos and Cassandra*, printed in 1578,[82] but there is further evidence to suggest that he has also read the prose version contained in *A Heptameron of Ciuill Discourses*, printed in 1582. The collection contains stories adapted from Cinthio, Bandello, and Boccaccio, and the tale of Promos and Cassandra is part of the fourth day, where it is related by a Madam Isabella. It is immediately preceded by 'the aduenture of Fryer *Inganno*', constructed loosely from two *novelle* in the *Decameron*,[83] in which the foolish country girl Farina is duped by the friar into believing that the spirit of Saint Fraunces is in love with her, in order to facilitate his own seduction of her. Farina is informed of Inganno's real intentions by the 'parrishe prieste', who sends an ugly maid, Leayda, in her place to the assignation with the friar. The priest's substitution of the two women in Whetstone's story is highly suggestive for the exchange of Mariana and Isabella, proposed by Duke Vincentio in his disguise as a friar, for the liaison with Angelo in *Measure for Measure*, which has no precedent in any of the direct sources.

The evidence points to the conclusion that Shakespeare is familiar with *both* the foreign and English versions of his source, and that he knows them in both their narrative and dramatic forms. This synthesis of all the available versions allows Shakespeare to explore fully the dramatic potential of the original Italian story. It demonstrates both the breadth of Shakespeare's reading, encouraged by the comparative parallel-text focus of his language-learning habits, in assimilating details of the plot from a disparate set of sources, and his ability to fashion this material into a coherent dramatic vision. Mowat argues that both *Measure for Measure* and *All's Well That Ends Well* are 'dramatic experiments in a more-or-less Guarinian mode'.[84] Their contemporaneity with the 1602 translation of *Il pastor fido*, and Marston's recasting of the Italian model in *The Malcontent*, suggests that they should indeed be viewed as part of a wider reaction to Guarini's play on the English stage. These plays are, equally, a direct response to the distinctive dramatic practice of Cinthio, with which Shakespeare also becomes familiar in the same period. He is the only playwright among his contemporaries who chooses to consider the theatrical possibilities of Guarini's tragicomedic dramaturgy in the light of Cinthio's earlier experiments in the form of *tragedia di fin lieto*. The result in the 'problem' comedies is a sustained exploration of aspects of both these Italian dramatic forms, which, through Shakespeare's skilful adaptations from his *novella* sources, creates a generically new, and continually unsettling, version of English romantic comedy.

Marston's *The Malcontent* and Guarinian tragicomedy

It is the dramatic device of the disguised duke, Shakespeare's most significant addition to the sources for *Measure for Measure*, which offers the clearest connection with Marston's *The Malcontent*. The two plays are among the earliest English experiments in the tragicomedic form, displaying a knowledge of and engagement with Guarini's *Il pastor fido*, and both are performed by the King's Men in 1604. Duncan-Jones argues that Shakespeare and the younger Marston share a close friendship and working relationship in the early years of the seventeenth century, but she does not consider that their twin responses to Italian tragicomedy might emerge directly from this period of collaboration.[85] The appearance of a disguised duke, who assumes dramatic control of the plot, and the emphasis on a corrupt urban rather than pastoral setting in each play suggests a similarity in their conception, which seems to be confirmed in a verbal echo in the expanded version of *The Malcontent*. In one of the additional passages that Marston writes for performance in the King's Men production, he has the court bawd, Maquerelle, respond to her final banishment to the suburbs in the same way that the brothel keeper, Mistress Overdone, reacts to her equivalent punishment in Shakespeare's play:

> O, good my lord, I have lived in the court this twenty year; they that have been old courtiers and come to live in the city, they are spitted at and thrust to the walls like apricots, good my lord. [V, ii, 185–188]

Good my lord, be good to me. Your honour is accounted a merciful man. Good my lord. [III, ii, 185–186][86]

Shakespeare strives to combine Guarinian tragicomedy and Cinthian *tragedia di fin lieto* in the dramaturgy of *Measure for Measure*, while Marston is simultaneously attempting a complete reworking of *Il pastor fido* for the English stage in his experimental play. *The Malcontent* is entered on the Stationers' Register in July 1604 as a 'Tragicomedia',[87] making it the earliest self-styled English tragicomedy. It is, therefore, significant that Marston chooses to borrow from the first self-styled Italian model, which is still provoking fierce literary debate in Italy at the turn of the century. Modern criticism, however, has underplayed the important link between these two plays, and the two dramatic traditions: 'Marston's play and its contemporary tragicomedies exhibit few connections with Italian theory and practice.'[88] In *The Malcontent* Marston produces an early model for tragicomedy on the public stage, which is different from both Fletcher's pastoral *The Faithful Shepherdess* (1608), often cited as the first English play to engage with Guarini's theory and practice, and the 'Romantic' type, written by Beaumont and Fletcher at the end of the decade.[89]

Marston's play is linked to Guarini's play and theory much more fundamentally than is usually acknowledged. Those who make the connection at all tend to stress a reductive, parodic design to Marston's use of Guarini. Hunter concludes that '*The Malcontent* is not, need I say, a simple reproduction of the mode of *Il Pastor Fido*; the surface appearance of the two plays could hardly be more distinct. The one is as much a critique of the other as an imitation.'[90] Hirst detects the presence of both Seneca and Guarini in the play, but concludes that Marston's attitude to both is equally parodic, suggesting that 'Marston creates a drama which is a perfect burlesque not merely of the revenge play but of the Guarinian model for tragicomedy'.[91] The relationship between *The Malcontent* and Guarini's play is deeper and more complex than such accounts would allow.[92]

The uncertain theatrical history of Marston's play creates some difficulties in assessing his numerous borrowings from the anonymous 1602 English translation of *Il pastor fido*. Webster's Induction, printed with the play in the third quarto of 1604, explains how the play enters the repertoire of the King's Men, implying that it was originally played by one of the boys' companies at the fashionable private theatres. Marston's *Antonio and Mellida* is certainly played by the Children of

St Paul's shortly after they reform in 1599, although *The Malcontent* is written for the Children of the Chapel Royal, who in 1604 become the Children of the Queen's Revels, performing at the Blackfriars theatre. The text of the third quarto is 'augmented', containing Marston and Webster's additional passages written for performance at the Globe. The borrowings from the translation of Guarini, however, are all present in the first two quartos, and thus seem to be aimed specifically at the 'coterie' audience of the private theatres, who would regard themselves as being *au fait* with contemporary theatrical fashion. Reavley Gair draws attention to Marston's 'technique of dramatic quotation, flattering his audience with his assumption of their intimate knowledge of contemporary theatre';[93] his earlier plays make free use of Shakespeare and Seneca, while *The Malcontent* draws heavily on Guarini and Seneca.

That the audience should be aware of the debt to Guarini, or at least to his English translator, is made clear by the dramatic situation for many of the borrowings, where characters themselves are clearly quoting from a fashionable source. Thus Ferneze, when pressing the ardour of his suit with Aurelia, deliberately adapts the language of the faithful shepherd Mirtillo, as he describes the effect that the sight of his beloved Amarillis has on him:

> But as for poor Ferneze's fixèd heart,
> Was never shadeless meadow drier parched
> Under the scorching heat of heaven's dog
> Than is my heart with your enforcing eyes.
> [I, ii, 35–38]

> But never was shadelesse meadow drier parcht
> Under the balefull fury of the heavenly dog,
> Then was my hart in sunshine of that sweet,
> Never so vanquisht as in victory.
> [II, i, 146–149][94]

Ferneze's image is taken almost verbatim from the translation, and Maquerelle's response to it, 'a hot simile!' [I, ii, 39], suggests both the borrowed artificiality and the appropriateness of the figure in his attempted wooing. Once Aurelia has succumbed but warned him of the danger of their meeting, Ferneze responds with another celebrated *sententia* from Guarini, where Amarillis in soliloquy confesses her love for Mirtillo:

she loves too litle that feares death,
Would gods death were the worst that's due to sin
[III, iv, 18–19]

His love is lifeless, that for love fears breath;
The worst that's due to sin, O would 'twere death.
[I, ii, 47–48]⁹⁵

Similarly, when the cuckolded Pietro tries to find the words to express his feelings at Aurelia's betrayal he chooses 'a good old simile' [III, i, 10] from Guarini, taken from an identical dramatic situation, as Mirtillo describes the effect Amarillis' apparent faithlessness has on him. The method of articulating emotion through borrowed figurative language creates a comic resonance to Pietro's complaint to Bilioso very different from the sense of genuine emotional upheaval conveyed in Guarini's original and its English translation:

> I am not unlike to some sick man
> That long desirèd hurtful drink; at last
> Swills in and drinks his last, ending at once
> Both life and thirst.
> [III, i, 11–14]⁹⁶

Marston, however, does not employ quotation merely to flatter the taste of his audience, but, more importantly, to stress the difference in the dramatic situations on the stage, and ultimately in the impact of these two model tragicomedies. In many respects Guarini's play informs the whole structure of Marston's tragicomedy,⁹⁷ although he uses it to produce a more explosive dramatic effect than that achieved in *Il pastor fido*. The example of Ferneze's use of Mirtillo's words to precipitate sexual seduction highlights the gulf between the worlds of the two plays. While Mirtillo may burn with passion for Amarillis in Arcadia, he remains passive, seeking only the opportunity for verbal contact. In the Genoese court of Marston's play, however, burning passion is clearly associated with the quest for sexual gratification. Aurelia's consent to Ferneze's suit leads to the immediate planning of their sexual liaison. Whereas in *Il pastor fido* Corisca's faithlessness stands alone against the fidelity of the other nymphs, in *The Malcontent* the situation is reversed. Infidelity is the norm, the 'courtlike' fashion encouraged by the promptings of Maquerelle, and it is against this that the fidelity of Maria for her banished husband Altofront in the final act shines.

The most sustained borrowing from Guarini in *The Malcontent* is Marston's transformation of the wanton nymph Corisca into the Genoese court bawd Maquerelle. Much of her court advice is derived directly from the language of Corisca,[98] highlighting important parallels in the dramatic function of the two characters, and thus demonstrating a connection between the seemingly incompatible worlds of Guarini's Arcadian pastoral and Marston's corrupt Genoese court. In *Il pastor fido* Corisca stands out as the only character to have been educated in modern city attitudes: in her first soliloquy she reveals what she has learnt from the example of a 'great Lady' of 'the Art of Love':

> Corisca, would she say, Let thy
> Lovers and thy garments be alike,
> Have many, use, weare but one, change often.
> [I, iii, 85–88][99]

In *The Malcontent* Maquerelle deliberately quotes this advice to the other court ladies, making apparent the link between city and court fashion:

> The more, the merrier! 'Twas well said, use your servants as you do your smocks; have many, use one, and change often, for that's most sweet and courtlike. [IV, i, 47–49][100]

The difference between the two dramatic worlds, pastoral and urban, is ultimately shown to be one of degree rather than type. Whereas Arcadia is threatened by the unsettling influence of one outsider promoting the 'arte di ben amar' [I, 652], the Genoese court has already been overtaken by an almost universal licentiousness, which matches sexual power with political power.[101] Marston gives his play a more overtly politicised setting than the Italian model, and the change from the pastoral to the satirical 'urban' mode of English tragicomedy helps to reinforce this.[102] The unspecific act of breaking faith in Arcadia leads to Diana's curse on the land. In *The Malcontent*, however, the chain of events follows a less abstract course; faithlessness is specifically adultery, making explicit the element of sexual betrayal that Guarini only hints at. The English play makes an overt connection between the private betrayal of adultery and the public betrayal involved in the usurpation of political power, as Malevole warns the cuckolded Pietro that Mendoza's usurpation of his bed is only the first step in the plot to usurp his role as Duke of Genoa:

Thou, closely yielding egress and regress to her, madest him heir, whose hot unquiet lust straight toused thy sheets, and now would seize thy state. Politician! Wise man! [III, ii, 52–54][103]

The role of Maquerelle in *The Malcontent* as plot catalyst is fundamental in a way that has not been fully considered by critics.[104] The sequence of events which leads finally to Altofront's return to rightful political power at the end of the play is set in motion by Maquerelle's promptings. Aurelia's decision to accept Ferneze as a lover is precipitated by Maquerelle's false claim that Mendoza has switched his amorous attentions to Bianca. This action exactly mirrors Corisca's attempts in *Il pastor fido* to persuade Mirtillo of Amarillis' faithlessness. Marston also develops Guarini's dramatic device of using the scheming comic character as an unwitting agent of good, hastening the comic denouement, despite intending a very different end. Clubb argues for the centrality of Corisca in Guarini's tragicomedy,[105] both as plot catalyst and, in her advocacy of promiscuity, as counterpoint to the faithful love and chastity of Mirtillo and Amarillis at the heart of the play. Guarini himself stresses the importance of this contrast between the two major female characters in his *Annotationi*:

> Se il valore d'vn animo virtuoso non può mostrarsi doue non è contrasto grandissimo, certissima cosa è ch' alla costanza di Amarilli era necessaria la maluagità di Corisca.[106]
>
> (If the value of a virtuous spirit cannot be demonstrated unless by complete contrast, then certainly it was necessary to show Corisca's wickedness to highlight Amarillis' constancy.)

Marston uses exactly this contrast in the scene between Maria and Maquerelle and Malevole, where the latter pair act as panders for Mendoza. Characteristically the old bawd borrows her language of persuasion directly from Corisca, conflating elements of her first soliloquy [I, iii], with her attempt to persuade Amarillis to break her contract with Silvio at the centre of the play [III, v]:

> Pish! Honesty is but an art to seem so. Pray ye, what's honesty? What's constancy? but fables feigned, odd old fools' chat, devised by jealous fools to wrong our liberty. [V, i, 70–72][107]

Maquerelle's appeal to their shared femininity, however, is ultimately unsuccessful, and this scene marks the end of Maquerelle's manipulations in the play.

Each of the four protagonists in *The Malcontent* corresponds to one of the central characters in *Il pastor fido*. Marston's creation of Maquerelle and Mendoza owes much, and not merely in the linguistic borrowings, to Guarini's conception of Corisca and the Satyr. Marston's play is more dramatically dynamic, and so it is not surprising that he finds the greatest opportunity for adaptation and expansion of his model in Guarini's proactive characters. The problem he encounters in recasting *Il pastor fido* for the English stage comes with the essential passivity of the central dramatic couple in Guarini's play. Mirtillo and Amarillis are largely powerless to act despite their mutual love, and the resolution is achieved through the emerging providential pattern, rather than through the workings of human agency within the play.

Marston's play demands a more active central dramatic focus. Even Maria, who represents Amarillis in the Guarinian pattern, although she only appears in the final act, needs to be more vigorous in her constancy to resist the demands made on her by Maquerelle and Mendoza. The most problematic area in this reading of *The Malcontent* comes with the required association of Malevole with the almost entirely passive Mirtillo. Marston makes this passivity one of the principal reasons for the Duke of Genoa's initial overthrow:

> I wanted those old instruments of state,
> Dissemblance and suspect. I could not time it, Celso;
> My throne stood like a point in midst of a circle,
> To all of equal nearness; bore with none,
> Reigned all alike; so slept in fearless virtue,
> Suspectless, too suspectless.
> [I, i, 212–217][108]

The passive Altofront assumes a more forceful and creative role in his disguise as Malevole, working towards his own final restoration. His return depends on an ability to assimilate the skills of both the politician and the actor; the 'instruments of state' become closely aligned in the play with the instruments of the stage. Altofront's advice to Celso to 'temporise' [IV, ii, 171], that is to wait for the opportune moment, has both political and dramatic relevance. It also suggests a connection between temporising and extemporising; timing and the ability to improvise are the skills of the actor that Malevole hones to perfection in the course of the play. 'Dissemblance', the ability to assume a different role convincingly, becomes central to Altofront's creed as both actor and politician, and his means to restoration by overcoming the other, ultimately inferior actors in the play, who embrace Corisca's code of dissembling from Guarini: 'Who cannot friendship faine, / Cannot truly hate' [II, iv, 14–15].

Malevole's *coup de théâtre* comes with his presentation of the Masque of the Genoan Dukes in the final scene, which restores him firstly to his wife, and ultimately to his rightful dukedom. In the masque Marston exploits the practice of showing the danger not the death ('il pericolo non la morte'), a central element of Guarinian tragicomic theory, as three of the male masquers are supposed dead by the watching Mendoza. The English playwright goes a stage further than the Italian model, which brings the protagonists to the point of seemingly unavoidable death before the final reversal, by allowing the illusion of death to stand within the dramatic structure. Thus Ferneze, like Dorinda in *Il pastor fido*, is wounded, but whereas she recovers, he appears to die. His subsequent recovery is witnessed only by Malevole, who intends to use Ferneze to help attain his own ends. The other 'deaths' are planned by Malevole himself, who is then able to show them as illusory in his final theatrical triumph. Pietro's 'suicide' and Mendoza's apparent poisoning of Malevole himself are only a part of Altofront's superior plotting as it sweeps towards its climax in his restoration at the end of the masque.

The practice of setting up a potentially tragic denouement only to undercut it with a different ending is central to the strategies of both playwrights. It is interesting that both draw heavily on the respective dominant tragic traditions in their countries to construct a new genre that goes beyond tragedy. For Guarini, writing shortly after the proliferation of commentaries on Aristotle's *Poetics* in Italy in the second half of the sixteenth century, Sophocles' *Oedipus Rex* is the prototypical tragedy, which he uses and adapts extensively in what is to become the prototypical tragicomedy. Similarly, Marston's play acknowledges the Senecan revenge tragedy, so popular on the English stage in the 1590s and early 1600s, where it reaches its apogee in Shakespeare's *Hamlet*, as the principal English model. Guarini's *Annotationi* record his frequent linguistic borrowings from both Classical and contemporary sources, and *Il Compendio della Poesia Tragicomica* registers a fundamental structural debt to Sophocles and Terence's comedy, *Andria*. It is clear that the denouement of *Il pastor fido* assimilates elements from both these sources into something generically new. In this way, Guarini mixes the confusions of identity of comedy with the more sober revelations of *Oedipus Rex*, creating a conclusion that ultimately promotes the 'ordine comico'. The framework of Sophocles' play is consciously used in the structuring of *Il pastor fido*: 'A child, as in *Oedipus Rex*, swept away in its cradle in a flood of twenty years before, and preserved for an agnition and a peripeteia.'[109]

Guarini alludes specifically to his Sophoclean model in the means of recognition, which must be through discussion, rather than the external signs of comedy. The purpose and impact of the reversal could not be more different, however, altering the course of the play from its apparently tragic movement to the surprising comic denouement, where all misunderstandings are resolved, and faithful love can finally flourish. Guarini employs 'the tragic effects of reversal (peripeteia) and recognition (anagnorisis) for purposes closer to comedy',[110] even using the figure of the blind prophet (Tirenio for Tiresias) as the means of explaining the revelations to the stunned characters on stage. The use of Sophocles structurally is central to Guarini's dramatic conception, but the most important element in his tragicomedy is the rejection of the tragic conclusion to *Oedipus Rex*.

The Malcontent works in an equivalent manner by alluding to, but ultimately rejecting, both the dramatic structure and the philosophy of the Senecan revenge play. As Guarini alludes to Sophocles and Terence, so Marston's principal points of reference are Seneca, and Guarini himself. As the 'ordine comico' triumphs over Sophoclean tragedy at the end of *Il pastor fido*, so in *The Malcontent* tragicomedy triumphs over revenge tragedy. The revenge ethos is espoused by the obvious villains, who consciously quote from Seneca in the same way that they allude to *Il pastor fido*; thus Mendoza in soliloquy misquotes *Thyestes*, as he plans the murder of Ferneze.[111] Malevole, however, merely assumes the language of the literate revenger as part of his manipulation of Mendoza, quoting the most celebrated of all Senecan tags on the Elizabethan stage, spoken by Clytemnestra in *Agamemnon*, and more recently by Hieronimo in Kyd's *The Spanish Tragedy*: '*Per scelera semper sceleribus tutum est iter*' [V, i, 165].[112] From the beginning, however, Malevole's desire for vengeance is distinguished from the desire for bloodshed characteristic of the revenge play: 'The heart's disquiet is revenge most deep' [I, i, 189].[113]

At the end of the play both Marston and Malevole consciously reject the ending of a revenge tragedy, an act that is fundamental to the status of *The Malcontent* as tragicomedy. The final scene of the play shows that all the politic 'killings' have only been illusory, and generically it is essential that Altofront does not invoke the death

'GIVE ME THE OCULAR PROOF'

penalty as a punishment for the traitors against his state. Michael Scott's reading of the play misunderstands the generic implications of the denouement, in criticising Altofront for not having Mendoza executed:

> Altofront merely kicks out Mendoza. This is an example of his affectation and self-adulation, and is consequently dangerous, since his role-play negates the possibility of his realising that the 'heart's disquiet' could lead Mendoza to more Machiavellian schemes.[114]

Death has no part in Guarinian or Marstonian tragicomedy, where the denouement deliberately denies the tragic ending by preventing death from entering the dramatic world. Marston, however, does not follow Guarini entirely in his stipulations for the ending of tragicomedy. Guarini's 'ordine comico' stresses the happiness of the entire social order at the end of the play; thus the vision of reharmonisation that concludes *Il pastor fido* includes Corisca, who repents of her attempted wrongdoings, and is freely forgiven by Mirtillo and Amarillis. Marston ultimately gives a more complex response in the re-establishment of political order at the Genoese court, by not allowing the easy repentance of the wrongdoers, who are summarily banished.

The dramatic worlds of the Arcadian pastoral and the corrupt Genoese court may seem initially remote, but this surface distinction should not conceal Marston's detailed exploration of a new generic model, in his attempt to produce a dramatically effective reworking of Guarini's play for the experimental stage of the private theatres. The play's transfer to the repertory of the King's Men at the Globe, where it is performed in the same year as Shakespeare's *Measure for Measure*, indicates Marston's immediate success with this new dramatic form, five years before the ill-fated appearance of Fletcher's version of English pastoral tragicomedy, *The Faithful Shepherdess*, on the stage in 1608.

'Non sono io quel che paio in viso': *Othello*, Cinthio, and *Orlando furioso*

After his experiments with tragicomedic dramaturgy in the 'problem' plays, Shakespeare turns to Cinthio's *novelle* again in 1603–4 for the composition of *Othello*, based on the tale of the Moor and Disdemona from the third decade of *Gli Hecatommithi* (III, 7). There is no prior Cinthian dramatic version for the tragedy as in the case of *Measure* for *Measure*, but Shakespeare still approaches this prose story by means of another Italian source and its English adaptation, discernible in the alterations and additions that he makes in his dramatisation of it. Maristella Lorch has suggested Ariosto's *Orlando furioso* as an important analogue for Shakespeare's *Othello*, with particular regard to the eponymous character's 'insanity' in the final three acts:

> If we choose to read *Othello* in the light of an Italian source, we should allow ourselves the freedom of looking outside the recognised direct source, in this case the *Hecatommiti*, and try to consider as worthy of Shakespeare some powerful expressions of Italian Renaissance thought.[115]

She is not the first critic to posit a connection between the play and Ariosto's poem, although previously the focus has been on minute verbal correspondences, in an attempt to demonstrate that Shakespeare knows the poem in Italian, as well as possibly in Harington's translation. Thus, Smart suggests that Othello's first account of the origin of the handkerchief that he has given to Desdemona, which has no equivalent in Cinthio's story, derives from Ariosto's description of the two-thousand-year-old pavilion embroidered by Cassandra, which Melissa transports to Paris for the wedding of Ruggiero and Bradamante in the final canto of the poem:

> Una donzella de la terra d'Ilia,
> ch'avea il furor profetico congiunto,
> con studio di gran tempo e con vigilia
> lo fece di sua man di tutto punto.
> [XLVI, lxxx, 3–6]

(A Trojan damsel with a prophetic gift, named Cassandra, had devoted long vigils to making it all with her own hand.)

> 'Tis true, there's magic in the web of it.
> A sibyl that had numbered in the world
> The sun to course two hundred compasses,
> In her prophetic fury sewed the work;
> [III, iv, 71–74][116]

Smart points out that 'in Harington's translation there is no mention of prophetic fury', and so the allusion in Shakespeare's lines is directly to the Italian original.[117]

More recently, Cairncross has detected verbal parallels between the play and another episode from Ariosto's poem, a connection he implies is triggered initially by a phrase in Cinthio's story, which occurs in an identical narrative situation in *Orlando furioso*. Muir quotes the Moor's warning to his Ensign from the *novella* as the source for Othello's demand of 'ocular proof' [III, v, 363] from Iago of Desdemona's infidelity, to demonstrate that Shakespeare has read the original Italian version, rather than, or possibly together with, Chappuys' French translation:

> Se non mi fai, disse, vedere cogl'occhi quello che detto mi hai, viviti sicuro, che ti farò conoscere, che meglio per te sarebbe, che tu fossi nato mutolo.
>
> (If you do not make me see with my own eyes what you have told me, be assured, I shall make you realise that it would have been better for you had you been born dumb.)[118]

Cairncross notes that the same phrase is found in exactly this situation in the fifth canto of Ariosto's poem, when Ariodante demands similar proof of Ginevra's infidelity from the scheming Polinesso:[119]

> ma ch'io tel voglia creder, non far stima,
> s'io non lo veggio con questi occhi prima.
> [V, xli, 7–8]
>
> (But don't imagine I'll believe what you said unless first I see it with my own eyes.)[120]

Shakespeare has already used Ariosto's tale as the source of the Claudio and Hero plot in *Much Ado About Nothing*, and his verbal association of it with another Italian tale of the wrongful and malicious accusation of female infidelity is immediately striking. Indeed, Cairncross cites another verbal parallel between *Othello* and Ariosto's Italian, which confirms the correlation and suggests retrospectively that Shakespeare's knowledge of the episode is direct, and not mediated solely through later versions by Bandello, Spenser, or Harington, when he first makes use of this material in the final years of the sixteenth century.[121]

Cairncross's model for Shakespeare's association, and then conflation, of different Italian sources into one play offers an interesting means of approaching *Othello*, although his particular example elucidates only one episode of the plot. It is possible to trace a similar, but more detailed, pattern for Shakespeare's use of Italian materials in the play, which concurs with Lorch's suggestion that it is necessary to look beyond Cinthio's story as a 'direct source', to demonstrate a greater correspondence between *Othello* and the primary narrative sequence of *Orlando furioso* than has previously been appreciated.

Shakespeare seems to be alluding playfully to Ariosto's poem in the central scene of *As You Like It*, where a character named Orlando inscribes the name of his beloved in the bark of the trees in the forest of Ardenne.[122] In the twenty-third canto of the Italian poem the discovery of the beloved's name, alongside that of Medoro, similarly carved on the trees of a French forest, is the first step in the eponymous hero's descent into madness, as he comes to understand that Angelica is in love with another soldier. It is one of the most instantly recognisable motifs of the *Orlando furioso*, and is given a key role in the plot of Robert Greene's loose adaptation for the stage of the central canto of Ariosto's poem, *The Historie of Orlando Furioso, One of the twelue Pieres of France*, performed in 1592, and printed in 1594. Shackford has suggested that Shakespeare borrows the carving motif from Greene's play, rather than from Ariosto directly, for his pastoral play.[123]

The theory that Greene's play may be an intermediary for Shakespeare between an Italian source and his own work opens up a range of interesting possibilities, which permits a reconsideration of the relationship between the two playwrights, most evident in Shakespeare's extensive use of Greene's prose romance *Pandosto, or the Triumph of Time* (1588) in *The Winter's Tale* (1610). From a series of semi-autobiographical pamphlets printed in the early 1590s it is clear that Greene travels to the continent, probably in the middle of the 1580s, where he spends time in both Spain and Italy. The connection with Italy is of particular interest, as half of the surviving plays that are attributed solely to him are indebted to Italian sources. The mere title of *The Historie of Orlando Furioso* advertises its Italian origin, although Greene is very free with his treatment of Ariosto's narrative in shaping his plot. In contrast, *The Scottish Historie of Iames the Fourth, slaine at Flodden*, printed posthumously in 1598, follows the outline of its Italian prose source quite closely. This source is the first story in the third decade of Cinthio's *Gli Hecatommithi* (1565), which of course also provides the story of the Moor and Disdemona.[124]

Greene's play is, after Whetstone's *Promos and Cassandra*, the earliest example of an adaptation for the English stage from Cinthio's *novelle*, and so it provides an important precedent for Shakespeare, who utilises the Italian prose collection in both *Othello* and *Measure for Measure*. The chronological proximity of the two Shakespeare plays suggests that they form a twin response to a recently discovered source.[125] Thus, some ten years after Greene's experiment in dramatising one of Cinthio's tales, Shakespeare attempts a similar process in two separate plays. Is the precedent merely coincidental, or does the later playwright become aware of what his predecessor had been doing, as his own familiarity with the Italian's work develops? Cinthio's tale of Astatio and Arrenopia, the basis of Greene's play, is part of the same decade as his tale of the Moor, and they share the already familiar theme of the wrongful accusation of infidelity, aimed at the central female character. Despite the radically different endings of the two stories, it is likely that Shakespeare recognises that Greene's source lay in the opening story of the decade dealing with infidelity and its consequences. This is not readily apparent from his dramatic treatment of the *Othello* story, but rather in his choice of a tale from another decade of the collection as the starting point for *Measure for Measure*.

The origin of Angelo's demand for Isabella's honour in exchange for her brother's life is the fifth story of the eighth decade of *Gli Hecatommithi*, and, equally significantly, Cinthio's own later dramatisation of the story as *Epitia*, as outlined earlier in this chapter.[126] The conclusion to Shakespeare's play, in which the seemingly dead brother is brought back to life, owes much to the alterations made between the two Italian versions, where Cinthio changes the original ending of the *novella* to comply with his dramatic conception of *tragedia di fin lieto*. The significance of Shakespeare's knowledge of *both* the narrative and the dramatic sources in Cinthio is that the situation is identical in the case of Greene's play. The tale of Astatio and the queen whom he deserts and tries to have killed, which already ends in restoration and reconciliation in the prose version, is dramatised in *Arrenopia*, also printed in 1583. Greene himself is not necessarily aware of the story in both of its forms,[127] but Shakespeare *is* in a position to detect the features of these narratives that are inherently suitable for dramatic treatment, through the prior examples of both Greene and Cinthio himself.

This triangular connection between Shakespeare, Greene, and Cinthio leads back to the original contention that Greene's version of *Orlando Furioso* works as an intermediary between Shakespeare's drama, and an Italian source. If Shakespeare's reading of Cinthio for *Measure for Measure* illuminates for him Greene's method of using Cinthio for *James IV*, then his reading of the Italian story for *Othello* seems to have called to mind Greene's treatment of Ariosto in another of his plays. Greene treats Ariosto's narrative with a good deal of dramatic freedom, and, in one decisive aspect, his alterations align the plot with the story of the Moor in the Italian *novella*. Once again, the dominant theme becomes the unfounded accusation of female infidelity.

The source for Greene's play is nominally the twenty-third canto of *Orlando furioso*, or more particularly the final forty stanzas of it, in which the narrator details Orlando's incipient madness as he realises that the scornful Angelica has given herself to the pagan soldier, Medoro, and is thus finally beyond his attainment. Greene's play also deals with the madness of its central character, but it is motivated in a vastly different way. In *The Historie of Orlando Furioso* Angelica is in love with, and faithful to, the paladin, Orlando, whom she has chosen in preference to the pagan kings gathered at the court of the Emperor Marsilius. One of the disappointed rivals, the County Sacrepant, seeks to undermine their relationship by spreading the false suggestion that Angelica is unfaithful to Orlando with her servant, Medor. He attempts this by carving their names on the trees, and hanging love poems in the wood where Orlando walks, the means of discovery taken directly from Ariosto:

> And on those trees that border in those walkes,
> Ile slily haue engraun on euerie barke
> The names of Medor and Angelica.
> Hard by Ile haue some roundelayes hung vp,
> Wherein shalbe some posies of their loues,
> Fraughted so full of fierie passions,
> As that the Countie shall perceiue by proofe,
> Medor hath won his faire Angelica.
>   [547–554][128]

His plan swiftly achieves its aim, and Greene's hero is reduced to a series of incoherent mutterings, which remind Honigmann of Othello in his Iago-prompted descent into madness:

Woods, trees, leaues; leaues, trees, woods: tria sequuntur tria. Ho Minerua, salue, God morrow how doo you to day? Tell me sweet Goddesse, will Ioue send Mercury to Calipso to let me goe. Will he? why then hees a Gentleman euerie haire a the head on him. [843–848][129]

'GIVE ME THE OCULAR PROOF'

The general outline of the plots, and, in particular, the correspondence in the central characters' insanity induced by their suspicions of cuckoldry hint at a connection between Greene's play and *Othello*, which can be confirmed by some verbal parallels in the opening scenes. Shakespeare seems consciously to recall Greene's characterisation of Orlando at the start of the play, as he arrives at the African court in his suit for Angelica, in his conception of Othello in Venice. In the first speeches, each character feels compelled to stress his lineage to counter the suggestion that he is unworthy of the affections of the beloved, Angelica and Desdemona respectively:

> Lords of the South, & Princes of esteeme,
> Viceroyes vnto the State of Affrica:
> I am no King, yet am I princely borne,
> Descended from the royall house of France,
> And nephew to the mightie Charlemaine,
> Surnamde Orlando the Countie Palatine.
> [99–104]

> 'Tis yet to know –
> Which, when I know that boasting is an honour,
> I shall promulgate – I fetch my life and being
> From men of royal siege, and my demerits
> May speak unbonneted to as proud a fortune
> As this that I have reached.
> [I, ii, 19–24][130]

Equally, both characters are eager to stress the unusual dangers that they have encountered in their military lives, and the recurrence of one particular word in *Othello* makes the link explicit. The *OED* cites Shakespeare's play for the first recorded use of 'anthropophagi' in English, but, in fact, Greene has already used the word over ten years earlier in Orlando's account of his arrival at the African court:

> The Seas by Neptune hoysed to the heauens,
> Whose dangerous flawes might well haue kept me backe;
> The sauage Mores & Anthropagei
> Whose lands I past might well haue kept me backe;
> [117–120]

Shakespeare's usage occurs in Othello's explanation to the Venetian Senate of how he has successfully wooed Desdemona with tales of his military exploits:

> Wherein of antres vast and deserts idle,
> Rough quarries, rocks and hills whose heads touch heaven
> It was my hint to speak – such was my process –
> And of the cannibals that each other eat,
> The Anthropophagi, and men whose heads
> Do grow beneath their shoulders.
>
> [I, iii, 141–146][131]

Othello's conclusion ('She loved me for the dangers I had passed / And I loved her that she did pity them' [168–169]) demonstrates the impact of his story-telling, and has a strong precedent in epic for the effect that it has on the auditor. Burrow argues that Ariosto conceives of the relationship between Angelica and Medoro as a reworking of that between Dido and Aeneas in *The Aeneid*, and he highlights the shared quality of pity felt by the female characters, inspired in each case by the autobiographical stories related by their future lovers:[132]

> insolita pietade in mezzo al petto
> si sentí entrar per disusate porte,
> che le fe' il duro cor tenero e molle,
> e piú, quando il suo caso egli narrolle.
>
> [XIX, xx, 5–8]

(An unaccustomed sense of pity stole into her breast by some unused door, softening her hard heart, the more so when he related his story to her.)[133]

Shakespeare, then, offers an epic dimension to Othello's self-conception of his relationship with Desdemona, although there is a conscious irony inherent in this Ariostan precedent. It is, of course, Angelica and Medoro's relationship that leads directly to Orlando's love-driven madness, a disease to which Othello himself will soon fall prey, through Iago's promptings, in Cyprus.

The emphasis so far has been on how Shakespeare makes use of Greene's version of Ariosto's narrative, but he also turns directly to the *Orlando furioso* in the process of composing *Othello*. Both Greene and Shakespeare emphasise the importance of story-telling as a theme in their plays, but each garners details independently from the Italian poem. Greene recasts the shepherd's true tale from Ariosto (XXIII, cxviii–cxx), which confirms to Orlando the love of Angelica and Medoro, by means of disguising Sacrepant's servant as a shepherd to misinform Orlando about Angelica and Medor:

'GIVE ME THE OCULAR PROOF'

> And when he heares a shepheards simple tale,
> He will not thinke tis faind.
> [563–564]

Shakespeare also understands the importance of the pastor's story in Ariosto, but he chooses to emphasise a different aspect of it. When the shepherd has concluded the account of the lovers' sojourn in his farmhouse, he produces a token from Angelica, left as a mark of her gratitude. This is a precious bracelet that Orlando had given to his beloved, and its appearance in another's possession has devastating consequences:

> All'ultimo l'istoria si ridusse,
> che 'l pastor fe' portar la gemma inante,
> ch'alla sua dipartenza, per mercede
> del buono albergo, Angelica gli diede.
>   Queste conclusion fu la secure
> che 'l capo a un colpo gli levò dal collo.
> [XXIII, cxx–cxxi]

(The herdsman ended his story by having the bracelet brought in – the one Angelica had given him on her departure as a token of thanks for his hospitality. This evidence shown in conclusion proved to be the axe which took his head off his shoulders at one stroke.)[134]

Earlier in the narrative Ariosto has implied that the bracelet has magical qualities, having originally been in the possession of the sorceress Morgana (XIX, xxxviii). It is the significance, and effect, of the bracelet in the Italian poem that suggests to Shakespeare the importance of the love-token in *Othello*, which has far greater weight than the handkerchief in Cinthio's story. This is conveyed predominantly through the elaborate history of the handkerchief that Othello describes to Desdemona when he first suspects that she has given it away.[135] This account contains an allusion to another part of Ariosto's poem, the description of the marriage pavilion in the final canto. Shakespeare uses Ariosto to imbue Othello's handkerchief with the associations of enchantment of both the bracelet and the pavilion. Equally important is the effect on the two central characters when confronted with evidence of the exchange of their love-tokens.

Iago has a precedent in Greene's Sacrepant, but in his adroit manipulation of Othello, especially with regard to the General's attachment to the handkerchief, his role also corresponds to that of the narrator in Ariosto's poem, whose timely production of the bracelet, the 'ocular proof' of Angelica's love, finally overthrows Orlando's mental stability. Iago re-introduces the theme of the lost handkerchief at the start of the fourth act to similarly grave effect, with Othello referring to it obsessively as his epilepsy begins:

> Handkerchief! confessions! handkerchief! – To confess, and be hanged for his labour! First to be hanged, and then to confess: I tremble at it. Nature would not invest herself in such shadowing passion without some instruction. It is not words that shakes me thus. Pish! Noses, ears, and lips. Is't possible? Confess! handkerchief! O devil! [IV, i, 37–43][136]

Shakespeare follows Ariosto rather than Greene in delineating carefully the steps of Othello's mental collapse,[137] and the trance that precedes his 'savage madness' recalls Orlando prostrate on the ground for three entire days, before the outbreak of his 'gran furor':

> Afflitto e stanco al fin cade ne l'erba,
> e ficca gli occhi al cielo, e non fa motto.
> Senza cibo e dormir cosí si serba,
> che 'l sole esce tre volte e torna sotto.
> Di crescer non cessò la pena acerba,
> che fuor del senno al fin l'ebbe condotto.
> [XXIII, cxxxii, 1–6]

(Weary and heart-stricken, he dropped on to the grass and gazed mutely up at the sky. Thus he remained, without food or sleep, while the sun three times rose and set. His bitter agony grew and grew until it drove him out of his mind.)[138]

Despite the different courses of the two protagonists' destructive insanity, Lorch claims that she 'cannot help sensing in this dramatic degradation of his great hero, ... the influence on Shakespeare of Ariosto's creation of a *folle* Orlando'. She supports this by suggesting that some of Othello's expressions in his madness 'are directly traceable to passages of the *Furioso*'.[139] The only verbal parallel cited, though, is from the final scene of the play, where Othello, in response to Lodovico's enquiry, echoes the conclusion of Orlando's great monologue on the verge of his breakdown:

> That's he that was Othello: here I am.
> [V, ii, 281]

'GIVE ME THE OCULAR PROOF'

> Non son, non sono io quel che paio in viso:
> quel ch'era Orlando è morto et è sotterra;
> la sua donna ingratissima l'ha ucciso:
> [XXIII, cxxviii, 1–3]
>
> (I am not who my face proclaims me; the man who was Orlando is dead and buried, slain by his most thankless lady.)[140]

If Orlando's declaration of his loss of identity is paralleled in Othello's confession, then the opening line of Ariosto's stanza is equally resonant in *Othello*, where the constant tension between seeming and being adds a dramatic dimension to the motivation for the action beyond anything found in Cinthio's story. The line is echoed in Desdemona's stunned reaction to Othello's insistence that she produce the apparently lost handkerchief ('My lord is not my lord, nor should I know him / Were he in favour as in humour altered' [III, iv, 125–126]), in the debate between Othello and Iago on the nature of Cassio's honesty ('Certain, men should be what they seem' [III, iii, 131]), and, most memorably, in Iago's declaration to Roderigo in the opening scene:

> For when my outward action doth demonstrate
> The native act and figure of my heart
> In complement extern, 'tis not long after
> But I will wear my heart upon my sleeve
> For daws to peck at: I am not what I am.
> [I, i, 60–64][141]

The switching of this line from Ariosto's epic protagonist to the play's arch manipulator is typical of the transformations of expectation that Shakespeare employs in *Othello*. The schematic reversal of the implied qualities of black and white in honest Othello and dishonest Iago is repeated in his adjustment to the central relationship of Ariosto's poem. There, the Christian knight, Orlando, is in love with the pagan princess, Angelica, where Shakespeare, in following Cinthio, has the Moorish soldier in love with a Christian woman.

Despite this reversal of situation, *Orlando furioso* clearly provides Shakespeare with an epic precedent for the doomed relationship, in which the hero is distracted from his habitual military life with tragic consequences, through an unaccustomed romantic infatuation. Many of the alterations that Shakespeare makes to Cinthio's original *novella* reflect his desire to lend to the play a heroic quality, and to raise the status of his story above that of the prose source. The Italian word 'novella' can convey the meaning of 'news' in a modern sense,[142] and there is an almost sensationalist aspect to the sordid conclusion in Cinthio, where the Moor and his ensign attempt to cover up their brutal murder of Disdemona. Shakespeare rejects this ending outright, and not merely because of the difficult stage business of having the roof collapse on the already murdered wife. His conception of the status and character of Othello does not allow for such a denouement, even if a trace of it is permitted in Othello's gleeful appearance as Iago wounds Cassio in the final act. This change of status is conveyed not simply by making the Moor a General instead of a Captain, as in Cinthio, but also by investing him with a fragile military nobility, for which Shakespeare finds a literary model in the figure of Orlando in both Ariosto's epic poem and Robert Greene's play.

The presence of *Orlando furioso* behind Shakespeare's treatment of Cinthio's story helps to account for his most significant addition to the material derived from the *novella*. The Turkish threat to Venetian Cyprus, which leads to Othello's urgent posting there as governor, is entirely Shakespeare's invention. Emrys Jones offers a plausible date for the historical setting of the action of *Othello* with reference to Richard Knolles's *Generall Historie of the Turkes*, printed in 1603. He argues that this historical specificity is intended to appeal directly to King James, whose interest in the ongoing European conflict with the Turks is evident in his poem *Lepanto*.[143] The addition also provides an epic dimension to the background of the play by highlighting the conflict between Christian and pagan powers, a theme central to the two great Italian epics of the sixteenth century, *Orlando furioso* and Tasso's *Gerusalemme liberata*. Ironically, of course, it is the fortunate destruction of the Turkish fleet in the storm off Cyprus that removes the military necessity of Othello's posting, and leaves him instead in the unfamiliar private sphere of personal relationships. *Othello* is a play based on a simple and sordid Italian prose tale of jealousy and murder, and has been described as 'embarrassingly domestic' in its frequent comparisons to the contemporary English domestic tragedy.[144] Shakespeare's central action, however, also deliberately echoes the celebrated portrayal of an epic hero, dislocated from his military context to the point of insanity, through the intense power of his affections:

> Farewell the neighing steed and the shrill trump,
> The spirit-stirring drum, th' ear-piercing fife,
> The royal banner, and all quality,

'GIVE ME THE OCULAR PROOF'

> Pride, pomp and circumstance of glorious war!
> And, O you mortal engines whose rude throats
> Th' immortal Jove's dread clamours counterfeit,
> Farewell: Othello's occupation's gone.
> [III, iii, 354–360]¹⁴⁵

Shakespeare revisits the theme of an unfounded and potentially destructive sexual jealousy in two plays written some five or six years after *Othello*. In both *Cymbeline* and *The Winter's Tale*, however, the tragic course of the earlier play is eventually averted as a result of what Robert Henke describes as Shakespeare's 'pastoral reformation of tragedy':

> In *The Tempest* and *The Winter's Tale*, and to a lesser extent in *Cymbeline*, tragedy is replayed and revised in a kind of pastoral theater, after the idea of Italian tragicomedy. In these plays, Shakespeare pursues something very similar to Guarinian tragicomedy in creating a variegated, capacious pastoral arena capable of incorporating tragic modalities.¹⁴⁶

Henke argues for a significant connection between Shakespeare's dramaturgy in these late plays and the techniques of Italian pastoral tragicomedy, but he is careful to avoid implying that this develops from the playwright's direct knowledge of Guarini's play and theory.¹⁴⁷ Where Duncan-Jones suggests that it is Marston who introduces Shakespeare to his Italian materials, Henke nominates John Fletcher as the collaborator who may have 'furnished Shakespeare with the most important source of information about Guarinian tragicomedy' a few years later.¹⁴⁸ Shakespeare's evident knowledge of Guarini's *Il pastor fido* in the composition of the earlier 'problem' plays, however, makes this tentativeness seem unnecessary. This chapter will conclude with a brief account of Shakespeare's use of Italian materials in two of his late plays to demonstrate the continuity in his approach and technique from the early years of the seventeenth century.

If *All's Well That Ends Well* and *Measure for Measure* together constitute Shakespeare's first formal experimentation with tragicomedy in a non-pastoral mode, then *Cymbeline* and *The Winter's Tale*, probably written simultaneously in 1609–10, can be considered as twin explorations of the theatrical possibilities of Guarini's pastoral form. The pastoral context of *The Winter's Tale* is already present in Shakespeare's direct source, Greene's *Pandosto*, though the playwright reverses the Bohemian and Sicilian locations of the prose original.

It is only in Shakespeare's version, however, that the switch to the pastoral mode in the second half of the plot presages the movement towards resolution into tragicomedy. The final 'tragical stratagem' in Greene's story, the suicide of Pandosto, overshadows the bringing together of his daughter Fawnia and Dorastus, whereas Shakespeare chooses instead to reunite Leontes with Hermione sixteen years after her apparent death. It is in the carefully orchestrated sense of wonder (Guarini's 'maraviglia') for both the onstage and offstage audiences at the revival of Hermione in the final scene that Shakespeare is closest in his dramaturgy to echoing the miraculous denouement of *Il pastor fido*, where it is discovered that the condemned Mirtillo is the long-lost son of the priest Montanus. Guarini's play resolves fully into the 'ordine comico' with the fulfilment of the opening oracle, as Mirtillo and Amarilli are united to lift the curse on Arcadia. Shakespeare's version of pastoral tragicomedy is more extreme: the happy vision of familial restoration at the end of *The Winter's Tale* is tempered by the deaths of Mamillius and Antigonus. For Guarini, tragicomedy is a distinct third genre that moderates the extremes of comedy, by avoiding clowning and coarse humour, and tragedy, by offering only a tempered image of the true terror ('rassomiglianza del terribile')[149] that tragedy inspires in its audience. Shakespeare challenges this Italian definition by attempting to combine unexpurgated versions of both comedy ('joy') and tragedy ('terror') within his own tragicomedy, as the opening of the pivotal Time chorus suggests:

> I that please some, try all: both joy and terror
> Of good and bad, that makes and unfolds error,
> Now take upon me, in the name of Time,
> To use my wings.
>
> [IV, i, 1–4][150]

The pastoral element in *Cymbeline* is Shakespeare's addition to the wager plot that he inherits from Boccaccio. Bullough has demonstrated that Shakespeare characteristically borrows details from both the Italian original (*Decameron*, II, 9) and an English adaptation of the story, *Frederyke of Jennen*, translated from a German version, and printed in 1518 and 1560.[151] In each case the falsely suspected wife flees the country by boat after being spared by her loyal servant. In Shakespeare's play Imogen instead seeks refuge in the pastoral retreat of Belarius and his two 'sons' in Wales. It is likely that the pastoral landscape, which offers solace to a distressed young woman in male attire, derives from the episode of *Erminia fra i pastori* in canto VII of Tasso's *Gerusalemme liberata*. The hospitality Belarius and his boys extend to Imogen recalls that of the old shepherd and his sons towards the disguised Erminia in Tasso's poem, which also provides a precedent for the satire on courtly values in Belarius' bitter recollections of his life at court (III, iii, 45–73). It seems that Shakespeare's desire to incorporate the pastoral mode into his tragicomedy, following the examples of Guarini and Tasso's *Aminta*, triggers an association between the latter's pastoral play and the other celebrated pastoral episode in his work, already imitated by Spenser in Book VI of *The Faerie Queene* (1596). In the following canto of Tasso's poem the decapitated corpse of a knight is mistakenly reported to be that of the Christian hero Rinaldo, a misunderstanding that may inspire the gruesome scene in which Imogen awakes next to what she believes is the headless body of her husband Posthumus (IV, ii, 291–332).

The elaborate dramatic climax of *Cymbeline*, with its extraordinary series of recognitions and reversals of circumstance, is equally as indebted to the denouement of *Il pastor fido* as is the final scene of *The Winter's Tale*. Both of Shakespeare's plays end with scenes of a royal family reunited after the fulfilment of an oracle, following the exact structural pattern of Guarini's play. Shakespeare strives for a different impact in the concluding scene of *Cymbeline*, however, through his frequent use of dramatic irony. Where the revelations in *Il pastor fido* and *The Winter's Tale* are a surprise to the theatrical spectators as well as the characters on stage, in *Cymbeline* most of the onstage recognitions have been signalled to the audience in advance. The alternative techniques displayed at the end of these twin pastoral plays suggest that they form part of Shakespeare's sustained response to Guarini's tragicomedic practice, an Italian model with which he continues to engage and experiment until the end of his dramatic career.

Notes

1 Charlotte Lennox first recognises Cinthio's *Hecatommithi* as a source for *Measure for Measure* in *Shakespear Illustrated* (1753), but by 1767 Richard Farmer is suggesting Whetstone's prose version of the story in English as Shakespeare's sole source, and quoting the opinion of his friend Mr Capell with regard to the playwright's use of French and Italian *novelle*: 'To say they are not in some English dress, prosaic or metrical, and perhaps with circumstances nearer to his stories, is what I will not take upon me to do:

nor indeed is it what I believe; but rather the contrary, and that time and accident will bring some of them to light, if not all.' Richard Farmer, *An Essay on the Learning of Shakespeare* (1767) in David Nichol Smith, ed., *Eighteenth-Century Essays on Shakespeare* (Clarendon Press, Oxford, 1963), pp. 151–202; p. 166 and pp. 186–7.

2. Naseeb Shaheen, 'Shakespeare's knowledge of Italian', *Shakespeare Survey* 47 (1994), 161–9; p. 161.
3. Nichol Smith, *Eighteenth-Century Essays*, p. xxvi.
4. John S. Smart, *Shakespeare: Truth and Tradition* (Edward Arnold and Co., London, 1928), p. 183.
5. Arthur Lytton Sells, *The Italian Influence in English Poetry: From Chaucer to Southwell* (Allen and Unwin, London, 1955), p. 204.
6. T. W. Baldwin, *William Shakspere's Small Latine and Lesse Greeke* (University of Illinois Press, Urbana, 1944).
7. See, for example, Yates, *John Florio*, pp. 35–8 and pp. 334–6; Frances Yates, *A Study of Love's Labour's Lost* (Cambridge University Press, Cambridge, 1936), pp. 27–49; Jonathan Bate, *The Genius of Shakespeare* (Picador, London, 1997), pp. 55–8. The tradition of linking Florio and Shakespeare stretches back to the mid eighteenth century when, in his edition of the plays, Warburton suggests that 'by *Holofernes* is designed a particular character, a pedant and schoolmaster of our author's time, one *John Florio*, a teacher of the *Italian* tongue in *London*': William Warburton, *The Works of Shakespear* (London, 1747), ii, pp. 227–8. Other modern critics who have focused only on the verbal parallels are Shaheen, 'Knowledge of Italian', pp. 162–3, Simonini, *Italian Scholarship*, pp. 87–103, and Mario Praz, 'Shakespeare's Italy', *Shakespeare Survey* 7 (1954), 95–106; p. 105.
8. Yates, *John Florio*, pp. 124–5.
9. Bate, *Genius of Shakespeare*, p. 55.
10. John Eliot's scathing attack on the teachers of Italian and French in London criticises the methods of their language lessons: 'I haue been scholer to one or two of them, but I like not their manner of teaching, for they will take mony before hand, and wen they are paide, they care little for their scholers profit, to instruct them the rudiments of their tongue a little, which is no great peece of worke. / / What is their order in teaching? / / Tis only to read some halfe side, and to construe it, which is no great matter, and will not stay aboue halfe an hower to make a lecture, so that they do all things by the halfes.' Eliot, *Ortho-epia Gallica*, pp. 4–5.
11. 'Venise, woo seeth thee not, praiseth thee not, but who seeth thee, it costeth hym wel': Florio, *First Fruites*, sig. 34r.
12. *Lombardia è il giardino del mondo*: Florio, *First Fruites*, sig. 31v.
13. All references from Shakespeare are from Stephen Greenblatt et al., eds, *The Norton Shakespeare* (W. W. Norton, New York, 1997) unless otherwise stated.
14. A. J. Hoenselaars, '"Under the dent of the English pen": the language of Italy in English Renaissance drama', in Michele Marrapodi et al., eds, *Shakespeare's Italy: Functions of Italian Locations in Renaissance Drama* (Manchester University Press, Manchester, 1993), pp. 272–91; p. 280.

'GIVE ME THE OCULAR PROOF'

15 The opening chapter contains the phrases 'Ben trovato caro fratello' and 'io vi ringratio con tutto il mio core' and the word for house ('casa'); chapter four has the expression 'Venite, voi sarete il ben venuto', which Shakespeare renders directly. Both forms of greeting are repeated at the start of chapter thirteen. Tranio the servant's phrase 'me perdonate' [I, i, 25] can be found in chapter eleven, entitled 'To speake to a servant': Florio, First Fruites, sig. 1, sig. 4r, and sig. 9r.
16 Shaheen, 'Shakespeare's knowledge', p. 161.
17 Grumio is described as 'the opportune scapegoat for monolinguists': Hoenselaars, 'Under the dent', p. 281.
18 Jean E. Howard suggests a date of 1592 or earlier: Greenblatt, Norton Shakespeare, p. 133.
19 'Small herbs have grace, great weeds do grow apace' [Richard III, II, iv, 13] recalls Florio's 'An ill weed groweth apace' [First Fruites, sig. 31v]; the inscription in the gold casket in The Merchant of Venice [II, vii, 65] echoes Florio's 'Al that glistreth is not gold' [First Fruites, sig. 32r], and Shylock's 'Fast bind, fast find – / A proverb never stale in thrifty mind' [II, v, 53–54] is taken from the opening chapter of the Second Frutes, which concludes with the observation 'Faste binde, faste finde. And he that shuts well, auoydeth ill luck' [p. 15]. Westmorland's description of the Scots 'playing the mouse in absence of the cat' in Henry V [I, ii, 172] brings to mind Florio's 'When the cat is abroad the mice play' [First Fruites, sig. 33r].
20 'There is an upstart Crow, beautified with our feathers, that with his *Tiger's heart wrapped in a Player's hide*, supposes he is as well able to bombast out a blank verse as the best of you': Greenes Groats-worth of Witte (London, 1592), sig. A3v.
21 Florio's description is itself taken from Petrarch: 'Questa umil fera, un cor di tigre o d'orsa / che 'n vista umana, o 'n forma d'angel vene' [152, 1–2]. (This humble wild creature, this tiger's or she-bear's heart that comes in human appearance and in the shape of an angel.) Durling, Petrarch's Lyric Poems, pp. 297–8.
22 The page numbering in the First Fruites is confused at this point, with page 28 preceding page 27, and page 26 immediately following it. The page numbering of the 1578 edition has been retained in references.
23 Florio returns to this theme in chapter twenty-eight: 'What a shame it is, that you shal see an English man come in company of straungers, who can neyther speake, nor vnderstand with them, but standes as one mute, & so is he mocked of them, and despised of al, and none wyl make account of hym?' [First Fruites, sig. 62v].
24 Some ten years after Shakespeare's reference, Jonson alludes to Florio's precepts in Peregrine and Sir Politic Would-be's conversation on travellers in Venice: see Volpone, II, i, 112–117.
25 Yates, Love's Labour's Lost, p. 54.
26 Florio, Second Frutes, p. 79.
27 Shaheen, 'Shakespeare's knowledge', p. 162, suggests a further parallel in Hamlet, when Hamlet greets the bare-headed Osric in V, ii. There is a similar exchange about the doffing of hats at the beginning of the seventh

chapter of the *Second Frutes*, which is a dialogue about fencing. Osric is, of course, about to deliver to Hamlet Laertes' challenge to a fencing contest.
28 'It is more than an analogy and Shakespeare must have had this passage in mind when he wrote Iago's speech': Simonini, *Italian Scholarship*, pp. 97-8. Desdemona's request for praise for 'a deserving woman' [II, i, 147] requires Iago to speak positively about women after his hitherto insistently negative comments. His ability to speak on both sides of a question does recall Florio's practice in the final chapter, where the positive and the negative views on women are clearly delineated in the two speakers (Silvestro and Pandolfo respectively).
29 Florio, *Worlde of Wordes*, sig. B2r.
30 Boccaccio's tale of Giletta of Narbonne provides the main plot for *All's Well That Ends Well*.
31 Geoffrey Bullough, *Narrative and Dramatic Sources of Shakespeare* (Routledge and Kegan Paul, London, 1957-75), ii, p. 61, argues for this date, as the play is not mentioned in Francis Meres's *Palladis Tamia*, printed in 1598, while the first quarto of 1600 occasionally gives the name 'Kemp', who leaves the Chamberlain's Men in early 1599, in the speech headings for Dogberry.
32 Miola details the similarities between the tale and play to argue that 'Shakespeare probably read the Italian original': 'The wooing of a lady in Belmont by means of a test, the friendship between adventurer and benefactor, the loan from a Jewish moneylender, the pound of flesh penalty, the imposture of the lady as a learned doctor, the trial and climactic discomfiture of the Jew, the ring switch and comic conclusion.' Robert S. Miola, *Shakespeare's Reading* (Oxford University Press, Oxford, 2000), p. 81. Bullough, *Narrative and Dramatic Sources*, ii, pp. 5-7, suggests that Shakespeare uses a different tale from Fiorentino for the duping of Falstaff plot in *The Merry Wives of Windsor*, probably composed in 1597. This almost simultaneous employment of more than one story from the same collection in two plays is consistent with Shakespeare's practice with *Gli Hecatommithi* in the early years of the seventeenth century.
33 R. P. Sorlien, ed., *The Diary of John Manningham of the Middle Temple, 1602-1603* (University Press of New England, Hanover, 1976), p. 48.
34 Bullough, *Narrative and Dramatic Sources*, ii, p. 271. He also points out the allusion to 'la notte di beffana', that is Twelfth Night, in the prologue.
35 In the mid nineteenth century Hunter discovered a copy of Gonzaga's play bound together with *Il sacrificio* and three other Italian comedies, including two by Girolamo Parabosco (*La notte* and *Il viluppo*), which are also consulted by Florio for the 1611 dictionary. The latter play contains a love-sick character called Orsino, leading Hunter to speculate on the provenance of this collection, though it seems more likely that it once belonged to the Italian teacher rather than the playwright himself: 'I could almost persuade myself that the very volume in which the *Sacrificio* was first found by me had once been Shakespeare's, and that it contained the identical copies of the *Ingannì* of Gonzaga and the *Ingannati* or *Sacrificio* of the Thunderstruck Academicians, which had been used by him. It was at least a singular

circumstance that they should be found bound together in the same volume, and the singularity was enhanced by the circumstance that another of the five comedies in the volume was the *Viluppo*, in which one of the characters is designated in the *personae* as *Orsino inamorata*.' Joseph Hunter, *New Illustrations of the Life, Studies, and Writings of Shakespeare* (London, 1845), i, p. 398.

36 Katherine Duncan-Jones, *Ungentle Shakespeare: Scenes from his Life* (Arden Shakespeare, London, 2001), p. 5 and pp. 114–15.
37 Duncan-Jones, *Ungentle Shakespeare*, p. 155.
38 *Ibid.*, p. 170.
39 The playwright's father John marries Marie Guarsi in 1575. She is the daughter of an Italian physician, who had moved to London to practise. It is not clear from the records of the marriage whether her mother is also Italian, or indeed if Marie was born in Italy or England.
40 Keith Sturgess, ed., *John Marston: The Malcontent and Other Plays* (Oxford University Press, Oxford, 1997), p. 41.
41 It is possible that Thomas Kyd writes Italian verse for the performance of Soliman and Perseda in the final act of *The Spanish Tragedy*, but the multilingual inset play is printed in English for the ease of the readers.
42 Sturgess, *The Malcontent*, p. 41, and translation, p. 309. Sturgess (p. xv) describes the exchange as 'a stretched Petrarchan sonnet'. The eighteen lines of the poem are constructed as three quatrains and two tercets, rather than the octave – sestet division of the regular Italian sonnet.
43 Sturgess, *The Malcontent*, p. 130. Florio, *First Fruites*, sigs 90v–91r. A direct borrowing from the *Second Frutes* in *Eastward Ho!* (1605) may confirm Marston's knowledge of that manual too. In the final scene Touchstone's words to Security clearly echo Caesar's description of a cuckolded husband in chapter nine: 'Againe, if you be a Cuckold, and know it not, you are an *Innocent*; if you know it, and endure it, a true *Martyr* [V, v, 195–196]'. 'If he knowe it, hee must needs be a patient, and therefore a martir, if hee knowes it not, hee is an innocent, and you know that martires and innocents shall be saved' [*Second Frutes*, p. 143]. The final scene of this collaborative play is usually attributed to Jonson, but Herford and Simpson suggest that 'the last lines of the scene . . . together with the epilogue, may be assigned to Marston': Herford and Simpson, *Ben Jonson*, x, p. 646.
44 Shaheen, 'Shakespeare's knowledge', p. 163.
45 Story Donno, *Renaissance Pastorals*, p. 75.
46 Philip J. Finkelpearl, *John Marston of the Middle Temple* (Harvard University Press, Cambridge, 1969), p. 179.
47 G. K. Hunter, 'Italian tragicomedy on the English stage', *Renaissance Drama* 6 (1973), 123–48; pp. 138–9.
48 Charles and Michelle Martindale, *Shakespeare and the Uses of Antiquity: An Introductory Essay* (Routledge, London, 1990), p. 5.
49 'What will you say if I can shew you that Shakespeare, when, in the favourite phrase, he had a Latin poet *in his Eye*, most assuredly made use of a Translation?': Nichol Smith, *Eighteenth-Century Essays*, p. 178.

50 Frank Kermode, ed., *The Tempest* (Methuen, London, 1954), p. 113; Nichol Smith, *Eighteenth-Century Essays*, p. 178.
51 Baldwin, *Shakspere's Small Latine*, ii, pp. 443–52; Virgil K. Whitaker, *Shakespeare's Use of Learning: An Inquiry into the Growth of his Mind* (Huntington Library, San Marino, 1953), p. 26.
52 Kermode, *The Tempest*, pp. 148–9; he argues that the phrase 'by whose aid' (V, i, 40) is a direct translation of Ovid's *quorum ope* (VII, 199).
53 The first recorded performed of *The Tempest* is at Whitehall on 1 November 1611.
54 Farmer accounts for the 'obscenity and nonsense' of the scene in French in *Henry V* by arguing that it is a non-Shakespearean addition: Nichol Smith, *Eighteenth-Century Essays*, p. 198.
55 Miola, *Shakespeare's Reading*, pp. 2–4. Martindale, *Uses of Antiquity*, p. 10, describes Shakespeare as 'opportunistic in his reading': 'Always on the lookout for material he could use for his own work. He knew some foreign languages, but often preferred to use translations; he did not necessarily read books all the way through; like all his contemporaries – like most scholars even – he used short-cuts to knowledge.'
56 J. M. Lothian and T. W. Craik, eds, *Twelfth Night* (Routledge, London, 1975), pp. xlii–xliii.
57 Cairncross suggests that the phrase 'naked in bed' [IV, i, 5] in the later *Othello* is a direct translation of Polinesso's words to Dalinda explaining how he intends to compromise Ginevra while she is 'nuda nel letto' [V, xxiv, 7]. Harington's translation of 1591 does not mention Ginevra's nakedness: Andrew S. Cairncross, 'Shakespeare and Ariosto: *Much Ado About Nothing, King Lear*, and *Othello*', *Renaissance Quarterly* 29 (1976), 178–82; p. 181.
58 Hunter, 'Italian tragicomedy', pp. 140–7.
59 See P. R. Horne, *The Tragedies of Giambattista Cinthio Giraldi* (Oxford University Press, Oxford, 1962), pp. 15–22, for the problems of dating Cinthio's plays.
60 Caroline Patey, 'Beyond Aristotle: Giraldi Cinzio and Shakespeare' in Sergio Rossi and Dianella Savoia, eds, *Italy and the English Renaissance* (Unicopli, Milan, 1989), pp. 167–85; p. 169.
61 Mary Lascelles, *Shakespeare's Measure for Measure* (Athlone Press, London, 1953), pp. 12–13. For details of Shakespeare's indebtedness to *Epitia* see the following source studies: Louis Albrecht, *Neue Untersuchungen zu Shakespeares Maß für Maß* (Berlin, 1914); Frederick E. Budd, 'Material for a study of the sources of Shakespeare's *Measure for Measure*', *Revue de Littérature Comparée* 11 (1931), 711–36; Robert H. Ball, 'Cinthio's *Epitia* and *Measure for Measure*' in E. J. West, ed., *Elizabethan Studies and Other Essays in Honor of George F. Reynolds* (University of Colorado Series, Boulder, 1945), pp. 132–46; Madeleine Doran, *Endeavors of Art: A Study of Form in Elizabethan Drama* (University of Wisconsin Press, Madison, 1954), pp. 385–9.
62 Two tales in the second tome of William Painter's *Palace of Pleasure*, printed in 1567, are based on *Gli Hecatommithi*.

'GIVE ME THE OCULAR PROOF'

63 It is not among the seventy-two titles in the book-list for the 1598 edition of *A Worlde of Wordes*, but does appear among the two hundred and fifty or so titles for the expanded *Queene Anna's New World of Words* in 1611.
64 Riche's story *Of Nicander and Lucilla* is based on the third tale of the sixth decade in Cinthio (VI, 3), that *Of Fineo and Fiamma* on II, 6, and that *Of Gonsales and his vertuous wife Agatha* on III, 5.
65 Kenneth Muir, *The Sources of Shakespeare's Plays* (Methuen, London, 1977), p. 182.
66 In his prefatory letter *To the Readers in generall* Riche describes how 'the third, the fourth, and the sixt: are Italian Histories, written likewise for pleasure by maister L. B.' [p. 19], who Malone conjectures is Lodowick Bryskett, responsible for another translation from Cinthio, *A Discourse of Civill Life*, printed in 1606, but probably written much earlier. See the introduction to the facsimile of the 1581 edition for the relationship between Riche and Bryskett: Thomas M. Cranfill, ed., *Rich's Farewell to Military Profession 1581* (University of Texas Press, Austin, 1959), pp. xxiii-xxviii, and also Donald Beecher, ed., *Barnabe Rich: His Farewell to Military Profession* (Dovehouse, Ottawa, 1992), pp. 50–1.
67 Horne, *Cinthio Giraldi*, pp. 57–60.
68 *Ibid.*, p. 62.
69 The stories in Painter are novels 38 and 39, out of 65, respectively. They do not appear consecutively in the *Decameron*, where the story of Giletta di Nerbona is the ninth in the third day, and that of Tancredi opens the fourth day.
70 'Of those who acquire something greatly desired, or recover something lost, through their own endeavours.'
71 Marvin T. Herrick, *Tragicomedy: Its Origin and Development in Italy, France, and England* (University of Illinois Press, Urbana, 1955), p. 241.
72 G. K. Hunter, ed., *All's Well That Ends Well* (Methuen, London, 1959), p. 77.
73 Bullough, *Narrative and Dramatic Sources*, ii, p. 381.
74 Hunter, 'Italian tragicomedy', pp. 144–5.
75 J. L. Klein, *Geschichte des Dramas* (Leipzig, 1867), p. 198, suggests that Helena's reluctance to ask Bertram for a kiss in II, v derives from Dorinda's similar coyness with regard to the scornful Silvio in *Il pastor fido* [II, ii]. In addition, Shakespeare recasts the celebrated debate between Amarilli and Corisca on the nature of love from the central act of Guarini's play [III, iv–v] by means of two new characters in the first act. Parolles' argument to Helena that virginity is 'against the rule of nature' [I, i, 133] recalls comically Corisca's specious reasoning as she tries to persuade Amarilli that her love for Mirtillo does not constitute infidelity, while the exchange between the Countess and Helena in the third scene as to how 'your Dian / Was both herself and love' [I, iii, 207–8] alludes, both linguistically and philosophically, to the similar argument on 'la legge di Diana o pur d'Amore' [III, v] in Guarini.
76 'It is surprise, incredulity, *maraviglia*, that are the effects aimed at by Giraldi's play [*Altile*] as well': Horne, *Cinthio Giraldi*, p. 66.

77 In his *Annotationi*, Guarini comments on the importance of Corisca in the final scene: 'Era necessaria da vna parte, che Corisca non rimanesse scontenta, anzi pure estremamente addolorata; percioché haurebbe il suo dolore contaminato il fin Comico, ouero che si sarebbe accostato al fine della Tragedia doppia, che dà buon fine à buoni; & cattiuo à cattiui; & non della Tragicommedia, che vuole tutti contenti.' ('It was important that Corisca should not have remained unhappy or in extreme distress, because her grief would have contaminated the comic denouement, or it would have brought it closer to the ending of a double tragedy, which ends happily for the good and unhappily for the bad, as opposed to tragicomedy, which requires all to be content.') Guarini, *Pastor fido*, p. 474.
78 Bullough, *Narrative and Dramatic Sources*, ii, p. 410.
79 Ball, '*Epitia* and *Measure for Measure*', pp. 133–4.
80 'But I will keep her ignorant of her good, / To make her heavenly comforts of despair / When it is least expected' [IV, iii, 108–110]. J. W. Lever, ed., *Measure for Measure* (Methuen, London, 1965), p. 116.
81 Lascelles, *Shakespeare's Measure for Measure*, p. 18, comments on the improbability of Whetstone knowing Cinthio's play.
82 Lever, *Measure for Measure*, pp. xli–xliii.
83 Boccaccio's stories are IV, 2, and VIII, 4. See Herbert G. Wright, *Boccaccio in England from Chaucer to Tennyson* (Athlone Press, London, 1957), pp. 166–7.
84 Barbara A. Mowat, 'Shakespearean tragicomedy' in Nancy Klein Maguire, ed., *Renaissance Tragicomedy: Explorations in Genre and Politics* (AMS Press, New York, 1987), pp. 80–96; p. 94.
85 Duncan-Jones, *Ungentle Shakespeare*, pp. 136–56. Henke argues that the younger playwright might be the source for Shakespeare's apparent knowledge of Italian tragicomedy, suggesting that 'Marston could well have furnished Shakespeare with an indirect account of Guarini's theories': Robert Henke, *Pastoral Transformations: Italian Tragicomedy and Shakespeare's Late Plays* (University of Delaware Press, Newark and London, 1997), p. 51.
86 Sturgess, *The Malcontent*, p. 174; Lever, *Measure for Measure*, p. 90.
87 Ristine, *English Tragicomedy*, p. 218.
88 Lee Bliss, *The World's Perspective: John Webster and the Jacobean Drama* (Rutgers University Press, New Brunswick, 1983), p. 16.
89 'Fletcher's *Faithful Shepherdess* introduced Guarini's theory, and thereafter many plays were called tragicomedies': Herrick, *Tragicomedy*, p. 218. See also Gordon McMullan and Jonathan Hope, eds, *The Politics of Tragicomedy* (Routledge, London, 1991), p. 2, and Eugene M. Waith, *The Pattern of Tragicomedy in Beaumont and Fletcher* (Yale University Press, New Haven, 1952), pp. 36–42.
90 Hunter, 'Italian tragicomedy', p. 134.
91 David L. Hirst, *Tragicomedy* (Methuen, London, 1984), p. 47.
92 'Every creative imitation mingles filial rejection with respect, just as every parody pays its own oblique homage': Greene, *Light in Troy*, p. 46.
93 W. Reavley Gair, ed., *Antonio and Mellida* (Manchester University Press, Manchester, 1991), p. 19. Kay stresses a specifically Jacobean context for the

'GIVE ME THE OCULAR PROOF'

Italian borrowings in the play, arguing that they 'may have functioned as intertextual allusions that flattered the sophistication of auditors capable of recognising them': W. David Kay, ed., *The Malcontent* (A. & C. Black, London, 1998), p. xviii.
94 All references to *The Malcontent* are from Sturgess, *The Malcontent*; p. 129. Story Donno, *Renaissance Pastorals*, p. 81.
95 Story Donno, *Renaissance Pastorals*, p. 108; Sturgess, *The Malcontent*, p. 129.
96 *Ibid.*, p. 144.
97 Kirsch writes of 'its overall response to Guarini's tragicomic ideas', although he fails to consider any of the structural similarities between the two plays: Arthur C. Kirsch, *Jacobean Dramatic Perspectives* (Virginia University Press, Charlottesville, 1972), p. 32.
98 See the textual notes to G. K. Hunter's edition of *The Malcontent* (Manchester University Press, Manchester, 1975); the introduction to Bernard Harris, ed., *The Malcontent* (Ernest Benn Ltd, London, 1967), pp. xxvi–xxvii; Leo Salingar, 'Elizabethan dramatists and Italy: a postscript' in J. R. Mulryne and Margaret Shewring, eds, *Theatre of the English and Italian Renaissance* (Macmillan, Basingstoke, 1991). pp. 232–5.
99 Story Donno, *Renaissance Pastorals*, p. 69.
100 Sturgess, *The Malcontent*, p. 153.
101 See T. F. Wharton, 'Sexual politics in Marston's *The Malcontent*' in T. F. Wharton, ed., *Drama of John Marston: Critical Re-visions* (Cambridge University Press, Cambridge, 2000), pp. 181–93; p. 182.
102 By the turn of the century Guarini himself acknowledges the possibility of urban tragicomedy when explaining the pastoral setting of his play in the *Annotationi sopra al Pastor Fido*: 'Et percioche poteua auuenire, che'l nome Tragicomico producesse nell'animo di chi legge di fauola cittadina, piacque al prouuido autore de leuar questo equiuoco con l'aggiunto di Pastorale.' ('And because it could happen that the name "tragicomedy" brings to the mind of the reader an urban fable, it has pleased the provident author to remove this equivocation with the addition of "pastoral"'.) Guarini, *Il pastor fido*, sig. A6r.
103 Sturgess, *The Malcontent*, p. 151.
104 She appears in six scenes altogether, including one additional scene printed in the third quarto, probably written by Webster. See Wharton, 'Sexual politics', p. 185.
105 Louise George Clubb, *Italian Drama in Shakespeare's Time* (Yale University Press, New Haven, 1989), p. 137.
106 Guarini, *Pastor fido*, p. 191.
107 Sturgess, *The Malcontent*, p. 164.
108 *Ibid.*, p. 124.
109 J. H. Whitfield, ed., *Battista Guarini: 'Il pastor fido' with 'The Faithful Shepherd' Translated* (Edinburgh University Press, Edinburgh, 1976), p. 17.
110 Hirst, *Tragicomedy*, p. 7.
111 *Unde cadis, non quo refert* [II, i, 26]: Sturgess, *The Malcontent*, p. 133.
112 J. R. Mulryne, ed., *The Spanish Tragedy* (A. & C. Black, London, 1989), p. 85: III, xiii, 6; Sturgess, *The Malcontent*, p. 167.

'WHO THE DEVIL TAUGHT THEE SO MUCH ITALIAN?'

113 Sturgess, *The Malcontent*, p. 123.
114 Michael Scott, *John Marston's Plays: Theme, Structure and Performance* (Macmillan, London, 1978), p. 31. See also David Pascoe, 'Marston's childishness', *Medieval and Renaissance Drama in England* 9 (1997), 92–111; p. 106.
115 Maristella de Panizza Lorch, 'Honest Iago and the lusty moor: the humanistic drama of *honestas/voluptas* in a Shakespearean context' in Mulryne and Shewring, *Theatre of the Renaissance*, pp. 204–20; p. 219.
116 Caretti, *Orlando furioso*, p. 1404; translation Waldman, *Orlando Furioso*, p. 566; E. A. J. Honigmann, ed., *Othello* (Nelson, Walton-on Thames, 1997), p. 245.
117 Smart, *Truth and Tradition*, p. 183.
118 Muir, *Shakespeare's Sources*, p. 183; translation Bullough, *Narrative and Dramatic Sources*, vii, p. 246.
119 Cairncross, 'Shakespeare and Ariosto', p. 181.
120 Caretti, *Orlando furioso*, p. 107; Waldman, *Orlando Furioso*, pp. 43–4.
121 Othello's outraged response to Iago's suggestion that he has discovered Desdemona and Cassio in bed together innocently ('Naked in bed, Iago, and not mean harm? [IV, i, 5]) recalls the phrasing of Polinesso's plan to entrap Ariodante's beloved in a compromsing situation by means of her servant Dalinda, 'quando allora Ginevra si ritrouva / nuda nel letto' [V, xxiv, 6–7].
122 'Run, run, Orlando; carve on every tree / The fair, the chaste, and unexpressive she' [III, ii, 9–10].
123 M. Hale Shackford, 'Shakespeare and Greene's *Orlando Furioso*', *MLN* 39 (1924), 54–6.
124 Greene's source was identified by P. A. Daniel in *Athenaeum* (October 1881), p. 465.
125 The earliest recorded performances of both plays are as part of the first Jacobean court season in 1604: *Othello* is performed at Whitehall on 1 November, and *Measure for Measure* on 26 December. Muir, *Shakespeare's Sources*, p. 182, suggests that the latter play 'was written about the same time as *Othello*'. Owing to the closure of the theatres in London between May 1603 and April 1604, there is the attractive possibility that Shakespeare is working on both plays simultaneously during this period of enforced inactivity.
126 Doran, *Endeavors of Art*, pp. 385–9, cites the features common to both *Measure for Measure* and *Epitia*, which are not found in any of the other possible sources.
127 In a modern edition of *James IV*, Sanders claims that he has 'been unable to find any verbal echoes to indicate that ... he [Greene] used Cinthio's own dramatic adaptation of the story, the neo-classical *Arrenopia*', which contains only the material found in the fifth act of Greene's play: Norman Sanders, ed., *The Scottish History of James the Fourth* (Methuen, London, 1970), p. xxx.

128 W. W. Greg, ed., *The History of Orlando Furioso, 1594* (Malone Society Reprints, Oxford, 1907).
129 Honigmann, *Othello*, p. 256, suggests that 'Othello's fit in some ways resembles . . . the raging of the hero in Greene's *Orlando Furioso*'.
130 *Ibid*., p. 129.
131 *Ibid*., p. 144.
132 Colin Burrow, *Epic Romance: Homer to Milton* (Clarendon Press, Oxford, 1993), pp. 66–7. Ariosto makes the connection between the two sets of lovers directly by means of the cave, where Angelica and Medoro's romantic liaison takes place: 'nel mezzo giorno un antro li copriva, / forse non men di quel commodo e grato, / ch'ebber, fuggendo l'acque, Enea e Dido, / de' lor secreto testimonio fido' [XIX, xxxv, 5–8]. ('At noontide a cave would shelter them, doubtless no less handy and hospitable than the one which offered Dido and Aeneas shelter from the rain and proved a trusty witness to their secrets.')
133 Caretti, *Orlando furioso*, p. 539; Waldman, *Orlando Furioso*, pp. 218–19.
134 Caretti, *Orlando furioso*, p. 693; Waldman, *Orlando Furioso*, p. 280.
135 'That handkerchief / Did an Egyptian to my mother give, / She was a charmer and could almost read / The thoughts of people. She told her, while she kept it / 'Twould make her amiable and subdue my father / Entirely to her love; but if she lost it / Or made a gift of it, my father's eye / Should hold her loathed and his spirits should hunt / After new fancies' [III, iv, 57–65]. Honigmann, *Othello*, p. 244.
136 *Ibid*., p. 256. Lorch, 'Honest Iago', p. 217, says of Othello that 'he acts out his madness in a language which seems to parallel Canto XXIII of the *Furioso*. In Shakespeare's play, however, the situation is quite different, since Iago is in perfect charge of Othello, replacing what in the *Furioso* I would define as the role of the poet Ariosto'.
137 Sammut criticises Greene's handling of Orlando's madness in comparison to the subtlety of Ariosto's original: 'Nella delineazione della pazzia del protagonista, ad esempio, ammiratissima in tutti i secoli per il meraviglioso crescendo, il Greene dimostra una completa carenza della psicologia dell'insanità mentale.' ('In the handling of the madness of the protagonist, for example, admired through the centuries for its marvellous development, Greene shows a complete lack of understanding of the psychology of insanity.') Alfonso Sammut, *La Fortuna dell'Ariosto nell'Inghilterra Elisabettiana* (Vita e Pensiero, Milan, 1971), p. 113.
138 Caretti, *Orlando furioso*, p. 696; Waldman, *Orlando Furioso*, pp. 281–2.
139 Lorch, 'Honest Iago', p. 216. There are no precise references to Ariosto's poem for the phrases that she suggests Shakespeare has taken from it.
140 Honigmann, *Othello*, p. 326; Caretti, *Orlando furioso*, p. 695; Waldman, *Orlando Furioso*, p. 281.
141 Honigmann, *Othello*, pp. 119–20.
142 See Janet L. Smarr, ed., *Italian Renaissance Tales* (Solaris Press, Rochester, 1983), pp. xvii–xxxiii, and Beecher, *Barnabe Rich*, pp. 30–1.

143 Emrys Jones, 'Othello, Lepanto, and the Cyprus wars', Shakespeare Survey 21 (1968), 47–52.
144 Dympna Callaghan, Woman and Gender in Renaissance Tragedy: A Study of King Lear, Othello, The Duchess of Malfi and The White Devil (Harvester, Hemel Hempstead, 1989), p. 35. See also David Farley-Hills, Shakespeare and the Rival Playwrights, 1600–1606 (Routledge, London, 1990), pp. 104–35.
145 Honigmann, Othello, pp. 231–2.
146 Henke, Pastoral Transformations, p. 103 and p. 106.
147 Henke's comparative methodology builds on Clubb's concept of 'theatergrams', whereby apparent correspondences between the Italian and English dramatic traditions are 'not primarily based on the assumption of direct Italian–English "influence" but on the presence of independent yet parallel historical, cultural, and theatrical developments': Henke, Pastoral Transformations, p. 18, and see also Clubb, Italian Drama, pp. 1–26.
148 Henke, Pastoral Transformations, p. 51.
149 Battista Guarini, Il Verato (1588) in G. A. Barotti and A. Zeno, eds, Delle opere del Caualier Battista Guarini (Verona, 1738), ii, p. 259.
150 J. H. P. Pafford, ed., The Winter's Tale (Methuen, London, 1963), p. 75.
151 Bullough, Narrative and Dramatic Sources, vii, pp. 17–19. The means of punishment for Ambrogiuolo in Boccaccio's story is transferred to The Winter's Tale, where Autolycus describes the appalling fate that awaits the shepherd's son in Bohemia: 'He has a son, who shall be flayed alive, then 'nointed over with honey, set on the head of a wasps' nest, then stand till he be three quarters and a dram dead' [IV, iv, 785–8]. Pafford, Winter's Tale, p. 132.

Conclusion: Seventeenth-century language learning

THERE IS no one seventeenth-century figure who proves to be as influential in the transmission of the Italian language and culture in England as John Florio. His legacy, however, goes on well beyond his death in 1625. One advantage of the printed language manuals is their long-term availability, and it is noteworthy that, with one exception,[1] there are no new Italian dialogue books printed between the end of the sixteenth century and the early 1640s. The start of that decade, though, sees the first printings of the work of another 'Italian, and Professor of the Italian Tongue in London'; Giovanni Torriano publishes three guides for the learning of Italian between 1640 and 1642.[2] It is some twenty years later in 1659, however, that Torriano's most significant work is printed, and its title page recognises Florio's substantial contribution to its genesis:

> Vocabolario Italiano & Inglese, A Dictionary Italian & English. Formerly Compiled by John Florio, and since his last Edition, Anno 1611. augmented by himselfe in His life time, with many thousand Words, and Thuscan phrases. Now Most diligently Revised, Corrected, and Compared, with 'La Crusca', and other approved Dictionaries extant since his Death; and enriched with very considerable ADDITIONS.
>
> Whereunto is added A Dictionary English and Italian, with Severall Proverbs and Instructions for the speedy attaining to the Italian Tongue. Never before Published.

In 'The Preface' Torriano explains exactly how he has come to produce an expanded version of the second edition of Florio's dictionary, *Queen Anna's New World of Words* (1611):

> This, notwithstanding being defective, and other Dictionaries and Italian Authors coming to his Hands, he collected out of them an Addition of many thousand Words and Phrases, relating to Arts, Sciences, and Exercises; intending (if he had lived) a third Edition, which he left behind him in a very fair Manuscript, perfected and ready for the Presse.
>
> This manuscript I have diligently perused, and in very many places supplyed, out of the generally approved Dictionary of the *Accademici della Crusca*, and severall others that have been set forth since his death. I have likewise much corrected the English Interpretations, and (where there was cause) reduced them to their genuine sense, as they are now used in these Modern Times.[3]

In the same preface the teacher suggests that there are still many good reasons to study Italian in England in the middle of the seventeenth century:

> When the Rarities of *Italy* (that Paradise of Art and Nature, that Academy and Garden of the World) do dayly call so many of the English Nation, and Forraigners, from all parts into it, when its excellent Books do travell into all Nations and find Universall Esteem; and when all Merchants that traffique into the *Levant*, must trade by that Language, it would be superfluous for me by a Studied Discourse to invite any to the Learning thereof.[4]

Torriano rehearses two familiar arguments for the continuing desire to learn Italian: the number of English travellers to Italy and the quantity and quality of books that can be read in the language. Indeed, he stresses that the Italian–English section of 'the precedent Dictionary is absolutely necessary for all such as are desirous to understand Italian Authors'. Torriano, however, also introduces a more pressing third reason to speak Italian: the need for English merchants in the eastern Mediterranean to carry out their trade in that language. Torriano's first book of Italian grammar, dedicated to the 'Company of Turkey Merchants' as well as an aristocratic patroness, draws attention to the 'infinite number' of merchants who have already learnt the language by the early 1640s.[5] The personal dedications in his later dictionary confirm this new emphasis on more practical motives for Italian language learning by the 1650s. There are dedications in Italian to 'Andrea Riccard' and 'Gulielmo Williams', who are respectively the 'governatore' and 'sotto-governatore dell'Honoratissima Compagnia de' Signori Negotianti di Turchia in London', and in English to 'Mr. James Stainer, Merchant in London' of the 'Right worshipful *Company of the Turkey Merchants'*. This also suggests a discernible decline by the middle of the seventeenth century in the characteristic prominence placed on learning the language by means of and in order to appreciate directly the riches of Italian literature, so evident in the works of teachers from William Thomas through to John Florio.[6]

It is in the context of a specifically literary seventeenth-century interest in Italian language learning, however, that it is worth considering the progress of John Milton's Italian studies in the 1620s and 1630s. It is through the repeated references to his youthful language learning in Milton's own writings that the importance of this aspect of his education becomes apparent. He first mentions his study of languages, at the insistence of his father, in the autobiographical preface to the second book of *The Reason of Church Government*, printed in 1642:

> I had from my first yeeres by the ceaselesse diligence and care of my father, whom God recompence, bin exercis'd to the tongues, and some sciences, as my age would suffer, by sundry masters and teachers both at home and at the schools.[7]

In the poem *Ad Patrem*, printed in the *Poemata* of 1645, Milton expounds on the languages, both ancient (Latin, Greek, and Hebrew) and modern (French and then Italian), in which he has been instructed:

> Tuo, pater optime, sumptu
> Cum mihi Romulae patuit facundia linguae,
> Et Latii veneres, et quae Iovis ora decebant
> Grandia magniloquis elata vocabula Graiis,
> Addere suasisti quos iactat Gallia flores,
> Et quam degeneri novus Italus ore loquelam
> Fundit, barbaricos testatus voce tumultus
> Quaeque Palaestinus loquitur mysteria vates.
> [78–85]

(When at your cost, dear father, I had become fluent in the tongue of Romulus, and had mastered the graces of Latin, and the lofty words of the magniloquent Greeks, which became the lips of Jove himself; you then persuaded me to add to these the flowers that Gallia boasts, and the language which the modern Italian pours from his degenerate mouth – a witness by his speech of the barbarian tumults – and the mysteries which the prophet of Palestine utters.)[8]

His father's educational programme leaves a deep impression on Milton, reflected in the promotion of both Classical and modern languages in his own tract, *Of Education*, printed in 1644. Despite the employment of private tutors to instruct the young Milton, there is no record of any particular Italian teacher who might have taught him in London. Unlike his predecessors Spenser and Daniel, who both seem to have started studying Italian during their years at university, Milton begins to learn the language *before* he goes up to Cambridge in 1625.[9] Even if Milton does benefit from the assistance of a personal Italian tutor, there is still the suggestion that his knowledge of the language may have been initially derived from printed sources. In a letter addressed to Benedetto Buonmattei, written during Milton's stay in Florence in September 1638, the English visitor pleads with his new friend to include a section on Italian pronunciation, specifically to help non-native speakers, in his forthcoming work on the Tuscan dialect, *Della Lingua Toscana*, which is eventually printed in 1643:

> uti jam inchoatis, majori etiam ex parte absolutis, velles, quantâ maximâ facilitate res ipsa tulerit, in nostram exterorum gratiam, de recta linguae pronuntiatione adhuc paululum quiddam adjicere. Caeteris enim sermonis vestri consultis in hunc usque diem id animi videtur fuisse, suis tantum ut satisfacerent, de nobis nihil soliciti. Quanquam ille meo quidem judicio, & famae suae, & Italici sermonis gloriae, haud paulo certius consuluissent, si praecepta ita tradidissent, ac si omnium mortalium referret ejus linguae scientiam appetere.

> (That you would be willing to add to your work, already begun and in large part completed, a little something on right pronunciation – as much as the work itself will bear, for the sake of us foreigners. For the intention of all previous authorities on your speech seems to have been to satisfy their own people, caring nothing about us. Although in my judgement they would have provided more surely for their own fame and the glory of the Italian speech if they had presented their precepts as if it were the business of all mortals to acquire the language.)[10]

While the letter confirms the author's ability in reading the language ('possum tamen nonnunquam ad illum Dantem, & Petrarcham aliosque vestros complusculos, libenter & cupide commessatum ire'),[11] it perhaps suggests that Milton's *spoken* Italian, which would have been encouraged by a native language teacher, is not at a particularly advanced level, at least not at the beginning of his year in Italy, between July 1638 and June 1639. In the same letter Milton is also bashful about the standard of his written Italian, although it appears that he is being a little disingenuous in this respect:

> De caetero, si forte cur in hoc argumento, Latinâ potius quam vestrâ Linguâ utar, miraris; id factum eâ gratiâ est, ut intelligas quam ego Linguam abs te mihi praeceptis exornandam cupio, ejus me plane meam imperitiam, & inopiam Latine confiteri.
>
> (Finally, if you should wonder why, on this subject, I use Latin rather than your tongue, I do it for this reason, that you may understand that I wish that Tongue clarified for me by your precepts, and to confess my awkwardness and ignorance plainly in Latin.)[12]

In his first collection of English poetry, printed in 1645, Milton includes five sonnets and a *canzone*, which are written in Italian. Until the beginning of the twentieth century it was habitually assumed that these poems dated from Milton's year in Italy, or from shortly after his return to England. His knowledge of Italian, however, clearly predates his visit, and so it is plausible that the Italian poems belong to an earlier period. In 1921 Smart argued that Milton composed them during his time at Cambridge, in around 1630; he refers to an annotated copy of the *Rime e Prose di Giovanni della Casa*, printed in 1563, which is autographed 'Jo. Milton, pre. 10d., 1629', demonstrating the poet's interest in the form and language of the Italian sonnet at that time.[13] He adds that Milton deliberately places the Italian poems before the seventh sonnet ('How soon hath Time, the subtle thief of youth, / Stolen on his wing my three-and-twentieth year!'), presumably written in either 1630 or 1631, in the carefully constructed 1645 volume, which further suggests an earlier date of composition. Both Smart and Prince cite della Casa as the most significant Italian precedent for the form and themes of Milton's *English* sonnets,[14] and yet it is only in the Italian poems that the author deals with the more characteristic sonnet theme of love. None of the five English sonnets printed in 1645 contains any amorous content, whereas, writing in Italian, the poet is constantly self-conscious about his unaccustomed romantic feelings, and his new and strange manner of expressing them:

> Cosi Amor mecu insù la lingua snella
> Desta il fior nuovo di strania favella,
> Mentre io di te, vezzosament altera,
> Canto, dal mio buon popol non inteso,
> E 'l bel Tamigi cangio col bel Arno.
>   [III, 6–10]

(So Love quickens on my swift tongue the new flower of a foreign speech, as I sing of thee, sweet and noble lady, – not understood by my own good people, – and change the fair Thames for the fair Arno.)[15]

In the following *Canzone* Milton continues to refer to the incomprehension of the young people who surround him, which again suggests to Smart that the poems are not composed during the poet's stay in Italy:

> Ridonsi donne e giovani amorosi,
> M'accostandosi attorno, e 'Perchè scrivi
> Perchè tu scrivi in lingua ignota e strana,
> Verseggiando d'amor, e come t'osi?'
>
> [1–4]

(Amorous youth and maidens gather about me with mirth, and 'Why dost thou write?' they ask, 'Why dost thou write in a strange and unknown tongue, making verses of love, and how dost thou dare?')[16]

Whatever the actual dates of composition of the Italian poems, Milton certainly presents them in his first collection as the works of a youthful poet. The *Poems* of 1645 also contains, at the end of the volume, his experiments with Italianate pastoral forms in the elegy *Lycidas*, written in 1637 and first printed in 1638, and the masque *Comus*, performed in 1634 and printed in 1637.[17] Both of these works clearly do predate his Italian visit,[18] but it is in Italy that Milton seems to begin to see the shape of his poetic career in terms of the model inspired by Tasso. Having tried his hand in both Italian lyric and pastoral forms before he leaves England in 1638, which he presents simultaneously after his return in the *Poems* of 1645, Milton first begins to consider seriously his own epic calling while in the country of Ariosto, and particularly Tasso.

Milton's experiences in Italy clearly instil in him a greater confidence in his chosen vocation as poet. In *The Reason of Church Government*, the first work to be issued, in 1642, under Milton's own name, the author explains the positive effect that his warm reception in Italian literary circles has on him:

> But much latelier in the privat Academies of *Italy*, whither I was favour'd to resort, perceiving that some trifles which I had in memory, compos'd at under twenty or thereabout (for the manner is that every one must give some proof of his wit and reading there), met with

acceptance above what was lookt for, ... which the Italian is not forward to bestow on men of this side of the *Alps*, I began thus farre to assent both to them and divers of my friends here at home, and not lesse to an inward prompting which now grew daily upon me, that by labour and intent study ... joyn'd with the strong propensity of nature, I might perhaps leave something so written to aftertimes, as they should not willingly let it die.[19]

Milton envisages this great work as a vernacular epic poem, and he considers it specifically in relation to the achievements of sixteenth-century Italian epic; he invokes Ariosto's example to explain his decision to write the poem in English, rather than Latin:

> There ought no regard be sooner had, then to Gods glory by the honour and instruction of my country. For which cause, and not only for that I knew it would be hard to arrive at the second rank among the Latines, I apply'd my selfe to the resolution which *Ariosto* follow'd against the perswasions of *Bembo*, to fix all the industry and art I could unite to the adorning of my native tongue; ... to be an interpreter & relater of the best and sagest things among mine owne Citizens throughout this Iland in the mother dialect.[20]

As he is pondering a subject for his own poem, Milton recounts Tasso's offer to Alfonso II, Duke of Ferrara, to compose an epic poem about either Godfrey, Belarius, or Charlemagne. Milton seems initially to conceive of a poem on the theme of a native English hero; while he is in Naples in December 1638, the English visitor meets, and is befriended by, Tasso's final patron, Giovanni Battista Manso, the Marquis of Villa.[21] Before he leaves again for Rome, Milton presents the Italian with a new poem *Mansus*, later printed in the *Poemata* of 1645, in which the young poet expresses his hope of finding as generous a patron as Manso for his own epic endeavours:

> O mihi si mea sors talem concedat amicum
> Phoebaeos decorasse viros qui tam bene norit,
> Siquando indigenas revocabo in carmina reges,
> Arturumque etiam sub terris bella moventem,
> Aut dicam invictae sociali foedere mensae
> Magnanimos Heroas, et – O modo spiritus adsit –
> Frangam Saxonicas Britonum sub Marte phalanges!
> [78–84]

> (If ever I recall in song my native kings, and Arthur setting wars in motion even beneath the earth; if ever I tell of the high-souled heroes in the social bond of the invincible Table; and – let the spirit be

present to aid me – if ever I break the Saxon phalanxes with British war; then may my lot grant me such a friend, one who knows so well how to honor the sons of Phoebus.)[22]

Both Masson and Arthos suggest that Milton's encounter with a figure so intimately connected with Tasso inspires him towards the fulfilment of his own epic ambitions.[23] When *Paradise Lost* finally appears almost thirty years later in 1667, it is a very different kind of poem from the one first imagined in *Mansus*. The prior example of Tasso's Christian epic remains highly significant for Milton's achievement, however, as the body of criticism that has traced the Italian element in his poetry through Tasso's epic theory and practice has shown.[24]

In spite of Milton's excellent knowledge of Italian, it is evident that he reads Tasso's poem in Fairfax's English translation as well as in the original language.[25] Weismiller draws attention to a series of parallels between *Paradise Lost* and Fairfax's translation, which are expanded upon in Lea and Gang's edition of *Godfrey of Bulloigne*: 'It is clear that while Milton nowhere sets out to imitate Fairfax or to allude to him, his poetry is shot through with recollections and echoes, probably often quite inadvertent ones of the *Godfrey*.'[26] Like William Drummond before him, Milton becomes familiar with the poem in both Italian and English versions, probably simultaneously. This indicates that the familiar technique of using parallel texts as a means of understanding and appreciating Italian poetry more readily, even if the reader already has prior knowledge of the language, is sustained well into the seventeenth century.

Milton is often regarded as something of a historical anomaly in terms of his continued engagement with Italian literary forms:

> When John Milton returned to the imitation of the Italian romantic epics in constructing his own great epic at the conclusion of the civil war period, he was writing idiosyncratically and anachronistically, and in this, like so many other things, he was alone.[27]

His modern language-learning habits and related techniques for reading Italian materials certainly recall those developed by Florio and other teachers in late sixteenth-century London. They also suggest that Milton is the last significant example in seventeenth-century England of a student learning the Italian language primarily to benefit from the wealth of its literary heritage, rather than for the more practical and increasingly popular motives of travel and trade.

CONCLUSION

Notes

1 *Il Passagiere, or the Passenger: of Benvenuto Italian, Professour of his Native Tongue, for these nine yeeres in London, . . . containing seauen exquisite Dialogues in Italian and English*, which is printed in 1612, and dedicated to Prince Henry. There is also a brief *Grammer or Introduction to the Italian Tongue* by John Sanford, the chaplain of Magdalen College, printed in Oxford in 1605.
2 His three publications are: *The Italian Tutor. Or a New and most compleat Italian Grammer* (London, 1640), dedicated to one of Florio's former pupils, Elizabeth Grey, the Countess of Kent, and 'To the Right Worshipfull and Now Most Flourishing Company of Turkey Merchants'; *New and Easie Directions for the Attaining the Thuscan Italian Tongue* (Cambridge, 1641); *Select Italian Proverbs: The most significant, very useful for Travellers, and such as desire that Language* (London, 1642). After the dictionary Torriano is also responsible for the *Piazza Universale di Proverbi Italiani* (1666), and *The Italian Reviv'd* (1670).
3 Giovanni Torriano, *Vocabolario Italiano & Inglese* (London, 1659), sig. A4r.
4 Torriano, *Vocabolario*, sig. A4r.
5 Torriano, *Italian Tutor*, sig. F4v.
6 The only merchant students anticipated by Florio are the 'Mercanti Italiani, che si dilettano de la lingua Inglese' in his *First Fruites*.
7 Don M. Wolfe, ed., *The Complete Prose Works of John Milton*, i (Yale University Press, New Haven, 1953), pp. 808–9.
8 Walter MacKellar, ed. and trans., *The Latin Poems of John Milton* (Yale University Press, New Haven, 1930), pp. 146–7.
9 See *Defensio Secunda* (1654): 'ita variis instructum linguis, & perceptâ haud leviter philosophiae dulcedine, ad Gymnasium gentis alterum, Cantabrigiam misit'; Eugene J. Strittmatter, ed., *The Works of John Milton*, viii (Columbia University Press, New York, 1933), p. 120. ('When I had thus become proficient in various languages, and had tasted by no means superficially the sweetness of philosophy, he sent me to Cambridge' (translation by Helen North in Wolfe, *Complete Prose*, iv, pp. 612–13).) It is at St Paul's School that Milton makes friends with Charles Diodati, the son of an immigrant Italian physician, Theodore, an acquaintance of Florio, and nephew of the theologian, Giovanni Diodati, whom Milton visits in Geneva in June 1639.
10 The letter is printed as the eighth epistle in *Joannis Miltonii Angli, Epistolarum Familiarium Liber Unus* (1674): Donald L. Clark, ed., *The Works of John Milton*, xii (Columbia University Press, New York, 1936), pp. 34–6; translation by W. Arthur Turner and Alberta T. Turner in Wolfe, *Complete Prose*, i, p. 331.
11 Clark, *Works*, pp. 34–6. ('Certainly I . . . am nevertheless glad to go for a feast to Dante and Petrarch, and to a good many of your other authors' (translation in Wolfe, *Complete Prose*, i, pp. 330–2).)
12 Clark, *Works*, pp. 34–8; translation in Wolfe, *Complete Prose*, i, pp. 330–2.

13 John S. Smart, ed., *The Sonnets of Milton* (Maclehose, Glasgow, 1921), p. 29. The edition is reprinted in Oxford in 1966.
14 See Smart, *Sonnets*, p. 27, and F. T. Prince, *The Italian Element in Milton's Verse* (Clarendon Press, Oxford, 1954), pp. 14–33 and pp. 89–107.
15 Smart, *Sonnets*, pp. 129–30.
16 *Ibid.*, p. 120 and pp. 131–2. Honigmann argues against Smart's interpretation, suggesting that the language is 'ignota e strana' to the poet, rather than his audience, and that he is, therefore, writing in Italy: E. A. J. Honigmann, ed., *Milton's Sonnets* (Macmillan, London, 1966), p. 79.
17 See Prince, *Italian Element*, pp. 70–88, for a consideration of the form and structure of *Lycidas* in relation to the Italian *canzone*. See Mario Praz, *The Flaming Heart: Essays on Crashaw, Machiavelli and other Studies of the Relations between Italian and English Literature from Chaucer to T. S. Eliot* (Doubleday Anchor, New York, 1958), p. 331, for the suggestion that Tasso's *Aminta* is Milton's 'real model' for his masque.
18 In the printing of *A Masque Presented at Ludlow Castle* for the 1645 volume, Milton includes as a preface the text of a letter from Sir Henry Wotton, the former ambassador to Venice under James I, who wrote to Milton in 1638 with some useful precepts for his forthcoming travels.
19 Wolfe, *Complete Prose*, i, pp. 809–10. Milton records the names of many of his Italian friends in *Defensio Secunda*: see Wolfe, *Complete Prose*, iv, pp. 616–17.
20 Wolfe, *Complete Prose*, i, pp. 810–12. Sir John Harington relates the same story in the *Life of Ariosto*, printed with his translation of *Orlando furioso* in 1591: see McNulty, *Orlando Furioso*, pp. 571, 33–44.
21 Manso is also an early patron of Marino, and Milton's praise of the 'dulciloquum... Marinum' [9] and his *L'Adone* (1623) in *Mansus* is characteristic of the high regard in which the Italian poet is held by English writers in the 1630s.
22 MacKellar, *Latin Poems*, pp. 156–9.
23 David Masson, *The Life of John Milton* (Boston, 1859), i, pp. 644–5; John Arthos, *Milton and the Italian Cities* (Bowes and Bowes, London, 1968), pp. 104–5.
24 See, for example, Prince, *Italian Element*; Praz, *Flaming Heart*, pp. 320–30; and Judith A. Kates, *Tasso and Milton: The Problem of Christian Epic* (Bucknell University Press, Lewisburg, 1983).
25 'A glance at the list of possible correspondences will show that for all his good Italian he had also enjoyed and profited from the English version': Lea and Gang, *Godfrey of Bulloigne*, p. 36.
26 Edward Weismiller, 'Materials dark and crude: a partial genealogy for Milton's Satan', *Huntington Library Quarterly* 31 (1967), 75–92; Lea and Gang, *Godfrey of Bulloigne*, pp. 49–52: p. 52.
27 Alistair Fox, *The English Renaissance: Identity and Representation in Elizabethan England* (Blackwell, Oxford, 1997), p. 24.

Appendix:
John Wolfe's Italian publications

John Wolfe has been described as 'one of the few genuinely internationalist Elizabethan stationers'.[1] He is a fascinating and important figure in the history of the reception of Italian writing in England, not least because his Italian publications involve the work of *both* generations of immigrant language teachers active in late sixteenth-century London. Wolfe is active in the printing of Italian texts only for a period of about twelve years (from 1579 to 1591), yet during this time he comes into contact with most of the significant Italian teachers, the notable exception being John Florio. Wolfe's immediate appeal to these Italians is his ability to print Italian texts accurately, a skill which he acquires during an apprenticeship at the Giunti press in Florence in the early 1570s,[2] and which is absent among other printers in his native London at the start of the 1580s. The dedicatory letters to the first two Italian publications to emanate from his presses both stress the significance of this development:

> L'opere Italiane non men si possono stampar felicemente in Londra, che le si stampino altroue (essendo questa la prima) per studio, & diligenza di Giouanni Wolfio suo cittadino; per la commodità del quale altre opere potrete hauer nella medesima lingua di giorno in giorno.[3]

> (Italian works can be printed no less easily in London than they are printed elsewhere (this being the first), through the skill and diligence of John Wolfe her own citizen, by whose efforts you could have other works in the same language day by day.)

APPENDIX

The letters are written by Italians long resident in England, but for whom Wolfe's return to London offers the first opportunity to see their works through the press. Wolfe's first Italian publication in 1579 or 1580 is Giacomo Aconcio's *Vna Essortatione al Timor di Dio, con alcune rime Italiane, nouamente messe in luce*, dedicated to the Queen by Giovan Battista Castiglioni, who is the author of the poems and responsible for the printing of the book. In the dedicatory letter he explains how his friend Aconcio left him some manuscripts on his deathbed, and that he liked one particular work so much that he has decided to have it printed, although it has taken some thirteen years, and the arrival of 'vn giouane di questa Città venuto di nuouo d'Italia, ou' ha con molta industria appreso l'arte de lo Stampare', to achieve his wish.[4] Aconcio spends the final seven years of his life in England,[5] where he becomes acquainted with Castiglioni, who has already established himself as Italian tutor to the Queen. He has been teaching Elizabeth the language since she was a princess, and, unlike Michel Angelo Florio, he remains in England throughout the reign of Queen Mary, apparently even enduring some time in prison for his Protestant beliefs. The edition of Aconcio is the only Italian work with which Castiglioni is directly associated, although he may also be responsible for recommending Wolfe's services to Alberico Gentili, the future professor of Civil Law at Oxford, recently arrived in London from Italy, accompanied by his younger brother Scipione, with letters of introduction to Castiglioni.[6] Wolfe is responsible for printing Alberico's legal disputations in Latin throughout the 1580s, and he also prints three editions of Scipione's Latin translation of the opening cantos of Tasso's *Gerusalemme liberata* in 1584.

The author of the second of Wolfe's Italian works, *La Vita di Carlo Magno Imperadore* (1581), has also been resident in England for a considerable time. Petruccio Ubaldini first visits London as early as 1545, spends time in Scotland in 1549, and suggests in a copy of later work dedicated to the Queen, also printed by Wolfe, that he has been in her service since 1564.[7] The life of Charlemagne is his first work to be printed, although there are seven surviving Italian manuscripts in his hand demonstrating his literary activity in England during the 1560s and 1570s.[8] The manuscripts are all gifts presented to members of the Elizabethan aristocracy, including at least three to the Queen herself, and they demonstrate the potentially restricted circulation of Italian materials in England before the advent of Wolfe's presses. The two manuscript copies of Michel Angelo Florio's *Regole de la Lingua*

APPENDIX

Thoscana in Cambridge University Library and the British Library, dedicated to the second Earl of Pembroke and Lady Jane Grey respectively, suggest a similar situation. For the first generation of immigrants the means of disseminating the Italian language and culture are limited. Michel Angelo Florio's Italian *Catechismo* is printed in England, by Stephen Mierdman in 1553, but this religious text is an isolated exception before the more secular activities of Wolfe in the 1580s.[9]

Wolfe's impact on the readership for Italian materials in London is almost immediate. A catalogue of the library of Francis Russell, the second Earl of Bedford, compiled a year before his death in 1585,[10] contains twelve Italian titles amongst the two hundred and twenty books; significantly it records copies of *both* of Wolfe's earliest Italian publications.[11] The emphasis so far has been on the publishing possibilities that Wolfe offers to immigrants like Castiglioni and Ubaldini, but clearly the printer would be unwilling to undertake such projects if he felt that there were an insufficiently developed market for the books in England. Of the twenty or so Italian titles that Wolfe prints between 1580 and 1591, over half are given false imprints. This suggests to Loewenstein that these works are intended mainly for export to the European book fairs, such as the six-monthly fair in Frankfurt, where attribution to an Italian printer would be taken as a mark of greater quality and authenticity.[12]

The majority of the falsely attributed books, though, contain material that is either politically or religiously sensitive or obscene, and it may be that the Italian imprints are intended equally as a cloaking device to disguise the genuine origins of these editions.[13] During the 1580s Wolfe systematically prints works by both Machiavelli and Pietro Aretino, which have been on the Inquisition's Index of Prohibited Books since 1559.[14] Clearly there *is* a gap in the European market for books that have been rigorously censored in Italy, but this should not lead to an underestimation of the demand for this outlawed material in London itself.

The popularity in England of Wolfe's editions of Machiavelli and Aretino can be demonstrated by a survey of the records of some important library holdings from the turn of the sixteenth century. The most popular of the illicit editions is, perhaps ironically, the only one that is printed under Wolfe's own name; there are at least five copies of Aretino's *Quattro Comedie* (1588) in contemporary collections. The copy in the British Library contains the signature of William Cecil, Lord

Burghley, and there are further copies in the possession of Gabriel Harvey, John Florio, William Drummond, and, by 1620, the Bodleian Library at Oxford. There are copies of both editions of Aretino's *Ragionamenti* in the collection of Sir Edward Coke, although they may have belonged originally to Sir Christopher Hatton. The 'Dialoghi o sei giornate dell'Aretino' cited in the book-list for Florio's *Worlde of Wordes* dictionary of 1598 probably refer to the same Wolfe editions. Machiavelli is equally popular in the Wolfe printings: the Coke–Hatton library contains a copy of the *Discorsi* (1584), along with an earlier Venetian edition, and 'Machiavells golden Asse', probably Wolfe's *Lasino doro* (1588), which has certainly been acquired for the Bodleian by 1620.[15] Stern suggests that Harvey possesses copies of the *Libro dell'arte della guerra* (1587), the *Discorsi*, and possibly other Wolfe-printed works by Machiavelli to which he refers frequently in his annotations.[16]

It is in the middle of the 1580s, when Wolfe begins printing the editions of Machiavelli and Aretino, that his output in Italian materials is at its most prolific. These years also mark the first appearance in London of Italian editions from the presses of other printers, which suggests a professional rivalry caused by the increasing demand for Italian books developing throughout the decade. In 1584 Wolfe prints a translation of a work by Lord Burghley, *Atto di Giustizia d'Inghilterra*, probably made by the language teacher Iacopo Castelvetro, who may also be responsible for translating Burghley's forged letter to Spain in the wake of the Armada's defeat in 1588.[17] In the following year a similar type of translation from a political pamphlet, *Dichiaratione delle cagioni che hanno mosso la reina d'Inghilterra a dar' auito alla difesa del popolo negli Paesi Bassi*, emerges from the press of Christopher Barker, the Queen's printer, and one of Wolfe's most vehement rivals until the latter's belated entry into the Stationers' Guild in 1583.[18] If it is uncertain whether such works are intended primarily for a native or a foreign readership, another publication printed in 1585 is clearly intended to appeal to the growing interest in Italy centred in London. This is an English version of an Italian letter about the death of Pope Gregory XIII, translated by John Florio, and printed by John Charlewood.[19] Although this letter is not printed in Italian, Charlewood *is* responsible at this time for the most significant body of Italian books to be printed in London which do not originate from Wolfe.

The connection between the names of Florio and Charlewood may be the key to explaining how the latter comes to print six works in Italian by the Neapolitan philosopher Giordano Bruno, during his two-year sojourn at the French embassy in London. Three of the four books by Bruno printed in 1584 are dedicated to the French ambassador, Michel de Castelnau de Mauvissière,[20] whose daughter Katherine is being tutored by Florio between 1583 and 1585, a period which coincides exactly with Bruno's stay at the embassy. Florio's friendship with Bruno, attested to in the letters 'To the curteous Reader', and to the Countess of Rutland and Lady Penelope Riche, in his translation of *The Essayes or Morall, Politike and Militarie Discourses of Lo: Michaell de Montaigne* (1603),[21] and his connection with Charlewood in 1585 suggest that he is responsible for presenting Bruno's works to the printer, and perhaps also helping to prepare them for the press. A professional association between Florio and Charlewood at this point, however brief, may explain why Florio's is the only significant name among the Italian teachers not to be linked to the activities of John Wolfe in the 1580s.

The dual role of translator and textual editor of Italian materials conjectured for Florio in relation to Charlewood corresponds with the simultaneous functions that another second-generation language teacher, Iacopo Castelvetro, fulfils for Wolfe. His part in the Italian translation of Burghley's pamphlet in 1584 has already been mentioned: the corrected working draft among the Italian's papers in the library of Trinity College, Cambridge, confirms either his authorship, or at least his revision of the work for the press. It is also likely that Castelvetro plays a part in the printing of Scipione Gentili's Latin translation of the first canto of Tasso's *Gerusalemme liberata* in the same year. He immediately sends a copy as a gift to the Duke of Ferrara, and then offers an impassioned defence of the translation and its author in a letter of 22 June 1584, in response to criticisms made by the Duke's Secretary, Lodovico Tassoni:

> Il saldo e modesto giudizio fatto da Vostra Signoria sopra il predetto libro, è non pure a me piaciuto, ma eziandio a questo valente giovinetto; ma le vo' però dire, che stimo, che quando meglio Vostra Signoria l'avrà considerato, che avrà altresi il furto trovato minore.[22]

> (The firm and modest judgement that you passed on the aforementioned book gave pleasure not only to me, but also to this worthy young man [Gentili]; but I would say that I think that, when you have considered it further, you will find the borrowings in it less conspicuous.)

APPENDIX

The working association between Castelvetro and Wolfe is certainly established by the beginning of 1584, and it becomes the most productive and long-lasting of the partnerships between the stationer and an Italian language teacher. Until the sudden termination of Wolfe's printing of Italian materials in 1591, there are at least a further five Italian and Latin publications with which Castelvetro is connected. His continued relationship with Wolfe throughout this period also makes him the most likely candidate in establishing the identity of the anonymous figure of 'Barbagrigia', who edits and writes the introductory material for Wolfe's 1584 editions of both Machiavelli and Aretino.[23] Ubaldini is the other possible candidate, but his connections with Wolfe are only intermittent, and involve the printing of his own work, rather than the publication of books of a wider literary and political interest.[24] Barbagrigia's work in the preparation of these texts for Wolfe in an editorial capacity certainly corresponds closely with that of Castelvetro at the same moment.

If Castelvetro is Barbagrigia, then it would seem to be the inherent literary interest in the works of Machiavelli and Aretino, rather than their censorship and the authors' scandalous reputations, that leads the Italian to become involved in the English publication of his compatriots' writings. A marked characteristic of Castelvetro's other publishing ventures with Wolfe is his desire to make available to the English reading public new or previously unattainable works by Italian authors, suggesting that the import trade into England of books by the best-known Italian writers is relatively active in the 1580s. This may partially explain why 'no English printers undertook to provide texts of any of the major authors in whom, a priori, they and their readers might have been supposed to have a legitimate interest: Dante, Petrarch, Boccaccio, Ariosto – writers who, except for Harington's translation of the *Orlando furioso*, were not even well represented in translation'.[25]

Castelvetro, however, does register an immediate interest in the most celebrated of contemporary Italian authors, Torquato Tasso, specifically through the medium of translation. His involvement in the printing of the first edition of Gentili's Latin translation of Tasso's epic in 1584, only three years after the initial Italian printing of *Gerusalemme liberata* in Parma, demonstrates his desire to make widely available a new version of what has already become a literary classic. The copy of the book sent to Alfonso II, Tasso's own literary patron, suggests that Castelvetro believes that there will be an inter-

APPENDIX

est in the translation in his native Italy,[26] but he clearly anticipates an equally enthusiastic response in England from a court readership, already familiar with Tasso's poem. A further two parts of Gentili's translation, with dedications to the Queen and Sir Philip Sidney respectively, are printed in separate editions by Wolfe in the same year, presumably with Castelvetro's continued assistance.[27]

Castelvetro's next acknowledged edition for the Wolfe press is another fragment of a previously unpublished Latin poem by an Italian writer. In 1585 he is responsible for the printing of two books of *Columbeidos*, an unfinished epic poem on Columbus's voyage of exploration by a Roman poet and nobleman, Giulio Cesare Stella. The poem was written some years earlier, but has never been printed until Castelvetro acquires a manuscript copy of it from a friend in Paris. The book is dedicated to Sir Walter Raleigh, whose interest in the poem's subject matter could be guaranteed. Rosenberg suggests that the friend who provides the manuscript is Richard Hakluyt, living in Paris between 1583 and 1588 as chaplain to the English ambassador, and for whom John Florio has already translated Ramusio's *Nauigations and Discoueries*, printed in 1580.[28] Hakluyt's influence may also be felt in other new works of discovery printed by Wolfe, such as Marco Antonio Pigafetta's *Itinerario* (1585), from Vienna to Constantinople, in which Castelvetro seems to play no direct part, and Francesco Avanzo's translation from Spanish of Mendoza's *L'Historia del Gran Regno della China*, printed in 1587. The Italian's connection with the latter volume is confirmed by a hand-written dedicatory letter to Sir Roger North, with whose son Castelvetro travelled in Italy between 1575 and 1577, in a presentation copy of the book, dated 27 June 1588:

> MI diterminai mandare a Vostra Signoria Illustre questa bella, e diletteuole historietta, fatta da me stampare, e da molti errori, scorsi nella primiera stampa, purgare.[29]
>
> (I determined to send to you this beautiful and delightful little history book, printed at my instigation, and to purge it of the many errors that were made in the first printing of it.)

The first Italian edition of the translation, printed by Andrea Muschio in Venice,[30] precedes Wolfe's version by only a year, and it is interesting to note how the editor stresses the greater accuracy of the English-printed edition over the Italian original.

APPENDIX

Castelvetro may have discovered the Muschio edition of Avanzo's translation at the Frankfurt Book Fair in September 1586, to which he travels as part of his professional association with Wolfe,[31] and it is certainly on the same trip that he acquires the manuscript for his next Wolfe publication. The Italian travels on from Germany to Basle, where he marries the widow of the Professor of Moral Philosophy, Erastus, early in 1587, before his return to England. His marriage presumably accounts for Wolfe's printing in 1589, with a decipherable fictitious imprint 'apud Baiocium Sultaceterum', of Erastus' treatise, *Explicatio gravissimae questionis*. This is the only one of the Wolfe editions with which Castelvetro is associated not to have any connection with Italy.

The two final Wolfe–Castelvetro collaborations revive their continued interest in Italian authors and works. In November 1590 Wolfe submits to the Stationers' Register an entry for Giovanni Battista della Porta's *De Furtivis Literarum Notis Vulgo. De Ziferis libri IIII*, which appears in print in May 1591, with a dedication by Castelvetro to Henry Percy, the 'Wizard' Earl of Northumberland, explaining that, because so many people have asked him about this learned work on cryptology, originally printed in Naples in 1563 but long since unavailable, he has decided to have it printed again at his own expense. A similar explanation is given in the dedicatory letter 'all'Illustre & nobile Caualiere il Signor Carlo Blunt', which precedes the dual edition of Battista Guarini's *Il pastor fido* and Tasso's *Aminta*, printed 'per Giouanni Volfeo, a spese di Giacopo Castelvetri' in June 1591. On this occasion it is the immediate fame of Guarini's pastoral play, printed only for the first time in Venice early in 1590, which creates a keen sense of anticipation among the readership of Italian materials in late Elizabethan England. Castelvetro's letter to Charles Blount demonstrates the lengths to which the editor and the printer are prepared to go in catering for the informed literary tastes of their readership in the early 1590s:

> La chiarissima fama di questa bella Pastorale del Pastor Fido . . . non contenta de termini della nobile Italia, li quali tosto hebbi scorsi, con velocissimo volo passò subito non pur di qua da monti, ma etiandio di qua del mare: onde ne petti di molti di questi singulari spiriti desto un non picciol desiderio de poterla vedere, & me pregarono di far si, che n'hauessero. Io, desideroso di compiacer loro, scrissi diuerse lettere, & varij amici pregai di farmene hauere alcuni essempi: ma con tutta la mia sollecitudine, non m'è pero stata da Dio conceduta

APPENDIX

cotal gratia, che d'alcuni pochi giorni in qua, de quali un solo *esempio* mi fu mandato. La lessi dunque subito che io l'hebbi, ne potrei cosi dire quanto piacere in leggerla prendessi, il quale fu cagione, che cominciassi a pensare, che non sarei male a farla qui ristampare: si per trouarla diletteuole, & anchora per vedere quanto malageuole fosse il poterne hauere. Non volli pertanto intraprender cosi fatta impresa, senza hauere prima il parere di persone, fornite di maggior litteratura, & di maggior acutezza d'ingegno, che io mi fia. Per la qual cosa la diedi a vedere a diuersi valenthuomini, li quali, tosto che l'hebbero gustata, non furono solamente della sentenza mia, anzi caldamente mi confortarono a farlo. Appresso stimai ben fatto di stampare seco l'Aminta del gran TASSO, per due ragioni, l'una è perche non pur a me, ma anchora a molti altri pare, che chi legge il Pastor Fido diuenghi volonteroso di veder l'Aminta, & poi anchora perche di lei si ritrouano hoggi pochissimi essempi da vendere.[32]

(The glowing reputation of this lovely pastoral, *Il pastor fido*, ... not content within the bounds of noble Italy, from where it so recently emerged, with swift flight has arrived here immediately not only by means of the mountains, but also from over the seas: where its reputation has awoken in the breasts of these singular spirits a not inconsiderable desire to be able to see the thing itself, and they have asked me to make it happen, if I could. Wishing to satisfy them, I have written many letters, and asked various friends to let me have some copies of the play: but, for all my promptness, God has not granted me that grace, except for a few days ago, when a single copy was sent to me. Therefore I read it as soon as I had it, and I cannot describe how much pleasure I took in reading it, which was the reason that I began to think that it would not be a bad idea to have the play reprinted here: both for the delight that I found in it, and also for having seen how difficult it was to procure a copy of it. I did not wish, however, to undertake such an enterprise, without first sounding out the opinions of certain people, more widely read than I am, and blessed with a greater keenness of wit. For this reason I gave the copy to various gentlemen to survey, who, as soon as they had sampled it, were not only of the same opinion as me, but also warmly encouraged me to print it. Later I considered it worthwhile to print the *Aminta* by the great Tasso along with it, for two reasons; firstly, because it seems, not only to me but to many others besides, that whoever wishes to read *Il pastor fido* would also be willing to look through the *Aminta*, and secondly, because today one finds so few copies of the latter available for sale.)

APPENDIX

The popularity of the two Italian pastoral plays, and the close association between them in English minds, anticipated by Castelvetro, is widely attested to throughout the late Elizabethan and early Jacobean periods. This is clear from both the number of copies of the plays in contemporary library collections, and equally from the sustained impact that the two works have on English literary activity in the period, by means of direct translation, and also imitation and adaptation. Gabriel Harvey owns a copy of the Wolfe edition, which he annotates carefully with footnotes and an index to the entire volume. Florio includes both plays in the book-list for his dictionary in 1611, and William Drummond possesses copies of the plays in both Italian and French. Perhaps more surprisingly, Henry Percy, the dedicatee of Wolfe's edition of della Porta, reads and annotates a copy of Guarini's play, printed in Paris in 1610, as he learns Italian during his incarceration in the Tower of London.[33]

After the printing of Tasso's *Aminta* in June 1591, Castelvetro's connections with Wolfe, and indeed the latter's publication of Italian materials, come to an abrupt end. There is a certain symmetry in that the Italian's association with the printer starts and finishes with editions of Tasso, from Gentili's Latin translation of his epic poem in 1584 to the pastoral drama in Italian in 1591. If Castelvetro's departure for Edinburgh in the early months of 1592 marks the definitive end of his activities in London, there is the lingering suspicion that his decision to leave may have been influenced by the acrimonious termination of his professional relationship with Wolfe. For in 1591 Wolfe is also responsible for printing an anonymous pamphlet of vicious Italophobia, *A Discovery of the great Subtilities and wonderful wisedome of the Italians*, after which his connections with the Italian immigrant community instantly cease. It is striking that Petruccio Ubaldini, for whom Wolfe has printed three books in Italian, immediately finds another printer for the remainder of the decade. Richard Field, the son-in-law of the immigrant printer Thomas Vautrollier, who both have a background in the publication of French materials, prints six Italian works by Ubaldini between 1592 and 1599.[34] The final edition in 1599 is a reprint, possibly posthumous, of *La Vita di Carlo Magno*, which is the last English publication to be printed in Italian in the sixteenth century, and indeed during Queen Elizabeth's reign. Again there is a pleasing symmetry, as, in the preface to the original Wolfe edition of 1581, Ubaldini claimed (although probably erroneously) that his was the first Italian work ever to be printed in England.

APPENDIX

The concentrated efforts to print Italian materials by Wolfe, Charlewood, and Field in the 1580s and 1590s are not repeated in the early seventeenth century. This does not necessarily imply a diminution in interest in Italian books in early Jacobean England, and it may rather indicate an increase in the availability of imported Italian titles. William Drummond purchases eighteen Italian books on his first visit to London from Edinburgh in 1606.[35] In the ten years between the first edition of his dictionary in 1598 and the publication date of the most recent work cited in the expanded version of 1611, John Florio consults an impressive one hundred and eighty Italian texts without, as far as is known, ever leaving England.[36] There are some isolated examples of Jacobean editions printed in Italian, which are usually works by immigrant writers living in England.[37] It is, however, only with the publications of John Bill (or Giovanni Billio, as he calls himself in his Italian editions) at the end of the second decade of the seventeenth century that the situation seems briefly to revert to the heyday of the 1580s. Bill spends time in Italy between 1602 and 1603 acquiring books for both Sir Thomas Bodley and Henry Percy, the Earl of Northumberland. In 1618 and 1619 he publishes three vastly different, but equally interesting, Italian titles. The first is a translation of Francis Bacon's *Essayes* of 1612 by Sir Tobie Matthew, *Saggi Morali del Signore Francesco Bacono*, dedicated to Cosimo II, the Grand Duke of Tuscany. In 1619 Bill prints a heroic poem, *La Caccia*, by Alessandro Gatti, whose *Madrigali* are consulted by Florio for his 1611 *New World of Words*. He is also responsible for the first printing of Paolo Sarpi's *Historia del Concilio di Trento*, dedicated to King James, and edited by the renegade Italian preacher Marc'Antonio de Dominis during his stay in England. Bill's three Italian publications demonstrate that there is, two decades into the seventeenth century, still a keen readership, both at home and on the continent, for previously unavailable Italian materials printed in England.

Notes

1 Joseph Loewenstein, 'For a history of literary property: John Wolfe's reformation', *ELR* 18 (1988), 389–412; p. 396. See also Joseph Loewenstein, *The Author's Due: Printing and the Prehistory of Copyright* (University of Chicago Press, Chicago, 2002), pp. 27–45.
2 Wolfe leaves for Italy in 1572, and by 1576 he has two books printed in Florence 'ad Instanzia di Giovanni Vuolfio Inglese', *La historia e oratione di Santo Stefano protomartire*, and the *Historia e vita di Santo Bernadino*. It is

APPENDIX

not certain when he returns from Italy, but he is active in London from 1579. See Clifford C. Huffman, *Elizabethan Impressions: John Wolfe and His Press* (AMS Press, New York, 1988), 'Re: John Wolfe', pp. 123-30, and 'John Wolfe and the Italian books', pp. 1-47.

3 Petruccio Ubaldini, *La Vita di Carlo Magno Imperadore* (London, 1581), p. 4.
4 'A young man of this City recently returned from Italy, where he has learnt with great industry the art of printing': *Timor di Dio*, p. 4.
5 Aconcio arrives in London in late 1559, and resides there until his death in 1566.
6 See Maria Grazia Bellorini, 'Le pubblicazioni Italiane dell'editore Londinese John Wolfe (1580-1591)', *Miscellanea* 1 (1971), 17-65; pp. 24-5.
7 Petruccio Ubaldini, *Le Vite delle Donne Illustri. Del Regno d'Inghilterra, & del Regno di Scotia* (London, 1591).
8 The earliest manuscript is dedicated to Edward VI. There are three, or possibly four, manuscripts presented to Queen Elizabeth. Another manuscript, *Relatione del come si debbino coronare in Aquisgrano gli Imperadori delle Diete Imperiale*, is presented to the Lord Chancellor, Sir Christopher Hatton, and forms part of his large collection of Italian materials, which passes into the library of Sir Edward Coke. A manuscript version of the *Psalter* in Italian, with illuminations by Ubaldini, is presented in 1565 to Henry Fitzalan, twelfth Earl of Arundel, the Italian's patron from 1562.
9 The only other work to be printed in Italian before 1580 is G. B. Agnello's *Espositione sopra un libro intitolato Apocalypsis spiritus secreti*, printed by John Kingston in 1566.
10 Russell travels in Italy between 1555 and 1557. His library also contains a copy of the *Historia di Pietro Bizari Della guerra fatta in Ungheria*, printed in Lyons in 1568, and dedicated to Bedford by the author.
11 The books are recorded as *The Life of Charles ye great by P. Ubaldino. Italian*, and *Exhortation to ye feare of God. Italian*. See M. St Clare Byrne and Gladys S. Thomson, 'The library of Francis Russell, Earl of Bedford, 1584', *RES* 7 (1931), 385-405.
12 Loewenstein, 'Literary property', p. 396. Hoppe suggests that there are some twenty titles, in both Latin and Italian, listed in catalogues of the Frankfurt book fair between 1581 and 1591, which correspond to editions printed by Wolfe: Harry R. Hoppe, 'John Wolfe: printer and publisher, 1579-1601', *The Library* 14 (1933), 241-89; p. 244.
13 Examples of editions of a potentially sensitive political nature are the *Auiso piaceuole dato alla bella Italia da un nobile giouanni Francese sopra la mentita data dal Re di Nauarra a Papa Sisto V*, printed by Wolfe in 1586, but attributed to a Giovanni Swartz in Monaco, and the *Esempio d'una lettera mandata d'Inghilterra a Don Bernadino di Mendoza*, probably written by Burghley and translated into Italian, on the subject of the Spanish Armada, printed in 1588 and attributed to Arrigo del Bosco in Leida. The only work with a false imprint that does not appear to have contained any controversial material is Ubaldini's *Descrittione del regno di Scotia*, allegedly printed in Anversa (Antwerp) in 1588.

APPENDIX

14 Wolfe's editions of Machiavelli's works are as follows: *Discorsi sopra la Prima Deca di Tito Livio* and *Il prencipe*, both printed in 1584 and attributed to 'Gli Heredi d'Antoniello degli Antonielli, Palermo'; *Libro dell'arte della guerra*, printed in 1587 with the same imprint as the 1584 volumes; *Historie fiorentine*, printed in 1587 with the imprint of 'Gli heredi di G. Giolito, Piacenza', and *Lasino doro con tutte l'altre sue operette*, allegedly printed in Rome in 1588. His editions of Aretino comprise the following works: *La prima parte de ragionamenti di M. Pietro Aretino*, which includes *La seconda parte de Ragionamenti*, and also Annibale Caro's pornographic *Commento di Ser Agresto*, all attributed to Bengodi and printed in 1584; *Quattro Comedie del Divino Pietro Aretino cioè Il Marescalco, La Cortegiana, La Talanta, l'Hippocrito*, registered in Wolfe's own name on the Stationers' Register in September 1588; *La terza et ultima parte de ragionamenti del divino Pietro Aretino*, attributed to Giovanni Andrea del Melograno in 1589.

15 See John L. Lievsay, *The Englishman's Italian Books, 1550–1700* (University of Pennsylvania Press, Philadelphia, 1969). For Burghley's library, which contains six Italian titles printed by Wolfe, see *Bibliotecha Illustris: sive Catalogus 1687*; for the Bodleian holdings see Thomas James, *Catalogus Universalis Librorum in Bibliotheca Bodleiana* (Oxford, 1620); for Drummond's library see MacDonald, *Library of Drummond*; Sergio Rossi gives an annotated version of Florio's book-list from the 1611 edition of the dictionary in *Ricerche sull'umanesimo e sul rinascimento in Inghilterra* (Vita e Pensiero, Milan, 1969), pp. 193–212; for the Coke–Hatton library, containing seven titles printed by Wolfe, see Hassall, 'Library of Sir Edward Coke'.

16 Stern, *Gabriel Harvey*, p. 268.

17 Burghley's pamphlet *The Execution of Justice in England for maintenance of public and Christian peace* is printed in 1583. For Castelvetro's connection with the translation see Butler, 'Giacomo Castelvetro', p. 10.

18 See Loewenstein, 'Literary property', pp. 396–403.

19 *A Letter lately written from Rome, by an Italian Gentleman, to a freende of his in Lyons in Fraunce . . . Newely translated out of Italian into English by I. F. Imprinted at London by Iohn Charlewoode* (London, 1585).

20 The three books dedicated to Mauvissière are *La Cena de le Ceneri, Dell'infinito Universo e Mondi*, and *De la causa, principio et Uno*. The fourth to be printed in 1584, *Spaccio de la Bestia Trionfante*, is dedicated to Sir Philip Sidney. A further two books, *De gl'eroici furori*, also dedicated to Sidney, and *Cabala del Cavallo Pegaso*, are printed in 1585. None of the works is given a genuine imprint: *La Cena* has no imprint, the next two are allegedly printed in 'Venetia', and the last three in 'Parigi'; Charlewood's printing of the editions is proved by Harry Sellers, 'Italian books printed in England before 1640', *The Library* 5 (1924), 105–28. All but the last of the Charlewood editions of Bruno's works are included in Florio's book-list for the 1611 edition of his dictionary. The Queen, extravagantly praised by Bruno as the 'Diva Elizabetta' in *De la causa, principio et Uno*, possesses a volume of Bruno's works, containing all four dialogues printed in 1584: see

APPENDIX

Rita Sturlese, *Bibliografia, censimento e storia delle antiche stampe di Giordano Bruno* (Olschki, Florence, 1987), pp. xxiv–xxv.
21 In the first letter Florio recalls the time that he, along with Samuel Daniel and 'N. W.', saw Bruno disputing at Oxford University in June 1583, when 'my olde fellow Nolano tolde me, and taught publikely, that from translation all science had its ofspring': J. I. M. Stewart, ed., *The Essayes of Montaigne: John Florio's Translation* (The Modern Library, London, 1931), p. xx.
22 The full letter is printed in Solerti, *Torquato Tasso*, ii, pp. 204–5.
23 See Eleanor Rosenberg, 'Giacopo Castelvetro: Italian publisher in Elizabethan London and his patrons', *Huntington Library Quarterly* 6 (1943), 119–48. Ottolenghi makes a strong case for Castelvetro's authorship of the prefatory material in Wolfe's 1584 Machiavelli editions: Paolo Ottolenghi, *Giacopo Castelvetro: esule modenese nell'Inghilterra di Shakespeare* (ETS, Pisa, 1982), pp. 38–47.
24 The suggestion that Ubaldini is 'Barbagrigia' is first made by Salvatore Bongi, *Annali di Gabriel Giolito de' Ferrari* (Rome, 1890–95), ii, pp. 418–24, and is followed by Sellers, 'Italian books'. Loewenstein argues that Ubaldini, rather than Castelvetro, is Wolfe's principal proofreader and collaborator for his Italian publications: Loewenstein, *Author's Due*, p. 48. After *La Vita di Carlo Magno* in 1581, Wolfe also prints Ubaldini's *Descrittione del Regno di Scotia*, dedicated to Walsingham, Hatton, and the Earl of Leicester, in 1588, and his *Le Vite delle Donne Illustri*, dedicated to the Queen, in 1591.
25 Lievsay, *Englishman's Italian Books*, p. 30. This is not an entirely fair assessment of Wolfe's Italian publications. In September 1587 there is an entry in the Stationers' Register for *Il decamerone di Boccaccio in Italian and the historie of China in Italian and English Aucthorised by The Archbishop of Canterbury*, licensed to Wolfe, although the former volume seems never to have appeared in print. In 1588 he does print a trilingual edition of one of the best known of all sixteenth-century Italian books, Castiglione's *Il Cortegiano*, in Italian, alongside English and French translations in parallel columns.
26 There is an edition of the translation of the first two books printed in Venice in 1585, and Tasso himself refers warmly to Gentili's version in a letter of 29 March 1587. With regard to Castelvetro's role in the dissemination of the poet's work in England, Ottolenghi suggests that 'il Tasso deve veramente contare l'intellettuale modenese tra i più convinti banditori dell'eccellenza delle sua poesia' ('Tasso should really consider the intellectual from Modena among the most convinced proclaimers of the excellence of his poetry'): Ottolenghi, *Giacopo Castelvetro*, p. 33.
27 The three editions of Gentili's translation, all attributed to 'J. Wolfius: Londini, 1584', are as follows: *Torquati Tassi Solymeidos liber primus, Latinis numeris expressus a S. Gentili*; *Scipii Gentilis Solymeidos libri duo priores de Torquati Tassi Italicis expressi*, dedicated to the Queen, and *Plutonis concilium. Ex initio quatri libri Solymeidos*, dedicated to Sidney.
28 Rosenberg, 'Giacopo Castelvetro', pp. 127–8.
29 *Ibid.*, p. 147. Wolfe is also responsible for printing an English version of Mendoza's history, translated by Robert Parke, in 1588.

APPENDIX

30 *Dell'Historia della China, descritta nella lingua spagnola dal P. Maestro Giovanni de Mendozza . . . e tradotta nell'Italiana dal Magn. M. Francesco Avanzo, cittadino originario di Venetia* (Venice, 1586).
31 Castelvetro also delivers letters from Lord Burghley and Sir Francis Walsingham to his acquaintance Horatio Pallavicino in Frankfurt on this occasion. Roberts suggests that the Italian also attends the Spring Fair at Frankfurt in 1589, as he has found an entry in the London Port Book for that year, recording the payment of petty customs on four crates of books (containing between 2,500 and 4,000 titles) that Castelvetro has imported from Germany: R. J. Roberts, 'New light on the career of Giacomo Castelvetro', *Bodleian Library Record* 13 (1990), 365–9.
32 Battista Guarini, *Il Pastor Fido* (London, 1591), sig. A2r-v.
33 See Stern, *Gabriel Harvey*, p. 146, p. 217 and plate F; Rossi, *Ricerche sull'umanesimo*, pp. 193–212; MacDonald, *Library of Drummond*; G. R. Batho, 'Library of the "Wizard" Earl', p. 256: 'The ninth Earl did not have any considerable interest in contemporary drama or literature, the only works of this kind annotated by him being two Italian pieces which he is known to have had with him in the Tower of London – Battista Guarini's sensuous play *Il pastor fido* and Sforza degli Oddi's *Comedie*.'
34 The six editions are: *Parte prima delle breui dimostrationi et precetti* (1592); *Lo Stato delle Tre Corti* (1594); *Scelta di alcune attione e di varii accidenti* (1595); *Rime* (1596); *Militia del Gran Duca di Thoscana* (1597); *La Vita di Carlo Magno* (1599).
35 See MacDonald, *Library of Drummond*, p. 40.
36 In the letter 'To the Reader' Florio explains how he intends 'to perfect [the dictionary] with addition of the French and Latine, and with the wordes of some twenty good Italian auctors, that I could neuer obtaine the sight of, and hope shortly to enjoy': Florio, *Worlde of Wordes*, sig. B2r.
37 The Jacobean publications in Italian are: *Rime di Antimo Galli all' illustrissima signora Elizabetta Talbot Grey*, the Countess of Kent, printed by M. Bradwood in 1609; *Raccolta, d'alcune rime, del cavaliere L. Petrucci, con la selva delle sue persecutioni*, dedicated to King James and the royal family, and printed in Oxford by Joseph Barnes in 1613; Francesco Peretto's *Gli Occhi. Oda. All' illustrimissima contessa Lucia Bedford: con altri vari componimenti heroici*, printed by George Purslowe in 1616.

Bibliography

Primary sources

Aconcio, Giacomo, *Una Essortatione al Timor di Dio, con alcune rime Italiane*, ed. Giovan Battista Castiglioni, London, 1579–80.
Anonymous, *Il Pastor Fido: or the faithfull Shepheard. Translated out of Italian into English* (1602), ed. Elizabeth Story Donno, *Three Renaissance Pastorals*, Medieval and Renaissance Texts and Studies, Binghamton, 1993.
Anonymous, *Second Part of the Return from Parnassus* (1601), ed. J. B. Leishman, *The Three Parnassus Plays (1598–1601)*, Ivor Nicholson and Watson Ltd, London, 1949.
Ariosto, Ludovico, *Orlando furioso* (1532), ed. Lanfranco Caretti, Einaudi, Turin, 1966.
Ariosto, Ludovico, *Orlando Furioso*, trans. Guido Waldman, Oxford University Press, Oxford, 1983.
Ascham, Roger, *The Scholemaster* (1570), ed. William A. Wright, *English Works of Roger Ascham*, Cambridge University Press, Cambridge, 1904.
Ascham, Roger, *The Schoolmaster (1570) by Roger Ascham*, ed. Lawrence V. Ryan, Cornell University Press, Ithaca, 1967.
Bembo, Pietro, *Rime*, Rome, 1548.
Bizari, Pietro, *Historia di Pietro Bizari, Della guerra fatta in Ungheria*, Lyon, 1568.
Boccaccio, Giovanni, *Decameron*, ed. Cesare Segre, Mursia, Milan, 1966.
Bonarelli, Guidobaldo, *Filli di Sciro*, Ferrara, 1607.
Bryskett, Lodowick, *A Discourse on Civill Life* (1606), ed. J. H. P. Pafford, *Literary Works of Lodowick Bryskett*, Gregg, Farnborough, 1972.
Campion, Thomas, *The Works of Thomas Campion*, ed. Walter R. Davis, Faber, London, 1969.
Carew, Richard, *Godfrey of Bulloigne, or The Recouerie of Hiervsalem*, London, 1594.
Castiglione, Baldassare, *Il cortegiano*, London, 1588.
Cinthio, Giambattista Giraldi, *De gli Hecatommithi*, Monte Regale, 1565.

BIBLIOGRAPHY

Cinthio, Giambattista Giraldi, *Le tragedie di M. Gio. Battista Giraldi Cinthio*, Venice, 1583.
Daniel, Samuel, *The Works of Samuel Daniel Newly Augmented*, London, 1601.
Daniel, Samuel, *The Whole Workes of Samuel Daniel Esquire in Poetrie*, London, 1623.
Daniel, Samuel, *The Queenes Arcadia*, London, 1606.
Daniel, Samuel, 'The Queenes Arcadia by Samuel Daniel, edited, with introduction and notes', ed. Lyle H. Butrick, PhD thesis, SUNY: Buffalo, 1968.
Daniel, Samuel, *Hymens Triumph*, London, 1615.
Daniel, Samuel, *Hymen's Triumph by Samuel Daniel*, ed. John Pitcher, Malone Society Reprints, Oxford, 1994.
Daniel, Samuel, *The Complete Works in Verse and Prose of Samuel Daniel*, ed. Rev. Alexander B. Grosart, London, 1885–96.
Daniel, Samuel, *Samuel Daniel: Poems and a Defence of Ryme*, ed. Arthur C. Sprague, Routledge and Kegan Paul, London, 1950.
Daniel, Samuel, *The Civil Wars by Samuel Daniel*, ed. Laurence Michel, Yale University Press, New Haven, 1958.
Daniel, Samuel, 'Samuel Daniel's occasional and dedicatory verse: a critical edition', ed. John Pitcher, DPhil thesis, Oxford, 1978.
Davison, Francis, *A Poetical Rhapsody* (1602), ed. Hyder E. Rollins, Harvard University Press, Cambridge, 1932.
Della Porta, Giovanni Battista, *De Furtivis Literarum Notis Vulgo*, ed. Iacopo Castelvetro, London, 1591.
Desportes, Philippe, *Les Amours d'Hippolyte* (1573), ed. Victor E. Graham, Droz, Geneva and Paris, 1960.
Desportes, Philippe, *Cléonice, Dernières Amours* (1583), ed. Victor E. Graham, Droz, Geneva and Paris, 1962.
Drummond, William, *The Poetical Works of William Drummond of Hawthornden*, ed. L. E. Kastner, William Blackwood, Edinburgh, 1913.
Du Bellay, Joachim, *L'Olive* (1549), ed. Ernesta Caldarini, Droz, Geneva, 1974.
Du Bellay, Joachim, *The Defence and Illustration of the French Language*, trans. Gladys M. Turquet, J. M. Dent, London, 1939.
Eliot, John, *Ortho-epia Gallica. Eliots Fruits for the French*, London, 1593.
Elizabeth I, *The Poems of Queen Elizabeth I*, ed. Leicester Bradner, Brown University Press, Providence, 1964.
Erondel, Peter, *The French Garden*, London, 1605.
Fairfax, Edward, *Godfrey of Bulloigne, or the Recouerie of Jerusalem*, London, 1600.
Fairfax, Edward, *Godfrey of Bulloigne*, eds K. M. Lea and T. M. Gang, Clarendon Press, Oxford, 1981.
Farmer, Richard, *An Essay on the Learning of Shakespeare* (1767), in David Nichol Smith, ed., *Eighteenth-Century Essays on Shakespeare*, Clarendon Press, Oxford, 1963.
Fletcher, John, *The Faithful Shepherdess*, ed. Fredson Bowers, *The Dramatic Works of Beaumont and Fletcher*, iii, Cambridge University Press, Cambridge, 1976.
Florio, John, *Florio his first Fruites*, London, 1578.

BIBLIOGRAPHY

Florio, John, *Florios Second Frutes*, London, 1591.
Florio, John, *A Worlde of Wordes, or most copious, and exact Dictionarie in Italian and English*, London, 1598.
Florio, John, *The Essayes or Morall, Politike and Millitarie Discourses of Lo: Michaell de Montaigne*, London, 1603.
Florio, John, *The Essayes of Montaigne: John Florio's Translation*, ed. J. I. M. Stewart, The Modern Library, London, 1931.
Florio, John, *Queen Anna's New World of Words, or Dictionarie of the Italian and English tongues*, London, 1611.
Fowler, William, *The Works of William Fowler*, eds H. W. Meikle, James Craigie, and John Purves, William Blackwood, Edinburgh, 1914–1940.
Fraunce, Abraham, *The Countess of Pembrokes Ivychurch*, London, 1591.
Gentili, Scipione, *Torquati Tassi Solymeidos liber primus, Latinis numeris expressus a S. Gentili*, London, 1584.
Gentili, Scipione, *Annotationi di Scipio Gentili sopra la Gerusalemme liberata di T. Tasso*, Leida, 1586.
Gosson, Steven, *Playes Confuted in fiue Actions*, London, 1582.
Greene, Robert, *Greenes Groats-worth of Witte*, London, 1592.
Greene, Robert, *The History of Orlando Furioso, 1594*, ed. W. W. Greg, Malone Society Reprints, Oxford, 1907.
Greene, Robert, *The Scottish History of James the Fourth*, ed. Norman Sanders, Methuen, London, 1970.
Groto, Luigi, *Il pentimento amoroso (1576)*, eds Giorgio Brunello and Antonio Lodo, *Luigi Groto: Opere*, Minelliana, Rovigo, 1987.
Groto, Luigi, *Rime*, Venice, 1587.
Guarini, Battista ed., *Rime degli academici eterei*, Padua, 1567.
Guarini, Battista, *Rime degli academici eterei*, ed. Lanfranco Caretti, Zara, Parma, 1990.
Guarini, Battista, *Il Pastor Fido*, ed. Iacopo Castelvetro, London, 1591.
Guarini, Battista, *Il pastor fido*, Venice, 1602.
Guarini, Battista, *Delle opera del Caualier Battista Guarini*, eds G. A. Barotti and A. Zeno, Verona, 1738.
Guarini, Battista, *Il pastor fido*, ed. Luigi Fassò, Einaudi, Turin, 1976.
Harington, Sir John, *Orlando Furioso in English Heroical Verse*, London, 1591.
Harington, Sir John, *Ludovico Ariosto's Orlando Furioso Translated in English Heroical Verse by Sir John Harington (1591)*, ed. Robert McNulty, Clarendon Press, Oxford, 1972.
Herbert, Mary, *The Collected Works of Mary Sidney Herbert, Countess of Pembroke*, eds Margaret P. Hannay, Noel J. Kinnamon, and Michael G. Brennan, Clarendon Press, Oxford, 1998.
Holyband, Claude, *The French Schoolemaister*, London, 1573.
Holyband, Claude, *Pretie and wittie historie of Arnalt & Lucenda*, London, 1575.
Holyband, Claude, *Campo di Fior, or else the Flourie Field of Foure Languages*, London, 1583.
Holyband, Claude, *The Italian Schoole-maister*, London, 1597.
James, Thomas, *Catalogus Universalis Librorum in Bibliotheca Bodleiana*, Oxford, 1620.

BIBLIOGRAPHY

Jones, William, *Nennio, or a Treatise of Nobility*, London, 1595.
Jonson, Ben, *Every Man in his Humour* (1601), eds C. H. Herford and Percy Simpson, *Ben Jonson*, iii, Clarendon Press, Oxford, 1927.
Jonson, Ben, *Volpone, or the Fox* (1607), eds C. H. Herford and Percy Simpson, *Ben Jonson*, v, Clarendon Press, Oxford, 1937.
Jonson, Ben, *Hymenaei* (1606), eds C. H. Herford and Percy Simpson, *Ben Jonson*, vii, Clarendon Press, Oxford, 1941.
Jonson, Ben, *Ben Jonson*, ed. Ian Donaldson, Oxford University Press, Oxford, 1985.
Kyd, Thomas, *The Spanish Tragedy*, ed. J. R. Mulryne, A. & C. Black, London, 1989.
Lyly, John, *John Lyly: Euphues*, ed. Edward Arber, A. Constable, London, 1904.
Marino, Giambattista, *Rime*, Venice, 1602.
Marino, Giambattista, *Rime*, Venice, 1608.
Marston, John, *The Malcontent*, ed. Bernard Harris, Ernest Benn Ltd, London, 1967.
Marston, John, *The Malcontent*, ed. G. K. Hunter, Manchester University Press, Manchester, 1975.
Marston, John, *The Malcontent, and Other Plays*, ed. Keith Sturgess, Oxford University Press, Oxford, 1997.
Marston, John, *The Malcontent*, ed. W. David Kay, A. & C. Black, London, 1998.
Marston, John, *Antonio and Mellida*, ed. W. Reavley Gair, Manchester University Press, Manchester, 1991.
Milton, John, *The Reason of Church Government* (1642), ed. Don M. Wolfe, *The Complete Prose Works of John Milton*, i, Yale University Press, New Haven, 1953.
Milton, John, *Poemata* (1645), ed. Walter MacKellar, *The Latin Poems of John Milton*, Yale University Press, New Haven, 1930.
Milton, John, *Defensio Secunda* (1654), ed. Eugene J. Strittmatter, *The Works of John Milton*, viii, Columbia University Press, New York, 1933.
Milton, John, *Joannis Miltonii Angli, Epistolarum Familiarium* (1674), ed. Donald L. Clark, *The Works of John Milton*, xii, Columbia University Press, New York, 1936.
Milton, John, *The Sonnets of Milton*, ed. John S. Smart, Maclehose, Glasgow, 1921.
Milton, John, *Milton's Sonnets*, ed. E. A. J. Honigmann, Macmillan, London, 1966.
Nichols, John, *The Progresses, Processions, and Magnificent Festivities, of King James the First*, London, 1828.
Painter, William, *The Palace of Pleasure*, London, 1566–67.
Pasquier, Etienne, *Etienne Pasquier: Les Recherches de la France*, ed. Marie-Madeleine Fragonard, Honoré Champion, Paris, 1996.
Petrarca, Francesco, *Petrarch's Lyric Poems*, ed. and trans. Robert M. Durling, Harvard University Press, Cambridge, 1976.
Petrarca, Francesco, *Trionfi*, ed. Guido Bezzola, Rizzoli, Milan, 1984.
Pettie George, *The Civile Conversation of M. Steeven Guazzo*, ed. Sir Edward Sullivan, Constable and Co, London, 1925.

BIBLIOGRAPHY

Reynolds, Henry, *Tasso's Aminta Englisht* (1628), ed. Elizabeth Story Donno, *Three Renaissance Pastorals*, Medieval and Renaissance Texts and Studies, Binghamton, 1993.
Riche, Barnabe, *Rich's Farewell to Military Profession 1581*, ed. Thomas M. Cranfill, University of Texas Press, Austin, 1959.
Riche, Barnabe, *Barnabe Rich: His Farewell to Military Profession*, ed. Donald Beecher, Dovehouse, Ottawa, 1992.
Ronsard, Pierre de, *Les sonnets pour Helene* (1573), ed. Georges Margolin, *Les Amours*, Delmas, Paris, 1954.
Sanford, John, *A Grammer or Introduction to the Italian Tongue*, Oxford, 1605.
Shakespeare, William, *The Works of Shakespear*, ed. William Warburton, London, 1747.
Shakespeare, William, *The Tempest*, ed. Frank Kermode, Methuen, London, 1954.
Shakespeare, William, *All's Well That Ends Well*, ed. G. K. Hunter, Methuen, London, 1959.
Shakespeare, William, *The Winter's Tale*, ed. J. H. P. Pafford, Methuen, London, 1963.
Shakespeare, William, *Measure for Measure*, ed. J. W. Lever, Methuen, London, 1965.
Shakespeare, William, *Twelfth Night, or What You Will*, eds J. M. Lothian and T. W. Craik, Methuen, London, 1975.
Shakespeare, William, *Othello*, ed. E. A. J. Honigmann, Thomas Nelson and Sons, Walton-on Thames, 1997.
Shakespeare, William, *The Norton Shakespeare*, eds Stephen Greenblatt, Walter Cohen, Jean E. Howard, and Katharine Eisamann Maus, W. W. Norton, New York, 1997.
Sidney, Sir Philip, *The Complete Works of Sir Philip Sidney*, ed. Albert Feuillerat, Cambridge University Press, Cambridge, 1912–1926.
Sidney, Sir Philip, *The Poems of Sir Philip Sidney*, ed. W. A. Ringler, Clarendon Press, Oxford, 1962.
Sidney, Sir Philip, *Sir Philip Sidney*, ed. Katherine Duncan-Jones, Oxford University Press, Oxford, 1989.
Spenser, Edmund, *The Faerie Queene* (1590–1596), ed. Edwin Greenlaw, *The Works of Edmund Spenser: A Variorum Edition*, Johns Hopkins Press, Baltimore, 1932–1957.
Spenser, Edmund, *The Faerie Queene*, ed. A. C. Hamilton, Longman, London and New York, 1977.
Spenser, Edmund, *The Yale Edition of the Shorter Poems of Edmund Spenser*, eds William A. Oram, Einar Bjorvand, Ronald Bond, Thomas H. Cain, Alexander Dunlop, and Richard Schell, Yale University Press, New Haven and London, 1989.
Sylvester, Joshua, *The divine weeks and works of Guillaume de Saluste, Sieur du Bartas, translated by Josuah Sylvester*, ed. Susan Snyder, Clarendon Press, Oxford, 1979.
Tasso, Torquato, *Gerusalemme liberata* (1581), ed. Lanfranco Caretti, Einaudi, Turin, 1971.
Tasso, Torquato, *Aminta*, ed. Iacopo Castelvetro, London, 1591.

Tasso, Torquato, *Aminta*, ed. B. T. Sozzi, Liviana Editrice, Padua, 1957.
Tasso, Torquato, *Rime del signor Torquato Tasso*, Mantua, 1591.
Tasso, Torquato, *Discorsi del Poema Eroico*, Naples, 1594.
Tasso, Torquato, *The Discourses on Heroic Poetry*, eds and trans. Mariella Cavalchini and Irene Samuel, Clarendon Press, Oxford, 1973.
Tasso, Torquato, *Poesie*, ed. Francesco Flora, Ricciardi, Milan, 1952.
Tofte, Robert, *The Blazon of Iealousie*, London, 1615.
Tofte, Robert, *Alba*, ed. Rev. Alexander B. Grosart, Manchester, 1880.
Tofte, Robert, *The Poetry of Robert Tofte, 1597–1620*, ed. Jeffrey N. Nelson, Garland, New York and London, 1994.
Torriano, Giovanni, *The Italian Tutor, or a New and Most Compleat Italian Grammer*, London, 1640.
Torriano, Giovanni, *New and Easy Directions for the attaining of the Thuscan Italian Tongue*, Cambridge, 1641.
Torriano, Giovanni, *Vocabolario Italiano e Inglese, A Dictionary Italian and English*, London, 1659.
Ubaldini, Petruccio, *La Vita di Carlo Magno Imperadore*, London, 1581.
Ubaldini, Petruccio, *Le Vite delle Donne Illostri. Dei Regno d'Inghilterra & del Regno di Scotia*, London, 1591.
Virgil, *Virgil's Georgics*, ed. R. A. B. Mynors, Clarendon Press, Oxford, 1990.
Wake, Isaac, *Rex Platonicus*, London, 1607.
Whetstone, George, *The right excellent and famous historye of Promos and Cassandra*, London, 1578.
Whetstone, George, *A Heptameron of Ciuill Discourses*, London, 1582.
Zabata, Cristoforo, ed., *Della Scelta di Rime, Di Diversi Eccellenti autori*, Genoa, 1579–1582.

Secondary sources

Adair, E. R., 'William Thomas: a forgotten clerk of the Privy Council' in R. W. Seton-Watson, ed., *Tudor Studies*, Longmans, London, 1924, pp. 133–60.
Adamany, Richard G., 'Daniel's debt to foreign literatures and *Delia* edited', University of Wisconsin PhD thesis, 1963.
Adams, Maurianne S., '"Ocular proof" in *Othello* and its sources', *PMLA* 79 (1964), 234–41.
Albrecht, Louis, *Neue Untersuchungen zu Shakespeares Maß fur*, Berlin, 1914.
Aquilecchia, Giovanni, 'Lo stampatore londinese di Giordano Bruno e altre note per l'edizione delle *Cena*', *Studi di filologia italiana* 18 (1960), 101–62.
Arthos, John, *Milton and the Italian Cities*, Bowes and Bowes, London, 1968.
Baldwin, T. W., *William Shakspere's Small Latine and Lesse Greeke*, University of Illinois Press, Urbana, 1944.
Ball, Robert H., 'Cinthio's *Epitia* and *Measure for Measure*' in E. J. West, ed., *Elizabethan Studies and other Essays in Honor of George F. Reynolds*, University of Colorado Series, Boulder, 1945, pp. 132–46.
Barasch, Frances K., 'Shakespeare puzzles, *Commedia* solutions: Italian intertexts in *Twelfth Night*' in Michele Marrapodi, ed., *Intertestualità Shakespeariane*, Bulzoni, Rome, 2003, pp. 207–28.

BIBLIOGRAPHY

Bate, Jonathan, *The Genius of Shakespeare*, Picador, London, 1997.
Batho, G. R., 'The library of the "Wizard" Earl of Northumberland, 1564–1632', *The Library* 15 (1960), 246–61.
Bell, Charles G., 'Fairfax's Tasso', *Comparative Literature* 6 (1954), 26–52.
Bellorini, Maria Grazia, 'Le pubblicazioni Italiane dell'editore Londinese John Wolfe (1580–1591)', *Miscellanea* 1 (1971), 17–65.
Béné, Charles, 'Marguerite de France et l'oeuvre de Du Bellay' in Louis Terreaux, ed., *Culture et pouvoir au temps de l'humanisme et de la Renaissance*, M. Slatkine and Honoré Champion, Geneva and Paris, 1978, pp. 223–41.
Benedetti, Anna, *L'Orlando Furioso nella vita intellettuale del popolo inglese*, Bemporad, Milan, 1914.
Benjamin, Andrew, *Translation and the Nature of Philosophy: A New Theory of Words*, Routledge, London, 1989.
Bennett, H. S., *English Books and Readers, 1558–1603*, Cambridge University Press, Cambridge, 1965.
Birrell, T. A., *English Monarchs and their Books: from Henry VII to Charles II*, British Library, London, 1987.
Bliss, Lee, *The World's Perspective: John Webster and the Jacobean Drama*, Rutgers University Press, New Brunswick, 1983.
Boas, F. S., *University Drama in the Tudor Age*, Clarendon Press, Oxford, 1914.
Boas, F. S., 'University Plays' in A. W. Ward and A. R. Waller, eds, *The Cambridge History of English Literature*, vi, Cambridge University Press, Cambridge, 1910, pp. 293–327.
Bongi, Salvatore, *Annali di Gabriel Giolito de' Ferrari*, Rome, 1890–95.
Boswell, Jackson C., *Milton's Library*, Garland, New York, 1975.
Braden, Gordon, '"Vivamus mea Lesbia" in the English Renaissance', *ELR* 9 (1979), 199–224.
Brand, C. P., *Torquato Tasso: A Study of the Poet and of His Contribution to English Literature*, Cambridge University Press, Cambridge, 1965.
Budd, Frederick E., 'Material for a study of the sources of Shakespeare's *Measure for Measure*', *Revue de Littérature Comparée* 11 (1931), 711–36.
Bullough, Geoffrey, *Narrative and Dramatic Sources of Shakespeare*, Routledge and Kegan Paul, London, 1957–75.
Burke, Peter, *The Italian Renaissance*, Polity, Cambridge, 1986.
Burke, Peter, *The Fortunes of the Courtier*, Polity, Cambridge, 1995.
Burrow, Colin, *Epic Romance: Homer to Milton*, Clarendon Press, Oxford, 1993.
Butler, Kathleen T., 'Two unpublished letters of Giambattista Marino', *MLR* 31 (1936), 550–5.
Butler, Kathleen T., 'Giacomo Castelvetro, 1546–1616', *Italian Studies* 5 (1950), 1–42.
Buxton, John, *Elizabethan Taste*, Macmillan, London, 1963.
Buxton, John, *Sir Philip Sidney and the English Renaissance*, Macmillan, London, 1964.
Byrne, M. St Clare, and Gladys S. Thomson, 'The library of Francis Russell, Earl of Bedford, 1584', *RES* 7 (1931), 385–405.
Cairncross, Andrew S., 'Shakespeare and Ariosto: *Much Ado About Nothing, King Lear*, and *Othello*', *Renaissance Quarterly* 29 (1976), 178–82.

Callaghan, Dympna, *Woman and Gender in Renaissance Tragedy: A Study of King Lear, Othello, The Duchess of Malfi and The White Devil*, Harvester, Hemel Hempstead, 1989.
Castelli, Alberto, *La Gerusalemme liberata nella Inghilterra di Spenser*, Vita e Pensiero, Milan, 1936.
Cecioni, Cesare G., *Thomas Watson e la tradizione petrarchista*, Messina G. Principato, Milan, 1969.
Chaudhuri, Sukantha, *Renaissance Pastoral and its English Development*, Clarendon Press, Oxford, 1989.
Clubb, Louise George, *Italian Drama in Shakespeare's Time*, Yale University Press, New Haven, 1989.
Cody, Richard, *The Landscape of the Mind: Pastoralism and Platonic Theory in Tasso's 'Aminta' and Shakespeare's Early Comedies*, Clarendon Press, Oxford, 1969.
Coleridge, Samuel Taylor, 'Note on Chalmer's Life of Daniel' in *The Literary Remains of Samuel Taylor Coleridge*, iii, ed. H. N. Coleridge, London, 1839, p. 360.
Coogan, Robert, 'Petrarch's *Trionfi* and the Renaissance', *Studies in Philology* 67 (1970), 306–27.
Dalla Valle, Daniela, *Pastorale barocca. Forme e contenuti dal Pastor fido al dramma pastorale francese*, Longo, Ravenna, 1973.
D'Amico, Jack, *Shakespeare and Italy: The City and the Stage*, University Press of Florida, Gainesville, 2001.
D'Amico, Jack, ed., *Petrarch in England: An Anthology of Parallel Texts from Wyatt to Milton*, Longo, Ravenna, 1979.
Dasenbrock, Reed Way, *Imitating the Italians: Wyatt, Spenser, Synge, Pound, Joyce*, Johns Hopkins University Press, Baltimore and London, 1991.
De Jongh, William F. J., *Western Language Manuals of the Renaissance*, University of New Mexico Press, Albuquerque, 1949.
Doran, Madeleine, *Endeavors of Art: A Study of Form in Elizabethan Drama*, University of Wisconsin Press, Madison, 1954.
Dubrow, Heather, *Echoes of Desire: English Petrarchism and its Counterdiscourses*, Cornell University Press, Ithaca and London, 1995.
Duncan-Jones, Katherine, *Sir Philip Sidney: Courtier Poet*, Yale University Press, New Haven, 1991.
Duncan-Jones, Katherine, *Ungentle Shakespeare: Scenes from his Life*, Arden Shakespeare, London, 2001.
Duncan-Jones, Katherine, 'Two Elizabethan versions of Giovio's treatise on Imprese', *English Studies* 52 (1971), 118–23.
Duncan-Jones, Katherine, 'Bess Carey's Petrarch: newly discovered Elizabethan sonnets', *RES* 50 (1999), 304–19.
Durling, Robert M., *The Figure of the Poet in Renaissance Epic*, Harvard University Press, Cambridge, 1965.
Eccles, Mark, 'Samuel Daniel in France and Italy', *Studies in Philology* 34 (1937), 148–67.
Einstein, Lewis, *The Italian Renaissance in England*, Columbia University Press, New York, 1902.

BIBLIOGRAPHY

Evans, Maurice, ed., *Elizabethan Sonnets*, Dent, London, 1977.
Farley-Hills, David, *Shakespeare and the Rival Playwrights, 1600–1606*, Routledge, London, 1990.
Farley-Hills, David, 'Giordano Bruno and Sidney's Astrophil', *MLR* 87 (1992), 1–17.
Ferguson, Margaret W., *Trials of Desire: Renaissance Defenses of Poetry*, Yale University Press, New Haven, 1983.
Finkelpearl, Philip J., *John Marston of the Middle Temple*, Harvard University Press, Cambridge, 1969.
Forster, Leonard, *The Icy Fire: Five Studies in European Petrarchism*, Cambridge University Press, Cambridge, 1969.
Fox, Alistair, *The English Renaissance: Identity and Representation in Elizabethan England*, Blackwell, Oxford, 1997.
Gabrieli, Vittorio, 'Lodovico Petrucci, soldato e poeta', *English Miscellany* 11 (1960), 287–332.
Gamberini, Spartaco, *Lo studio dell'italiano in Inghilterra nel '500 e nel '600*, Casa Editrice G. d'Anna, Messina and Florence, 1970.
Garganò, Giuseppe S., *Scapigliatura Italiana a Londra sotto Elisabetta e Giacomo I*, L. Battistelli, Florence, 1923.
Gatti, Hilary, *The Renaissance Drama of Knowledge: Giordano Bruno in England*, Routledge, London, 1989.
Gatti, Hilary, 'Giordano Bruno and the Stuart court masques', *Renaissance Quarterly* 48 (1995), 809–42.
Goldberg, Jonathan, *Desiring Women Writing: English Renaissance Examples*, Stanford University Press, Stanford, 1997.
Greenblatt, Stephen J., *Renaissance Self-Fashioning: From More to Shakespeare*, University of Chicago Press, Chicago and London, 1980.
Greene, Thomas M., *The Descent from Heaven: A Study in Epic Continuity*, Yale University Press, New Haven and London, 1963.
Greene, Thomas M., *The Light in Troy: Imitation and Discovery in Renaissance Poetry*, Yale University Press, New Haven and London, 1982.
Greg, W. W., *Pastoral Poetry and Pastoral Drama: A Literary Inquiry, with Special Reference to the pre-Restoration English Stage*, A. H. Bullen, London, 1905.
Grillo, Ernesto M., *Shakespeare and Italy*, Maclehose, Glasgow, 1949.
Guggenheim, Josef, *Quellenstudien zu Samuel Daniels Sonnettencyclus 'Delia'*. Berlin, 1898.
Hale, John R., *England and the Italian Renaissance*, Faber and Faber Ltd, London, 1954.
Hannay, Margaret P., *Silent but for the Word: Tudor Women as Patrons, Translators, and Writers of Religious Works*, Kent State University Press, Kent, 1985.
Hannay, Margaret P., *Philip's Phoenix: Mary Sidney, Countess of Pembroke*, Oxford University Press, Oxford, 1990.
Hassall, W. O., 'A catalogue of the library of Sir Edward Coke', *Yale Law Library Publications* 12 (1950).
Hatchwell, Richard, 'A Francis Davison/William Drummond conundrum', *Bodleian Library Record* 15 (1996), 364–7.

BIBLIOGRAPHY

Henke, Robert, *Pastoral Transformations: Italian Tragicomedy and Shakespeare's Late Plays*, University of Delaware Press, Newark and London, 1997.

Herrick, Marvin T., *Tragicomedy: Its Origin and Development in Italy, France, and England*, University of Illinois Press, Urbana, 1955.

Hirst, David L., *Tragicomedy*, Methuen, London, 1984.

Hoenselaars, A. J., *Images of Englishmen and Foreigners in the Drama of Shakespeare and his Contemporaries*, Fairleigh Dickinson University Press, Rutherford, 1992.

Hoenselaars, A. J., '"Under the dent of the English pen": the language of Italy in English Renaissance drama' in Michele Marrapodi, ed., *Shakespeare's Italy: Functions of Italian Locations in Renaissance Drama*, Manchester University Press, Manchester, 1993, pp. 272–91.

Hoppe, Harry R., 'John Wolfe, printer and publisher, 1579–1601', *The Library* 14 (1933), 241–89.

Horne, P. R., *The Tragedies of Giambattista Cinthio Giraldi*, Oxford University Press, Oxford, 1962.

Huffman, Clifford C., *Elizabethan Impressions: John Wolfe and His Press*, AMS Press, New York, 1988.

Hulse, Clark, *Metamorphic Verse: The Elizabethan Minor Epic*, Princeton University Press, Princeton, 1981.

Hunter, G. K., *Dramatic Identities and Cultural Tradition*, Liverpool University Press, Liverpool, 1978.

Hunter, G. K., 'Elizabethans and foreigners', *Shakespeare Survey* 17 (1964), 37–52.

Hunter, G. K., 'Italian tragicomedy on the English stage', *Renaissance Drama* 6 (1973), 123–48.

Hunter, Joseph, *New Illustrations of the Life, Studies, and Writings of Shakespeare*, London, 1845.

Jack, Ronald D. S., *The Italian Influence on Scottish Literature*, Edinburgh University Press, Edinburgh, 1972.

Jardine, Lisa, and Anthony Grafton, '"Studied for action": how Gabriel Harvey read his Livy', *Past and Present* 129 (1990), 30–78.

Jayne, Sears R., *Library Catalogues of the English Renaissance*, University of California Press, Berkeley, 1956.

Jayne, Sears R., and Francis R. Johnson, *The 1609 Catalogue of the Lumley Library*, British Museum, London, 1956.

Jeffery, Violet M., *John Lyly and the Italian Renaissance*, Honoré Champion, Paris, 1928.

Jeffery, Violet M., 'Italian and English pastoral drama of the Renaissance, III: sources of Daniel's *Queen's Arcadia* and Randolph's *Amyntas*', *MLR* 19 (1924), 435–44.

Jeffery, Violet M., 'Italian influence in Fletcher's *Faithful Shepherdess*', *MLR* 21 (1926), 147–58.

Jones, Emrys, 'Othello, Lepanto, and the Cyprus wars', *Shakespeare Survey* 21 (1968), 47–52.

Kastner, L. E., 'The Elizabethan sonneteers and the French poets', *MLR* 3 (1908), 268–77.

Kastner, L. E., 'The Italian sources of Daniel's *Delia*', *MLR* 7 (1912), 153–6.

BIBLIOGRAPHY

Kates, Judith A., *Tasso and Milton: The Problem of Christian Epic*, Bucknell University Press, Lewisburg, 1983.

Kau, Joseph, 'Samuel Daniel and the Renaissance *Impresa*-makers: sources for the first English collection of *Imprese*', *Harvard Library Bulletin* 18 (1970), 183–204.

Kau, Joseph, '*Delia*'s gentle lover and the eternizing conceit in Elizabethan sonnets', *Anglia* 92 (1974), 334–48.

Kennedy, William J., *Authorizing Petrarch*, Cornell University Press, Ithaca and London, 1994.

Keynes, Geoffrey, *Bibliography of Dr. John Donne*, Clarendon Press, Oxford 1973.

Kirkpatrick, Robin, *English and Italian Literature from Dante to Shakespeare: A Study of Sources, Analogy, and Divergence*, Longman, London, 1995.

Kirsch, Arthur C., *Jacobean Dramatic Perspectives*, Virginia University Press, Charlottesville, 1972.

Klein, J. L., *Geschichte des Dramas*, Leipzig, 1867.

Klein, Lisa M., *The Exemplary Sidney and the Elizabethan Sonneteer*, University of Delaware Press, Newark, 1998.

Kostic, Veselin, *Spenser's Sources in Italian Poetry*, Filoloski fakultet Beogradskog univerziteta, Belgrade, 1969.

Krontiris, Tina, *Oppositional Voices: Women as Writers and Translators of Literature in the English Renaissance*, Routledge, London, 1992.

LaBranche, Anthony, 'Imitation: getting in touch', *MLQ* 31 (1970), 308–29.

Lamb, Mary Ellen, 'The myth of the Countess of Pembroke', *Yearbook of English Studies* 11 (1981), 194–202.

Lamb, Mary Ellen, 'The Countess of Pembroke's patronage', *ELR* 12 (1982), 162–79.

Lambley, Kathleen R., *The Teaching and Cultivation of the French Language in England during Tudor and Stuart Times*, Manchester University Press, Manchester, 1920.

Lascelles, Mary, *Shakespeare's Measure for Measure*, Athlone Press, London, 1953.

Lawrence, Jason, '"The whole complection of *Arcadia* chang'd": Samuel Daniel and Italian lyric drama', *Medieval and Renaissance Drama in England* 11 (1999), 143–71.

Lee, Sidney, *Elizabethan Sonnets*, Archibald Constable and Co Ltd, London, 1904.

Lee, Sir Sidney, *Elizabethan and Other Essays*, ed. F. S. Boas, Clarendon Press, Oxford, 1929.

Leedham-Green, Elizabeth, and Robert J. Fehrenbach, *Private Libraries in Renaissance England: A Collection and Catalogue of Tudor and Early Stuart Book-lists*, Medieval and Renaissance Texts and Studies, Binghamton, 1992–.

Leishman, J. B., *Themes and Variations in Shakespeare's Sonnets*, Hutchinson, London, 1961.

Lever, J. W., *The Elizabethan Love Sonnet*, Methuen, London, 1956.

Levin, Harry, *The Myth of the Golden Age in the Renaissance*, Indiana University Press, Bloomington, 1969.

Levith, Murray J., *Shakespeare's Italian Settings and Plays*, Macmillan, Basingstoke, 1989.

Lewalski, Barbara K., *Writing Women in Jacobean England*, Harvard University Press, Cambridge, 1993.
Lievsay, John L., *Stefano Guazzo and the English Renaissance, 1575–1675*, University of North Carolina Press, Chapel Hill, 1961.
Lievsay, John L., *The Elizabethan Image of Italy*, Cornell University Press, Ithaca, 1964.
Lievsay, John L., *The Englishman's Italian Books, 1550–1700*, University of Pennsylvania Press, Philadelphia, 1969.
Lievsay, John L., 'Italian *favole boscarecce* and Jacobean stage pastoralism' in Richard Hosley, ed., *Essays on Shakespeare and Elizabethan Drama in Honour of Hardin Craig*, Routledge and Kegan Paul, London, 1963, pp. 317–26.
Loewenstein, Joseph, 'For a history of literary property: John Wolfe's reformation', *ELR* 18 (1988), 389–412.
Loewenstein, Joseph, *The Author's Due: Printing and the Prehistory of Copyright*, University of Chicago Press, Chicago, 2002.
Lorch, Maristella de Panizza, 'Honest Iago and the lusty moor: the humanistic drama of *honestas/voluptas* in a Shakespearean context' in J. R. Mulryne and Margaret Shewring, eds, *Theatre of the English and Italian Renaissance*, Macmillan, Basingstoke, 1991, pp. 204–20.
Lytton Sells, Arthur, *The Italian Influence in English Poetry: From Chaucer to Southwell*, Allen and Unwin, London, 1955.
Lytton Sells, Arthur, *The Paradise of Travellers: The Italian Influence on the Englishman in the Seventeenth Century*, Allen and Unwin, London, 1964.
McCoy, Richard C., *The Rites of Knighthood: The Literature and Politics of Elizabethan Chivalry*, University of California Press, Berkeley, 1989.
MacDonald, R. H., *The Library of Drummond of Hawthornden*, Edinburgh University Press, Edinburgh, 1971.
McKerrow, Ronald B., *Dictionary of Printers and Booksellers in England, Scotland and Ireland, and of Foreign Printers of English Books, 1557–1642*, Blades, East and Blades, London, 1910.
McMullan, Gordon, and Jonathan Hope, eds, *The Politics of Tragicomedy*, Routledge, London, 1991.
McPherson, David, 'Ben Jonson's library and marginalia: an annotated catalogue', *Studies in Philology* 71 (1974), 1–106.
McWilliam, G. H., *Shakespeare's Italy Revisited*, Leicester University Press, Leicester, 1974.
Maguire, Nancy Klein, ed., *Renaissance Tragicomedy: Explorations in Genre and Politics*, AMS Press, New York, 1987.
Majelli, Barbara, 'Riscrivendo "l'alfieri": Cinthio, Greene e la figura di Iago in *Othello*' in M. Marrapodi, ed., *Intertestualità Shakespeariane*, Bulzoni, Rome, 2003, pp. 255–73.
Marotti, Arthur F., '"Love is not love": Elizabethan sonnet sequences and the social order', *ELR* 49 (1982), 396–425.
Marrapodi, Michele, ed., *Shakespeare's Italy: Functions of Italian Locations in Renaissance Drama*, Manchester University Press, Manchester, 1993.

BIBLIOGRAPHY

Marrapodi, Michele, and A. J. Hoenselaars, eds, *The Italian World of English Renaissance Drama: Cultural Exchange and Intertextuality*, University of Delaware Press, Newark, 1998.
Marrapodi, Michele, ed., *Shakespeare and Intertextuality*, Bulzoni, Rome, 2000.
Marrapodi, Michele, ed., *Intertestualità Shakespeariane: il Cinquecento italiano e il Rinascimento inglese*, Bulzoni, Rome, 2003.
Martindale, Charles, and Michelle Martindale, *Shakespeare and the Uses of Antiquity: An Introductory Essay*, Routledge, London, 1990.
Masson, David, *The Life of John Milton*, Boston, 1859.
Matthiesen, F. O., *Translation: An Elizabethan Art*, Harvard University Press, Cambridge, 1931.
Melzi, Robert C., *Robert Tofte's 'Discourse' to the Bishop of London*, Slatkine, Geneva, 1989.
Minta, Stephen, *Petrarch and Petrarchism: The English and French Traditions*, Manchester University Press, Manchester, 1980.
Miola, Robert S., *Shakespeare's Reading*, Oxford University Press, Oxford, 2000.
Mirollo, James V., *The Poet of the Marvelous: Giambattista Marino*, Columbia University Press, New York and London, 1963.
Mitchell, Dennis S., 'Samuel Daniel's *Delia*: a critical edition', Princeton University PhD thesis, 1969.
Mortimer, Anthony, *Petrarch's Canzoniere in the English Renaissance*, Minerva Italica, Bergamo, 1975.
Mowat, Barbara A., 'Shakespearean tragicomedy' in N. K. Maguire, ed., *Renaissance Tragicomedy*, AMS Press, New York, 1987, pp. 80–96.
Muir, Kenneth, *Shakespeare's Sources*, Methuen, London, 1957.
Muir, Kenneth, *The Sources of Shakespeare's Plays*, Methuen, London, 1977.
Mulryne, J. R., and Margaret Shewring, eds, *Theatre of the English and Italian Renaissance*, Macmillan, Basingstoke, 1991.
Neely, Carol T., 'The structure of English Renaissance sonnet sequences', *ELH* 45 (1978), 359–89.
Neri, Nicoletta, *Il pastor fido in Inghilterra*, Giappichelli, Turin, 1963.
Oakeshott, Sir Walter, 'Ralegh's Library', *The Library* 23 (1968), 285–327.
Obertello, Alfredo, *Madrigali italiani in Inghilterra*, V. Bompiani, Milan, 1949.
Orr, David, *Italian Renaissance Drama in England before 1625: The Influence of Erudite Tragedy, Comedy, and Pastoral on Elizabethan and Jacobean Drama*, University of North Carolina Press, Chapel Hill, 1970.
Orsini, Napoleone, *Studi sul rinascimento italiano in Inghilterra*, G. C. Sansoni, Florence, 1937.
Osborn, James M., *Young Philip Sidney, 1572–1577*, Yale University Press, New Haven and London, 1972.
Ottolenghi, Paola, *Giacopo Castelvetro: esule modenese nell'Inghilterra di Shakespeare*, ETS, Pisa, 1982.
Parker, Brian, 'Jonson's Venice' in J. R. Mulryne and Margaret Shewring, eds, *Theatre of the English and Italian Renaissance*, Macmillan, Basingstoke, 1991, pp. 95–112.
Parks, George B., *The English Traveller to Italy*, Edizioni di storia e letteratura, Rome, 1954.

Parry, Graham, *The Golden Age Restored: The Culture of the Stuart Court, 1603–1642*, Manchester University Press, Manchester, 1981.

Partridge, A. C., 'Shakespeare and Italy', *English Studies in Africa* 4 (1961), 117–27.

Pascoe, David, 'Marston's childishness', *Medieval and Renaissance Drama in England* 9 (1997), 92–111.

Patey, Caroline, 'Beyond Aristotle: Giraldi Cinzio and Shakespeare' in S. Rossi and D. Savoia, eds, *Italy and the English Renaissance* (Unicopoli, Milan, 1989), pp. 167–85.

Patterson, Annabel, *Pastoral and Ideology: Virgil to Valery*, University of California Press, Berkeley, 1988.

Pavlock, Barbara, *Eros, Imitation and the Epic Tradition*, Cornell University Press, Ithaca, 1990.

Peck, Linda Levy, *Court Patronage and Corruption in Early Stuart England*, Unwin Hyman, Boston, 1990.

Peck, Linda Levy, ed., *The Mental World of the Jacobean Court*, Cambridge University Press, Cambridge, 1991.

Pellegrini, Giuliano, *John Florio e il Basilicon Doron di James VI: un esempio inedito di versione elisabettiana*, Feltrinelli, Milan, 1961.

Pellegrini, Giuliano, *Un fiorentino all corte d'Inghilterra nel Cinquecento: Petruccio Ubaldini*, Bottega d'Erasmo, Turin, 1967.

Perella, Nicholas J., *The Critical Fortune of Battista Guarini's Il Pastor Fido*, Olschki, Florence, 1973.

Perella, Nicholas J., 'Amarilli's dilemma: the *Pastor fido* and some English authors', *Comparative Literature* 12 (1960), 252–68.

Perry, Curtis, *The Making of Jacobean Culture: James I and the Renegotiation of Elizabethan Literary Practice*, Cambridge University Press, Cambridge, 1997.

Pettegree, Andrew, *Foreign Protestant Communities in Sixteenth Century London*, Clarendon Press, Oxford, 1986.

Pitcher, John, *Samuel Daniel: The Brotherton Manuscript: A Study in Authorship*, University of Leeds School of English, Leeds, 1981.

Pitcher, John, 'Essays, works and small poems: divulging, publishing and augmenting the Elizabethan poet, Samuel Daniel' in Andrew Murphy, ed., *The Renaissance Text: Theory, Editing, Textuality*, Manchester University Press, Manchester, 2000, pp. 8–29.

Policardi, Silvio, *John Florio e le relazioni culturali Anglo-Italiane agli arbori del XVII secolo*, Biblioteca di saggi e lezioni accademiche, Venice, 1947.

Potter, Lois, 'Pastoral drama in England and its political implications' in M. Chiabò and F. Doglio, eds, *Sviluppi della Drammaturgia Pastorale nell' Europa del Cinque-Seicento*, Centro studi sul teatro medioevale e rinascimentale, Rome, 1992, pp. 159–79.

Praz, Mario, 'Shakespeare's Italy', *Shakespeare Survey* 7 (1954), 95–106.

Praz, Mario, *The Flaming Heart: Essays on Crashaw, Machiavelli and Other Studies of the Relations between Italian and English Literature from Chaucer to T. S. Eliot*, Doubleday Anchor, New York, 1958.

Prescott, Anne Lake, *French Poets and the English Renaissance: Studies in Fame and Transformation*, Yale University Press, New Haven, 1978.

BIBLIOGRAPHY

Prince, F. T., *The Italian Element in Milton's Verse*, Clarendon Press, Oxford, 1954.
Proctor, Johanna, 'The Queen's Arcadia and Hymen's Triumph: Samuel Daniel's court pastoral plays' in J. Salmons and W. Moretti, eds, *The Renaissance in Ferrara and its European Horizons*, University of Wales Press, Cardiff, 1984, pp. 83–109.
Pruvost, René, *Matteo Bandello and Elizabethan Fiction*, Honoré Champion, Paris, 1937.
Pursglove, Glyn, 'Robert Tofte, Elizabethan translator of Boiardo' in J. Salmons and W. Moretti, eds, *The Renaissance in Ferrara and its European Horizons*, University of Wales Press, Cardiff, 1984, pp. 111–22.
Quint, David, *Origin and Originality in Renaissance Literature: Versions of the Source*, Yale University Press, New Haven, 1983.
Raab, Felix, *The English Face of Machiavelli: A changing Interpretation, 1500–1700*, Routledge and Kegan Paul, London, 1964.
Rebora, Piero, *L'Italia nella dramma inglese, 1558–1642*, Modernissima, Milan, 1925.
Rebora, Piero, *Civiltà italiana e civiltà inglese*, Felice Le Monnier, Florence, 1936.
Rees, D. G., 'Petrarch's *Trionfo della Morte* in English', *Italian Studies* 7 (1952), 82–96.
Rees, Joan, *Samuel Daniel: A Critical and Biographical Study*, Liverpool University Press, Liverpool, 1964.
Reynolds, Barbara, ed., *The Translator's Art*, Penguin, Harmondsworth, 1987.
Rhodes, Dennis E., *Short-title Catalogue of Books Printed in Italy and of Italian Books Printed in Other Countries from 1465–1600, Now in the British Library*, British Library, London, 1990.
Ristine, Frank H., *English Tragicomedy: Its Origin and History*, Russell and Russell, New York, 1910.
Roberts, R. J., 'New light on the career of Giacomo Castelvetro', *Bodleian Library Record* 13 (1990), 365–9.
Roche, Thomas P., *Petrarch and the English Sonnet Sequences*, AMS Press, New York, 1989.
Rosenberg, Eleanor, 'Giacopo Castelvetro: Italian publisher in Elizabethan London and his patrons', *Huntington Library Quarterly* 6 (1943), 119–48.
Ross Murray, James, *The Influence of Italian upon English Literature during the Sixteenth and Seventeenth Centuries*, Cambridge, 1886.
Rossi, Sergio, *Ricerche sull'umanesimo e sul rinascimento in Inghilterra*, Vita e Pensiero, Milan, 1969.
Rossi, Sergio, and Daniella Savoia, eds, *Italy and the English Renaissance*, Unicopli, Milan, 1989.
Rossi, Vittorio, *Battista Guarini ed Il Pastor Fido*, Turin, 1886.
Salingar, Leo, *Shakespeare and the Traditions of Comedy*, Cambridge University Press, Cambridge, 1974.
Salingar, Leo, 'Elizabethan dramatists and Italy: a postscript' in J. R. Mulryne and Margaret Shewring, eds, *Theatre of the English and Italian Renaissance*, Macmillan, Basingstoke, 1991, pp. 232–5.
Sammut, Alfonso, *La Fortuna dell'Ariosto nell'Inghilterra Elisabettiana*, Vita e Pensiero, Milan, 1971.

BIBLIOGRAPHY

Sammut, Alfonso, 'Per una storia della critica sulla fortuna Inglese del Petrarca' in Renzo Crivelli and Luigi Sampietro, eds, *Il passaggiere italiano: saggi sulle letterature di lingua inglese in onore di Sergio Rossi*, Bulzoni Editore, Rome, 1994, pp. 41–57.

Schaar, Claes, 'A textual puzzle in Daniel's *Delia*', *English Studies* 40 (1959), 382–5.

Schaar, Claes, *An Elizabethan Sonnet Problem*, Gleerup, Lund, 1960.

Schaar, Claes, *Elizabethan Sonnet Themes*, Gleerup, Lund, 1962.

Schelling, Felix E., *Foreign Influences in Elizabethan Plays*, Harper & Brothers, New York, 1923.

Sciarrino, Silvana, 'Da John Florio a Giovanni Torriano: l'insegnamento della lingua italiana nel Rinascimento inglese' in M. Marrapodi, ed., *Intertestualità Shakespeariane*, Bulzoni, Rome, 2003, pp. 31–46.

Scott, Janet G., *Les sonnets élisabéthains*, Honoré Champion, Paris, 1929.

Scott, Mary A., *Elizabethan Translations from the Italian*, Houghton Miffin, Boston, 1916.

Scott, Michael, *John Marston's Plays: Theme, Structure and Performance*, Macmillan, London, 1978.

Sellers, Harry, 'Italian books printed in England before 1640', *The Library* 5 (1924), 105–28.

Seronsy, Cecil, *Samuel Daniel*, Twayne Publishers, New York, 1967.

Shackford, M. Hale, 'Shakespeare and Greene's *Orlando Furioso*', *MLN* 39 (1924), 54–6.

Shaheen, Naseeb, 'Shakespeare's knowledge of Italian', *Shakespeare Survey* 47 (1994), 161–9.

Simonini, Rinaldo C., *Italian Scholarship in Renaissance England*, University of North Carolina Press, Chapel Hill, 1952.

Simonini, Rinaldo C., 'Italian–English language books of the Renaissance', *Romanic Review* 42 (1951), 241–4.

Smarr, Janet L., ed., *Italian Renaissance Tales*, Solaris Press, Rochester, 1983.

Smart, John S., *Shakespeare: Truth and Tradition*, Edward Arnold and Co., London, 1928.

Solerti, Angelo, *La Vita di Torquato Tasso*, Turin and Rome, 1895.

Sorlien, R. P., ed., *The Diary of John Manningham of the Middle Temple, 1602–1603*, University Press of New England, Hanover, 1976.

Spriet, Pierre, *Samuel Daniel: sa vie, son oeuvre*, Didier, Paris, 1968.

Starnes, De Witt T., 'Bilingual dictionaries of Shakespeare's day', *PMLA* 52 (1937), 1005–18.

Steiner, George, *After Babel: Aspects of Language and Translation*, Oxford University Press, Oxford, 1992.

Stern, Virginia F., *Gabriel Harvey: A Study of His Life, Marginalia, and Library*, Clarendon Press, Oxford, 1979.

Sturlese, Rita, *Bibliografia, censimento e storia delle antiche stampe di Giordano Bruno*, Olschki, Florence, 1987.

Svensson, Lars-Hakan, *Silent Art: Rhetorical and Thematic Patterns in Samuel Daniel's 'Delia'*, Gleerup, Lund, 1980.

Symonds, John A., *Renaissance in Italy: Italian Literature*, London, 1898.

BIBLIOGRAPHY

Thomson, Patricia, 'Sonnet 15 of Samuel Daniel's *Delia*: a Petrarchan imitation', *Comparative Literature* 17 (1965), 151–7.
Viglione, Francesco, *L'Italia nel pensiero degli scrittori inglesi*, Fratelli Bocca, Milan, 1946.
Waith, Eugene M., *The Pattern of Tragicomedy in Beaumont and Fletcher*, Yale University Press, New Haven, 1952.
Wall, Wendy, *The Imprint of Gender: Authorship and Publication in the English Renaissance*, Cornell University Press, Ithaca, 1993.
Watson, Foster, *The Beginnings of the Teaching of Modern Subjects in England*, London, 1909.
Watson, George, *The English Petrarchans: A Critical Bibliography of the Canzoniere*, Warburg Institute, London, 1967.
Weinberg, Bernard, *A History of Literary Criticism in the Italian Renaissance*, University of Chicago Press, Chicago, 1961.
Weismiller, Edward, 'Materials dark and crude: a partial genealogy for Milton's Satan', *Huntington Library Quarterly* 31 (1967), 75–92.
Wharton, T. F., ed., *Drama of John Marston: Critical Re-visions*, Cambridge University Press, Cambridge, 2000.
Wharton, T. F., 'Sexual politics in Marston's *The Malcontent*' in *Drama of John Marston: Critical Re-visions*, Cambridge University Press, Cambridge, 2000, pp. 181–93.
Whitaker, Virgil K., *Shakespeare's Use of Learning: An Inquiry into the Growth of His Mind*, Huntington Library, San Marino, 1953.
White, Harold O., *Plagiarism and Imitation during the English Renaissance*, Harvard University Press, Cambridge, 1935.
Williams, Franklin B., 'Robert Tofte', *RES* 13 (1937), 282–96 and 405–24.
Williamson, C. F., 'The design of Daniel's *Delia*', *RES* 19 (1968), 251–60.
Woodfield, D. B., *Surreptitious Printing in England, 1550–1640*, Bibliographical Society of America, New York, 1973.
Woolfson, Jonathan, *Padua and the Tudors: English Students in Italy, 1485–1603*, University of Toronto Press, Toronto, 1998.
Woudhuysen, Henry R., *Sir Philip Sidney and the Circulation of Manuscripts, 1558–1640*, Clarendon Press, Oxford, 1996.
Wright, Herbert G., *Boccaccio in England from Chaucer to Tennyson*, Athlone Press, London, 1957.
Yates, Frances A., *John Florio: The Life of an Italian in Shakespeare's England*, Cambridge University Press, Cambridge, 1934.
Yates, Frances A., *A Study of Love's Labour's Lost*, Cambridge University Press, Cambridge, 1936.
Yates, Frances A., 'Italian teachers in Elizabethan England', *Journal of the Warburg Institute* 1 (1937–38), 103–16.

Index

Note: Literary works are listed under authors' names, and 'n.' refers to a note number.

Aconcio, Giacomo 56n.33, 188
  Essortatione al Timor di Dio, Vna 56n.33, 188
Anne of Denmark 7, 8, 62
Aretino, Pietro 189, 190, 192, 199n.14
  Quattro Comedie 189, 199n.14
  Ragionamenti 190, 199n.14
Ariosto, Ludovico 13, 29, 45, 47, 49, 67, 88, 90, 113n.96, 136, 152–63, 170n.57, 175n.132, 182, 183, 186n.20
  Orlando furioso 13, 29, 45, 47, 109n.33, 112n.72, 113n.96, 114n.98, 136, 151–63, 170n.57, 174n.121, 175n.132
Ascham, Roger 1, 2, 3, 5, 6, 15n.4, 17n.12, 22–6, 29, 31, 32, 37
  Scholemaster, The 1, 3, 5, 6, 15n.4, 17n.12, 22–6, 32, 37

Baldwin, T. C. 119, 134
Bandello, Matteo 16n.4, 47, 127, 135, 137, 141, 153
  Novelle 16n.4, 127, 128
Bate, Jonathan 120–1, 126

Belleforest, Francois de 47, 127, 135, 137
  Histoires Tragiques 47
Bembo, Pietro 5, 37, 41–2, 48, 52–3
  Asolani, Gli 48, 53
  Prose della Volgar Lingua 5
  Rime 52–3
Bizari, Pietro 31, 56n.32
Boccaccio, Giovanni 2, 15n.4, 88, 99, 127, 136, 138, 139, 141, 164, 172n.83, 176n.151, 200n.25
  Decameron 2, 15n.4, 127, 138, 139, 141, 164, 171n.69, 200n.25
Bruno, Giordano 18n.21, 191, 199n.20
Bryskett, Lodowick 10, 14, 17n.20, 171n.66
Bullough, Geoffrey 139, 140, 164, 168n.31
Buonmattei, Benedetto 180

Cairncross, Andrew 152–3, 170n.57
Campion, Thomas 92, 94
  Book of Ayres 92
  Observations in the Art of English Poesy 92

INDEX

Carew, Richard 60n.85
Carey, Elizabeth 13, 35–7, 58n.47, 66
Castelvetro, Iacopo 4, 7, 8, 13, 17n.14, 190–6, 200n.23, 201n.31
'Barbagrigia' 192, 200n.24
Castiglione, Baldassare 16n.5, 43, 99, 200n.25
Cortegiano, Il 16n.5, 43, 47, 200n.25
Castiglioni, Giovan Battista 4, 6, 13, 16n.9, 31–2, 35, 56n.33, 188, 189
Catullus 92
Chappuys, Gabriel 43, 44, 47, 59n.71, 127, 153
Roland furieux 47, 59n.71
Charlewood, John 69, 190–1, 197, 199n.20
Cicero 5, 24, 26
Cinthio, Giambattista Giraldi 127, 129, 133, 137–42, 151–6, 159, 161–2, 170n.59, 171n.64
Arrenopia 155
Epitia 136, 137, 140–1, 155, 172n.81, 174n.126
Hecatommithi, Gli 127, 129, 137–40, 151–6, 168n.32, 170n.62
tragedia di fin lieto 136, 137–40, 142, 143, 155
Coleridge, Samuel Taylor 106, 117n.162

Daniel, Samuel 9, 10, 12, 15, 36, 38–41, 50, 54, 62–106, 110n.44, 133, 180, 200n.21
Civil Warres, The 88–9, 91
Complaint of Rosamond, The 50, 60n.88, 87–8
Defence of Ryme, The 92, 94
Delia 15, 36, 38–41, 43, 50–1, 54, 57n.46, 60–1n.91, 62, 63–86, 91, 98, 105, 109n.40, 110n.52, 112n.78, 113n.89
Hymens Triumph 61n.95, 62, 92, 102–6, 117n.149
immortality sonnets 75–86
Musophilus 91
Pastorall, A 91–7, 114–15n.112

Queenes Arcadia, The 92, 97–102, 103
Tragedie of Cleopatra, The 87
Davison, Francis 12, 50
Poetical Rhapsody, A 12, 50
Desportes, Philippe 36, 39, 45, 47, 57n.46, 59n.71, 63, 64, 75, 76–8, 82–4, 107n.7, 108n.18
Amours de Diane, Les 39, 65, 107n.9
Amours d'Hippolyte, Les 57n.46, 64, 107n.9, 110n.53, 113n.86
Cléonice 64, 76, 110n.53
Roland furieux 47, 59n.71
Drummond, William 11, 12, 37–8, 41–3, 46–54, 66, 133, 184, 190, 196, 197
Hawthornden manuscripts 37, 41, 46, 51
library collection 46–9
Poems: by W. D. 38, 46, 51
du Bellay, Joachim 12, 63, 66–9
Antiquitez de Rome, Les 12, 67
L'Olive 66–9, 108n.16, 112n.72
Duncan-Jones, Katherine 14, 35–6, 58n.47, 128, 129–30, 142, 163
Dymoke, Sir Edward 63, 71, 78, 95

Eliot, John 6, 24–5, 27, 29, 56n.23, 166n.10
Ortho-epia Gallica 25, 55n.10, 56n.23, 166n.10
Elizabeth I 6, 7, 13, 14, 16n.9, 31–4, 188

Fairfax, Edward 47, 48, 89–90, 184
Godfrey of Bulloigne 47, 48–9, 90, 184
Farmer, Richard 118, 119, 133–4, 135, 165n.1
Essay on the Learning of Shakespeare, An 118, 133, 166n.1, 169n.49
Field, Richard 128–9, 196, 197
Fiorentino, Ser Giovanni 127, 130, 135
Pecorone, Il 127, 130, 135
Fletcher, John 143, 151, 163, 172n.89

INDEX

Faithful Shepherdess, The 143, 151, 172n.89
Florio, John 1, 3–6, 8, 9–12, 16n.9, 17n.13, 19, 21, 26–8, 29, 44, 48, 62, 67, 70, 75, 99, 100, 107n.2, 108n.25, 119–28, 130, 131, 137, 166n.7, 167n.21, 168n.28, 177, 179, 184, 185n.6, 187, 190, 191, 193, 197, 200n.21
 Essayes of Montaigne, The 62, 100, 107n.2, 191
 First Fruites 3, 9, 11, 12, 16n.9, 20, 21, 26–8, 29, 54n.4, 55n.10, 119, 121–3, 131, 166n.11, 167n.15
 Giardino di Recreatione 62
 Queen Anna's New World of Words 8, 18n.21, 107n.3, 126, 127, 171n.63, 177, 197
 Second Frutes 1, 11, 18n.21, 27, 29, 55n.10, 108n.25, 110n.41, 119, 121, 123–6, 167n.19, 169n.43
 Worlde of Wordes, A 16n.11, 48, 54n.2, 99, 120, 126, 171n.63, 190, 201n.36
Florio, Michel Angelo 4, 6, 16n.9, 188, 189
 Catechismo 189
 Regole de la Lingua Thoscana 16n.9, 188
Fowler, William 10, 11, 34, 45, 57n.40, 71, 72, 74, 75, 109n.35, 110n.44
 Tarantula of Love, The 11, 72, 74
Fraunce, Abraham 92–3, 96, 115n.115
 Countesse of Pembrokes Yvychurch, The 92–3, 115n.115

Gl'Ingannati 128
Gl'Inganni 128, 129
Golding, Arthur 118, 134
Gosson, Steven 2, 3, 4, 9
 Playes confuted in fiue Actions 2, 3
 School of Abuse, The 3
Grantham, Henry 16n.10
 Italien Grammer 16n.10, 17n.21
Greene, Robert 123, 154, 155–8, 159, 160, 163, 174n.127, 175n.137

Grenes Groats-worth of Witte 167n.20
 Historie of Orlando Furioso, The 154–8
 Pandosto 154, 163–4
 Scottish Historie of James IV 154, 155, 174n.127
Greene, Thomas 37, 45, 58n.48, 66, 67, 84, 108n.16, 172n.92
 eclectic imitation 66, 75, 78
 heuristic imitation 84
 reproductive imitation 66
 types of imitation 66, 107n.14
Greg, W. W. 102–3, 116n.129
Groto, Luigi 50, 59n.81, 98
 Pentimento amoroso, Il 59n.81, 98–9, 101, 116n.129
Guarini, Battista 48, 54, 61n.95, 74, 78, 95–6, 97, 99, 100, 132–3, 137, 139–40, 142, 143–51, 163–5, 171n.75, 172n.77, 173n.102
 Madrigali 59n.81
 Pastor fido, Il 8, 48, 59n.81, 61n.100, 78, 95–6, 97, 99, 101, 115n.124, 116n.129, 132–3, 136, 137, 139–40, 142, 143–51, 163–5, 171n.75, 194–5
 Rime degli academici eterei 78, 110n.51, 113n.89
Guazzo, Stefano 44, 47, 99
 Civil conversatione, La 44, 47
Gwynne, Matthew 9, 54n.2
 Candido, Il 9, 54n.2

Harington, Sir John 47, 57n.37, 60n.85, 153, 170n.57, 186n.20
 Orlando Furioso 60n.85, 186n.20
Harvey, Gabriel 9, 12, 13, 17n.21, 28, 190, 196
Henke, Robert 163, 172n.85, 176n.147
Herbert, Mary Countess of Pembroke 14, 15, 34, 57n.37, 68–9, 86, 87, 93, 110n.41
 Trionfo della Morte 14, 34
 Wilton circle 94, 115n.118
Hoby, Sir Thomas 16n.5, 43, 47

221

INDEX

Holyband, Claude 6, 9, 13, 16n.10, 17n.13, 22, 48, 55n.10
   Arnalt and Lucenda 16n.10, 17n.21, 55n.10, 59n.79
   Campo di Fior 25, 43, 55n.17
   French Schoolemaister, The 6, 16n.10, 22, 55n.10
   Italian Schoole-maister, The 6, 16n.10, 48, 55n.10
Horne, P. R. 138, 170n.59, 171n.76
Hunter, G. K. 133, 136, 139, 143

Italian verse anthologies 11, 72, 74–5, 107n.7, 109n.35, 110n.51
   Fiori delle Rime, I 74–5, 110n.51

Jack, Ronald 38, 45, 52, 57n.40, 61n.101, 110n.44
James VI and I 7, 8, 17n.14, 162, 197
   Lepanto 162
Jonson, Ben 99–100, 110n.41
   Every Man in his Humour 110n.41
   Volpone 99–100, 116n.134, 167n.24

Kastner, L. E. 53, 80, 113n.86
Kau, Joseph 44, 80, 111n.70
Klein, Lisa 81, 111n.67

language-learning techniques
   bilingual parallel-text manuals 4, 6, 11, 20, 22, 24–9
   private instruction 4, 5, 6, 7, 10, 12, 13, 19, 119, 121
   private language schools 9, 13, 20
   reading knowledge 11, 21, 22, 126
   self study 11, 12, 20, 23, 58n.51, 119, 121–6
   travel 3, 6, 10, 12, 19
Languet, Hubert 10, 24
Lee, Sidney 64, 76, 91
Leishman, J. B. 77, 78, 79, 80
Lievsay, John 44, 57n.40
literary imitation 9, 12, 15, 37, 65–6
   complex imitation 86
   imitatio 37
   simple imitation 66, 86
   see also Greene, Thomas

Lorch, Maristella 152, 153, 160, 175n.136
Lotti, Ottaviano 8, 17n.15
Lyly, John 30
   Euphues and his England 30

MacDonald, R. H. 46, 48, 49
Machiavelli, Niccolo 28, 45, 189, 190, 192, 199n.14
   Discorsi 28, 190, 199n.14
   Lasino doro 190, 199n.14
   Libro dell'arte della Guerra 190, 199n.14
   Principe, Il 45, 199n.14
Manners, Roger Earl of Rutland 8, 54n.2, 120
Manningham, John 127–8, 129, 136
Marino, Giambattista 38, 51, 53–4, 186n.21
   Rime 53–4, 61n.92
Marston, John 13, 129–33, 136, 142–51, 163, 169n.39
   Antonio and Mellida 130, 143
   Malcontent, The 130–3, 136, 137, 142–51, 173n.104
Milton, John 13, 179–84
   Comus 182, 186n.18
   Defensio Secunda 185n.9
   Of Education 180
   Paradise Lost 184
   Poemata 179, 183
   Poems 1645 181–2
   Reason of Church Government, The 179, 182
Miola, Robert 134, 168n.32
Mitchell, Dennis 41, 63, 74, 82, 107n.7
Mozzarello, Giovanni 75, 110n.52
Muir, Kenneth 138, 153, 174n.125

Newman, Thomas 39, 57n.46, 63, 74, 83
Noci, Carlo 103
   Cinthia, La 103

Painter, William 16n.4, 138–9, 170n.62, 171n.69

INDEX

Palace of Pleasure, The 16n.4, 138, 170n.62
Parker, Henry Lord Morley 15n.4, 57n.40
  Tryumphes of Fraunces Petrarcke, The 15n.4, 57n.40
Pasquier, Etienne 41–3
  Recherches de la France, Les 41
Percy, Henry Earl of Northumberland 18n.21, 194, 196, 197, 201n.33
Petrarch 2, 5, 11, 13, 14, 15n.4, 29, 30–6, 39, 48, 51, 63, 65, 67, 68, 70, 74, 84–6, 88, 105–6, 107n.7, 167n.21
  Canzoniere 13, 15n.4, 30, 35–6, 39–41, 48, 51, 70, 84, 117n.160
  Trionfi 2, 11, 14, 15n.4, 29, 30, 32–4, 36, 45, 57n.37, 72
Pettie, George 44, 47
Pitcher, John 8, 61n.95, 91, 95
Proctor, Johanna 117n.149

Quint, David 89, 90

Reynolds, Henry 97
  Aminta Englisht 97
Riche, Barnabe 129, 138, 171n.64
  Riche his Farewell to Militarie Profession 129, 135, 137
Roche, Thomas 111n.56, 114–15n.112
Ronsard, Pierre de 41–2, 47, 78, 112n.73
  Sonnets pour Helene, Les 79–81, 112n.73
Rota, Bernadino 70, 109n.35, 110n.52
Russell, Lucy Countess of Bedford 8, 54n.2, 57n.37, 120

Schaar, Claes 70, 72, 109n.35
Second Part of the Return from Parnassus 85–6
Seneca 143, 144, 150
  Agamemnon 150
  Thyestes 150
Shaheen, Naseeb 122, 131, 167n.27
Shakespeare, William 11, 12, 118–43, 144, 149, 151–65

All's Well 133, 136, 138–40, 163, 171n.75
Cymbeline 163, 164–5
Hamlet 125, 149
King John 124–5
Love's Labour's Lost 120–1, 123
Measure for Measure 127, 133, 136, 140–2, 143, 151, 154, 155, 163, 172n.80, 174n.125
Merchant of Venice, The 123–5, 127, 135
Much Ado about Nothing 127, 135, 153
Othello 125, 127, 129, 133, 136, 151–63, 174n.121, 175n.135
Romeo and Juliet 124
Taming of the Shrew, The 12, 121–2, 123, 125
Tempest, The 134, 163, 170n.53
Twelfth Night 127, 129, 130, 135, 137
Two Gentlemen of Verona, The 121, 123
Winter's Tale, The 154, 163–4, 165, 176n.151
Sidney, Sir Philip 6, 7, 10, 14, 17n.20, 24, 110n.44, 193, 199n.20
  Astrophil and Stella 39, 57n.46, 63, 69, 74, 75, 108n.25
Simonini, Rinaldo 20, 125, 168n.28
Smart, John 152, 166n.4, 181, 182, 186n.16
Sophocles 149, 150
  Oedipus Rex 149, 150
Spenser, Edmund 12, 29, 49, 53, 88, 112n.73, 153, 165, 180
  Amoretti 53
  Colin Clouts Come Home Againe 88
  Faerie Queene, The 13, 29, 112n.73, 165
Theatre for Voluptuous Worldlings, A 12
Stanford, Henry 13, 35–6, 58n.47
Stringer, Philip 100, 117n.140
Sturm, Johannes 24
Svensson, Lars-Hakan 65, 83, 92, 112n.84, 114–15n.112

223

INDEX

Tansillo, Luigi 51, 75, 107n.7, 110n.52
Tasso, Torquato 7, 14, 47, 48–9, 53, 54, 65, 72–4, 76, 77–8, 81, 88, 90, 91–8, 99, 112n.73, 113n.89, 162, 165, 182, 183, 188, 191, 200
   Aminta 47, 48, 61n.95, 91–7, 98, 101, 102, 103–5, 115n.124, 165, 194–5, 196
   Gerusalemme liberata 14, 47, 48–9, 60n.88, 79, 80, 83, 89, 90, 112n.73, 162, 165, 188, 191, 192
   Rime 53, 65, 77–8, 82, 112n.78
   Rinaldo, Il 53
Tebaldeo, Antonio 37–8, 41–3, 52, 64, 84, 113n.86
Thomas, William 3, 18n.21, 28, 179
   Historie of Italie, The 3, 18n.21
   Principal Rules of the Italian Grammar 3, 4, 5, 18n.21, 28
Tofte, Robert 10, 69–70, 71, 73–4, 108n.29
   Blazon of Iealousie, The 71, 109n.33
   Laura 69–70, 73–4, 109n.40
   Two Tales 70, 109n.33
Torriano, Giovanni 19, 20, 22, 62, 177–8, 185n.2
   Italian Tutor, The 23, 55n.10, 185n.2
   Vocabolario Italiano & Inglese 177, 178
translation
   conferring 25, 27
   double translation 5, 6, 24
   literary translation 91–7

parallel-text reading 11, 43, 45, 48–9, 58n.51, 132–4, 141, 184
paraphrastic translation 37–41
translation exercises 5, 12, 13, 15, 24, 26, 29, 30–6, 37–43, 66–7, 97
translation into target language 25–6

Ubaldini, Petruccio 4, 16n.9, 128, 188, 189, 192, 196, 198n.8, 200n.24, 201n.34
   Vita di Carlo Magno, La 188, 196, 200n.24, 201n.34

Vautrollier, Thomas 16n.10, 17n.21, 128, 196
Virgil 67, 88, 90
   Aeneid 158
   Georgics 90

Whetstone, George 141, 154
   Heptameron of Ciuill Discourses, A 141
   Promos and Cassandra 141, 154
Wolfe, John 4, 6, 7, 43, 56n.33, 129, 187–97
Woudhuysen, Henry 69, 78, 108n.25
Wriothesley, Henry Earl of Southampton 8, 10, 19, 120
Wyatt, Sir Thomas 3, 15n.4

Yates, Frances 8, 17n.13, 120, 124

Zabata, Cristoforo 72
   Della Scelta di Rime 72, 74

EU authorised representative for GPSR:
Easy Access System Europe, Mustamäe tee 50,
10621 Tallinn, Estonia
gpsr.requests@easproject.com

www.ingramcontent.com/pod-product-compliance
Lightning Source LLC
Chambersburg PA
CBHW070941230426
43666CB00011B/2520